Praise for *Surrounded by Energy Vampires*

"With his trademark humor and practical insights, Erikson will help you vanquish the 'energy vampires' in your life—even when it turns out you're the villain! Using his wildly successful behavior-based system, you'll learn how self-awareness is the key to preserving your time, energy, and sanity—no matter what comes your way."

—Gay Hendricks, bestselling author of
The Big Leap

"Thomas Erikson just gets it—this book is equal parts logical, emotionally astute, and gut-wrenchingly funny. His observations are studied in a way that don't come across as either snarky or preachy—he's one of us and sees what we have always known—vampires are real! This book gives you tools to ward off those who would try to suck out your joy. Buy it!"

—Jim McPartlin, author of *The
Enneagram at Work*

Praise for *Surrounded by Narcissists*

"Outstanding . . . Erikson impresses with his trademark facility for making research-based discussions accessible and entertaining, and readers will appreciate the insightful guidance. This is another home run from Erikson."

—*Publishers Weekly* (starred review)

Praise for *Surrounded by Bad Bosses*

"[An] encouraging treatise . . . The dual focus on both employee and manager separates this from the pack."

—*Publishers Weekly*

Praise for *Surrounded by Psychopaths*

"A guidebook for deflecting psychological manipulators . . . Bluntly cautionary and applicable advice on the importance of vigilance."

—*Kirkus Reviews*

"This easy-to-read guide will calm fears by arming readers with practical tactics for thwarting a psychopath's strategies. Adults in the workplace and at home would benefit from Erikson's advice on how to recognize and understand different behaviors, as well as how to recognize red flags in all types of relationships."

—*Booklist*

Praise for *Surrounded by Idiots*

"A useful guide to communicating with the uncommunicable . . . clearly, dynamically presented and easy to grasp."

—*Publishers Weekly*

"Readers will be delighted. Most everyone can benefit from this book, especially those in the workplace. In addition, parents, educators, and students will find these insights valuable."

—*Booklist* (starred review)

Surrounded by Energy Vampires

Also by Thomas Erikson

Surrounded by Idiots

Surrounded by Psychopaths

Surrounded by Bad Bosses

Surrounded by Setbacks

Surrounded by Narcissists

. . . .

Surrounded by Energy Vampires

How to Slay the Time, Joy, and Soul Suckers in Your Life

Thomas Erikson

ST. MARTIN'S
ESSENTIALS
NEW YORK

Published in the United States by St. Martin's Essentials,
an imprint of St. Martin's Publishing Group

SURROUNDED BY ENERGY VAMPIRES. Copyright © 2023 by Thomas Erikson.
Translation © 2023 by Jan Salomonsson. All rights reserved.
Printed in the United States of America. For information, address
St. Martin's Publishing Group, 120 Broadway, New York, NY 10271.
Translation. Copyright © 2023 by Jan Salomonsson.

www.stmartins.com

The Library of Congress Cataloging-in-Publication Data is available upon request.

ISBN 978-1-250-90756-1 (trade paperback)
ISBN 978-1-250-83847-6 (ebook)

Our books may be purchased in bulk for promotional, educational, or business use.
Please contact your local bookseller or the Macmillan Corporate and
Premium Sales Department at 1-800-221-7945, extension 5442, or
by email at MacmillanSpecialMarkets@macmillan.com.

First published in Sweden by Book Mark in 2022

First U.S. Edition: 2023

10 9 8 7 6 5 4 3 2 1

Contents

Surrounded by
Energy Vampires

The Time I Almost Gave Up

O nce, many years ago, I was sitting on a spongy office chair in my local bank branch, working away, oblivious to the fact that my life was about to take a drastic turn. Strangely enough, I can't recall exactly what I was doing on this particular occasion, but it's safe to assume it was something that wouldn't have any effect at all on anybody's life.

All I can say for certain is that I was following some corporate order or other. I was simply toiling away, carrying out my everyday tasks without giving too much thought to how or why.

This already raises an interesting question: Why was I doing this?

The purpose behind my mere presence at the office where I was employed was shrouded in the deepest of mysteries. Even to this day, more than thirty years later, I remain unable to give any insightful explanation as to why I buried myself in that soul-draining work. I was only there because of a series of chance events.

I would get up in the mornings, wake my family, make breakfast, go to work, do my work, go home, make dinner, watch television for an hour, and then go to bed.

Surely, that was more or less the life most people led? So what was the problem?

The problem was a rather subtle one. It's not that there was anything terribly wrong with my work. It just didn't feel rewarding to me at all. And, because of that, it wasn't right for me. To be absolutely frank with you, I was often unmotivated at work. You could even say I was lethargic. I can assure you, this state of mind did nothing to boost my performance.

When you're feeling listless and drained of energy, the challenge is identifying the true cause. In my case, as I would eventually become keenly aware, there wasn't just one problem, but several.

The main one was that my actual work tasks were largely mind-numbingly dull. I may have been able to put up with that if it weren't for the fact that the entire banking sector in Sweden was undergoing a crisis at the time. The banking slump was the result of a deep recession, which mainly impacted the financial system but also the real estate market.

What about the banking sector itself? Those of us who worked in bank branches bore the brunt of it all, as we were the ones who had to listen to angry customers' reactions to events and decisions that we didn't understand any better than they did. Nobody had asked us if we wanted to lay waste to several billions' worth of capital. We were overworked and underpaid, which did nothing to improve my motivation.

For the record, mistakes had been made in the banking sector. There's no denying that. Huge, painfully expensive mistakes. But this had all gone on so far above our own heads that we had no influence at all over the decisions being made.

All these events, which went on for several years, were exhausting for me. I was stuck in my seat, unable to do any-thing about the whole disaster. It was like living in a state of mental limbo. If energy drinks could have helped, I would have chugged them endlessly.

When the crisis passed and the dust settled, people ended up losing their jobs, our clients went bankrupt, and families were driven out of their homes. My role, which involved in-teracting with the least fortunate of these, saw me witnessing men and women breaking down in tears on a daily basis.

Even so . . .

Perhaps I could have coped with all that if I hadn't also had the misfortune of working with a number of colleagues who habitually drained me of an almost unbelievable amount of energy. Some days, their attitudes and ways of responding to and handling the situation left me feeling as if I had been robbed of my entire will to live.

In fact, any of these situations would probably have been manageable one at a time. I'm a fairly stable person, and I've been to hell and back more than once. My experiences have strengthened me, but at the time I was still a fairly young man, who hadn't developed any real strategies for tackling this. Most difficult of all, I still lacked any real understanding of where this hopelessness I was feeling really came from. All I knew was that I would come home at night feeling drained and that I was irritable and frustrated much of the time.

One serious cause was that I was doing the wrong kind of work. Anybody who has been in the wrong job before knows how exhausting it can be to try to feel even the mildest enthusiasm when you're constantly aware of how much you detest the work you need to do.

To further complicate things, corporate leadership wasn't interested at all in listening to the frustrations of their work-force. Instead of providing us with clear guidance and strong leadership, they sent us to motivational seminars. In many cases, these were actually quite entertaining. I laughed in recognition at a lot of stuff, as did most of the other people in the room.

But as it turned out, inspirational seminars, however in-spiring, solved absolutely none of our actual problems. Lis-tening to some bundle of energy on a big stage explain to us how all we had to do was apply some *positive thinking* was certainly captivating, but, strangely, it did nothing to help us handle being the object of our clients' fits of rage. If you've ever had a boss who tried to give you a pep talk when what you really needed was specific answers, I'm sure you know the feeling.

However, the most interesting thing was the fact that sev-eral of my colleagues exhibited some rather unusual behavior. One woman was so work averse that she used to begin nearly every workweek with a sick day. Her accounts of her various ailments became more and more fanciful as the months went by. As you are no doubt aware, accusing a coworker who may be sick of putting on an act might be perceived as less than helpful. However, I had to draw the line when she returned from a two-week leave of absence because a ladybug bit her thumb. She hated taking directions, and she tried to get away with doing the bare minimum whenever she was given a task to do. Now, I've learned that she was displaying what psy-chologists call passive-aggressive behavior, which involves seeking to avoid all personal responsibility. As far as I know, she's still at it today.

We were in an open office of sorts. The guy I shared desks with never seemed to shut up. It didn't matter if he was busy working or pouring coffee down his throat; his mouth was always running, ceaselessly. For the life of me, I couldn't tell you what he was actually talking about—all of my energy was spent trying to block him out of my mind. He was loud, bombastic, and highly needy in terms of other people's attention. Whenever some of our more notable clients would visit, he unleashed his entire repertoire. He was a bona fide drama queen, a type you'll be reading more about later on in this book.

Another of my coworkers seemed to be incredibly dedicated to sabotaging our attempts to meet deadlines. He would slow the entire team down, thanks to his horrendous sense of discipline. I still find him popping up in my mind whenever I find myself thinking about inefficient people. He never did what he was told to do, or, at least, never on time. He never took any notes, and he rarely remembered what was said. He was completely clueless. According to his wife, he was just the same at home. How he was able to keep his life together at all astonishes me. One thing, however, was beyond all doubt: Having to work with him felt a lot like being punished.

Worse than all that, however, was his habit of constantly trying to shift the blame and paint himself as the victim of unfortunate circumstances. If he hadn't been given incomplete instructions, he'd run afoul of some unreasonably angry clients. When he wasn't complaining about how management didn't appreciate his work, he was harping on about how he'd been unable to sleep since childhood and how this had made him chronically exhausted. And considering how bad his pay was, what could anyone really expect? He displayed telltale signs of chronic victimhood, although he wasn't the worst offender. One thing was clear, though: Nobody really had any clue how to handle him.

So far, I haven't even mentioned the coworker who refused to do any real work at all, probably because they were busy having an affair with the office manager.

As the crisis deepened, I was assigned clients who had been designated as financially troubled. That is, the ones who had had their houses and homes taken because of unpaid credit. Days without meetings with teary-eyed clients were few and far between. The mental pressure was unbearable. I hadn't even turned thirty yet, and I was certainly not a therapist.

The whole situation, with my difficult colleagues, angry clients, and a leadership team preoccupied with the goings-on in the stratosphere of upper management, was bad enough in itself. I was also consuming all the news I could get my hands on and constantly reading about the seeming avalanche of unfolding disasters within the banking world. One of the major evening tabloids in Sweden ran a series of anti-banking campaigns that made me feel like a criminal. My mood fell even further, and the whole mess ended up having a serious, negative impact on my marriage. I became ill-tempered and stressed out, and I struggled with a deep sense of hopelessness.

In the long term, my marriage crumbled, too. My work and the difficult conditions I had to contest with weren't the only causes, of course, but they definitely helped give a good strong push in the wrong mental direction. I don't think it's an unreasonable assumption that I would have succumbed to some kind of depression if I had carried on like that.

This situation was a hard one, but I want to be clear that

I'm not claiming to be a victim here. I still had my job, after all. I was able to feed my family. I was young and strong. I had my whole future ahead of me. But I would be lying if I claimed it wasn't hard going.

What would have happened if someone had sat down and explained to me why the people around me were behaving as they were? If I had understood how these coworkers were draining me, and most of the people they interacted with, of so much energy?

If I had been given an introduction to the subject of this book, I bet my attitude would have changed significantly. I suspect I wouldn't have reacted as strongly to the behaviors of certain coworkers. I also think I could have been of more use to myself, my clients—and my family.

1

How to Spot an Energy Vampire

Sometimes nothing works. Nothing at all. It doesn't matter what you do; everything you touch just falls to pieces. Everything goes wrong. Regardless of how hard you try. It still goes wrong.

Fortunately, there are other days when things work out a bit better. You make your way through the day and actually end up achieving a great deal. There aren't any impending disasters ahead, even though you might be wishing things were working even better.

Other days still, everything just seems to flow. You're inspired, passionate, motivated. You find yourself spotting opportunities where, weeks earlier, all you could see was doom and gloom. This could all depend on the weather, of course, but it's more likely that you're in a state of positive flow, you're *in the zone,* the planets suddenly have aligned, or it's just one of those days.

In the moment, it's not too important where all the positive energy is coming from. What matters is that it's there, making you feel good inside. It comes over you, and for a few magical moments you realize how simple it all really is. You wonder why you never thought of it before. The world is yours for the taking. Just get it done!

The sense that you're absolutely invincible. The realization that you can do whatever you want. You've cracked the code, found the right opening, and your energy gushes forth. This is the moment! The feeling that this is it—things are about to go down!

However, strangely enough, just ten minutes later—or thirty seconds later—all of your profound ideas are gone, just like that. Every last thought of a new, bright future has been ground to dust. Your grand ambitions are all shattered.

The prospects that looked so promising only moments ago suddenly seem completely insurmountable. You're all washed-out. All you see is darkness, and all your strength has disappeared. You don't feel up to anything right now.

How is it possible to make that transition from exhilaration and delight to bleak nothingness in just a few minutes? Where did all that boisterous boldness and energy go, exactly? Did it all go down some mental inner drain, never to be seen again? And if it did—why? Your day, or week, or year started out so great, and now it all just feels hopeless.

The answer is simple.

You encountered a vampire. A vampire whose calling in life it is to quickly and efficiently extinguish people's dreams, obscuring anything that so much as resembles a bright future.

An energy vampire crossed your path.

An energy vampire is an uninvited mental squatter, who seems to live to drain everybody around them of all their energy. Energy vampires are sometimes referred to as psychic vampires, too.

Despite your change in mood, you know that what you had planned—a new business venture, a trip you wanted to go on, a relationship you wanted to tell somebody about, a house in the country you found, or whatever it was that was feeding you that amazing energy—was actually not a bad idea. It was all entirely realistic, actually. It's just that now . . . you can't even bring yourself to think about it. Somebody helped convince you it was hopeless.

And as a result, you file it all away in mental storage under "Ideas for the Future." You'll have to see. Maybe another time. Maybe never. The idea has been effectively quashed and may never return to you. We all carry countless such ideas around, like mental debris.

Imagine a person who always responds the same way, no matter what you've suggested: *Weeell, I'm not sure that's quite right. I think you missed a comma right there.* If it happens once, that might not be too bad. You could probably even live with it happening twice, or even three times. But *always* being corrected, no matter what you're talking about—how frustrating is that? It even happens when you're discussing subjects you have a pretty good handle on. Stoneface simply furrows their brow and proceeds to ask twelve different questions, which all convey the same, consistent insinuation: *You have no idea what you're doing.* In the end, you'll hardly dare open your mouth, in case some pedantic bully tries to shut you up.

For another example, consider this: You return home from the hospital after a stay you wouldn't have wished upon your worst enemy (this is actually a silly expression, as this is exactly the kind of misfortune you might be happy having your worst enemy endure). Perhaps you're not actively seeking sympathy, but when you explain how sick you've been and how scared you were somebody will tell you all about how they actually suffered *far worse health issues, thank you very much!* They'll then proceed to deflect all attention from you by relating some lengthy anecdote that you don't believe a single word of. If you had pneumonia, you can bet this person had *double* pneumonia! How frustrating is that?

Or how about this: A numbingly complex project has been tossed your way by your optimistic boss, and she is cheerfully celebrating *the amazing job you're about to do on it! Whoop-de-doo!* But the more you learn about it, the more you realize that in addition to lacking any kind of plan, the project has such ridiculously overambitious targets that it would take at least a violation of the laws of physics and the participation of two Nobel Prize winners to even seem plausible. When you ask for further instructions, your boss looks at you as though you came from another planet. Rather than support and assist you, she asks you, with ill-concealed displeasure, if you're sure that you're still happy to be working there? *You've seemed so negative lately, you know?*

Or, perhaps, it's just a simple garden project. You're going to build a new patio. Nothing too huge. It shouldn't take more than a couple of days. But then your neighbor interferes. He grins at you from across the fence, hurling some carefully aimed comments at you. And then, just like that, the patio has turned into a hazy mirage.

A real-life example: A good friend of mine heard that I

had managed to purchase my dream home after thirty years of hard work. An eighteenth-century house that required a ridiculous number of renovations—just the kind of project my wife and I wanted! I was hoping this person might respond along these lines: *What fun! I know this has always been a dream of yours! I'd love to come by and see it.* Something like that. Instead, I got this: *Oh, really?* And then we moved on to another subject.

Was I asking for too much? Well, maybe. But it disappointed me. This was somebody I had been looking forward to sharing the news with. Instead, the conversation gave me a lot to consider, including how envy can change people.

All of these examples illustrate how energy vampires can completely deflate your excitement with a single sentence. It's crazy when you think about it.

It could also be a matter of navigating an average day, when you're not facing any particular challenges. That is, until you run into the wrong person on your way from the coffee machine. Suddenly, everything seems to be lost.

Energy vampires can rob you of your enthusiasm without the slightest effort.

But how can you tell you've been hit by an energy vampire, and are there ways to prevent it from happening?

An energy drain could be a job, a group, a phenomenon, or anything that's causing difficulty in your life. However, surprisingly often, the culprit is a flesh-and-blood human being, who has made a habit of raining on other people's parades. Some of them are energy vampires because they genuinely enjoy seeing people fail. Maybe it makes them feel big and important to put others down. Others, however, bumble around in other people's lives like proverbial elephants in china shops, causing irreparable harm without even knowing it.

This phenomenon impacts all of our lives from time to time. We've all had moments when we've gone from full speed ahead to making no headway at all in the course of a few hours. All that lovely energy must have gone somewhere, right? Wouldn't you love to know how to steer clear of those obstacles?

Imagine if there was a way to evade situations and people who rob you of your positive energy, leaving you feeling empty and confused! Imagine if you could see and discover the warning signs ahead of time and know how to gracefully weave your way around the worst energy drains.

This book is about energy vampires, or psychic vampires, or emotional vampires—all three labels are sometimes applied to this same phenomenon. The term "energy vampires" doesn't exist in every language, but the English phrase gives a pretty accurate idea of what it's all about:

Individuals—energy vampires—who feast on your life force and leave you drained and dry, practically a member of the walking dead. They also leave you in danger of doing the same to others.

It might all sound a bit bonkers, but when you think about it, it's actually quite an apt allegory. The mythological vampire drains their victim's life force by drinking their blood, and an energy vampire does the same by robbing people of their confidence, their motivation, and sometimes even their desire to live.

I don't want us to get bogged down in semantics here, but I do find the similarity amusing. The main difference, I suppose, is that fairy-tale vampires know what they're doing and can't help themselves, while real-life energy parasites aren't always aware of the impact they have on others.

Also, different people lose their energy in different ways. Usually, we don't all respond to an event the exact same way, and that's probably a good thing.

Some people might be completely exhausted by just a minor dispute over something trivial, like a travel destination, while others might actually gain energy from the same situation. Getting to engage in a little verbal hand-to-hand seems to wake them up. On the other hand, having to wait drives them insane, while the first group might not mind that in the slightest. Identical situations, but wildly different reactions.

While some might only be mildly annoyed—if at all—by the sluggishness of their colleagues, others might cancel entire projects if people don't express sufficient enthusiasm right away. If they don't get the acceptance and appreciation they feel entitled to, they won't bother. On the other hand, they will respond positively to novelty and change, both things the first group will strongly dislike. Identical situations, but again, wildly different reactions.

Some of us just need a break sometimes, a chance to sit down and regroup before we go at it again. If we skip too many breaks, we simply won't have the energy to see something through. In contrast, others hate sitting still and resting and need to be even more active in their leisure time in order to recover. If they don't get to roar along at full throttle, they will quickly run out of steam and get into a bad mood. And how about this: While some people need to interact with others in order to fill up their gas tank, others might find that people and conversations drain them completely. If they don't get to spend some time by themselves now and then they can become absolutely impossible to deal with.

Energy comes and goes in different ways in different people, and that goes for both positive and negative energy. Neither way is right or wrong, but knowing what triggers these reactions in yourself—and why—can be very valuable. It can help you avoid major missteps and preserve your energy for the right things.

It's complicated. However, it's often a matter of who you are and what personality traits you possess. We'll be taking a closer look at these things in the section titled "The DISC Theory: A Study in Energy Loss." Most of these challenges can be solved, you see.

Regardless of what you react to personally, you might want to consider what it would be worth to you to dodge as many of these energy drains as possible. What would you give to be able to maintain your energy at peak capacity when you need it the most? Or why not all the time?

In this book, I'll be detailing a series of different kinds of energy vampires, how to spot them, the effects they can have on you, and how they do it.

At this point, I should mention that this isn't the only book out there on energy vampires. I've read a large number of the ones that are already available, and some of them offer suggestions that I actually suspect may be of no use at all.

This book focuses on everyday situations, the kinds of things you and I both encounter quite commonly. However, I will also address how basically anybody can protect themselves if they encounter somebody who is a bad influence on them.

Who falls victim to energy vampires? Well, the truth is, everyone does. But each type of energy vampire will have different effects on different people. And that makes sense, really. For instance, you might tell a friend how *Johnny is such a pain to deal with*. But your friend just doesn't see it. *Johnny? He's fabulous!*

Usually, there are no simple explanations when it comes to human behavior. Somebody your partner might find annoying and unruly, because they can never seem to sit still, might seem energetic and stimulating to you. Another person might seem very strange to you, because he hardly ever says a word—what an energy vampire! But others might appreciate this individual's ability to refrain from blathering on about stuff.

We can all fall victim to energy vampires, but it tends to happen in different ways. Naturally, there are some varieties that seem to cause near-universal offense—pathological liars, for instance, don't tend to have many allies.

Different types of energy vampires will also affect us to varying degrees. It might range from bemusement or mild annoyance all the way to post-traumatic stress. It's a very wide spectrum. You often won't know what happened until afterwards.

One thing that's clear, however, is that your own insight into who you are can help you evade the influence of specific types. Self-awareness may well be the key here; it could even be the best protection available against energy vampires.

If you've read any of my books before, you'll know by now that I will, sooner or later, discuss the DISC theory and its four colors. This is a simplified map of human behavior, but it shouldn't be viewed as a full, in-depth understanding of 100 percent of another individual's inner workings. As you make your way through the book, you'll see me refer to this system repeatedly. In a later section, I'll also be giving you more details and explain how the different color types themselves can actually cause you serious energy loss—depending on your own personality.

What sets this book apart from my previous titles is that it focuses on behaviors and mannerisms that don't really have anything to do with the four colors. However, realizing how you function personally will give you important tools for managing different varieties of energy vampires.

Here, though, I'd like to give a brief introduction to the system, just to make sure any readers who have never encountered it before will know how to approach the subject. If you feel that this is all familiar ground to you, feel free to skip ahead, but I'd suggest you give yourself a quick reminder as to who's Red and who's Green and why it's useful to know.

The four colors are based on the widely disseminated DISC theory, which is used in contexts such as recruiting, sales training, and leadership but can also be helpful to individuals seeking to better understand themselves. Personally, I've used this system for more than thirty years, often complementing it with other tools to get a more complete picture.

It's based on the matrix on the following page.

The system divides people into the following categories: introverts versus extroverts, and task-oriented versus relationship-oriented. The various types of behavior are outlined in the image on pg. 20.

Red people tend to gain energy from activity and bustle and from staying on the move. However, they tend to lose energy when people ask them to sit down and relax. Losing control is the worst thing that can happen to them. They are good at handling other people, however they don't feel any particular need for constant company.

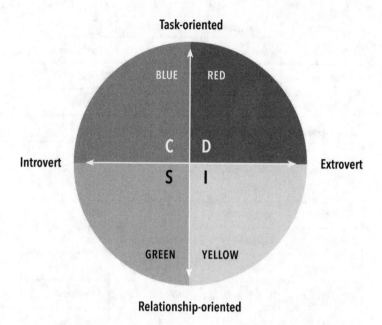

Yellows love to socialize and revel at being the center of everyone's attention. They always like to offer their opinions on things, and they gain energy from bringing about change. The worst energy drain for Yellows is social isolation. It's a severe stressor for them. A lack of human contact can be exhausting for them.

Greens tend to prefer the status quo more than anything. They thrive when everything is the way it usually is. Their most serious energy drainage, as you might expect, is caused by frequent change—it's even worse if the change is random or unmotivated. That can be an incredible stressor for them. They need to have people around them, but not just anyone. They rely on people they know well, who won't stir up any trouble.

RED	YELLOW	GREEN	BLUE
Aggressive	Talkative	Patient	Conscientious
Ambitious	Enthusiastic	Relaxed	Systematic
Strong-willed	Persuasive	Self-controlled	Distant
Goal-oriented	Creative	Reliable	Correct
Pushing	Optimistic	Composed	Conventional
Problem-solver	Social	Loyal	Seems insecure
Pioneer	Spontaneous	Modest	Objective
Decisive	Expressive	Understanding	Structured
Innovator	Charming	Long-winded	Analytical
Impatient	Full of vitality	Stable	Perfectionist
Controlling	Self-centered	Prudent	Needs time
Convincing	Sensitive	Discreet	Reflecting
Performance-oriented	Adaptable	Supportive	Methodical
Powerful	Inspiring	Good listener	Seeks facts
Result-oriented	Needs attention	Helpful	Quality-oriented
Initiator	Encouraging	Producer	Scrutinizes
Speed	Communicative	Persistent	Follows rules
Timekeeper	Flexible	Reluctant	Logical
Intense	Open	Thoughtful	Questioning
Opinionated	Sociable	Conceals feelings	Meticulous
Straightforward	Imaginative	Considerate	Reflecting
Independent	Easygoing	Kind	Reserved

Finally, Blues prefer it when things are neat and orderly. They spend much of their cool and steady energy checking the details. This is where they find security, and being wrong about something, i.e., not being clued in, is probably the worst thing a Blue person can imagine. Other people are more or less a necessary evil, and although Blues can attend parties, they need some time to recuperate afterwards.

As you can no doubt guess, few people will exclusively display only one of these basic personality aspects. The most common arrangement—which covers around 80 percent of individuals, in my experience—is a profile consisting of two colors. Some even possess three. Very few people only exhibit a single color. But they're out there!

As I mentioned, I'll be providing more details on the different colors and how they tend to interact later on in this book. By learning about your own colors, you can also figure out how you will respond to the various kinds of energy vampires you're about to read about. It's simply a matter of knowing yourself.

The main point of reading this book is to help you—regardless of who you are and why—to preserve more of your energy reserves for more important things than just handling people and situations that only complicate your life. That's what this book is about.

Now, while we're on the topic of self-knowledge . . .

While I've been writing this book, I've discovered things about myself I didn't expect to find. What I learned is that although I found doing research and writing about the behaviors of others interesting, the most significant learning experience for me was recognizing aspects of myself in no fewer than two of the complex varieties of energy vampires.

Maybe not to a high degree, but nonetheless, I found tendencies in my behavior that I had never reflected on before. Maybe we're all energy vampires, to some degree, depending on whom we ask? Be that as it may, I definitely possess some rather unflattering traits of the control freak type, which you'll be learning more about in a moment.

It's not exactly something I'm proud of.

It also made me think, because I most definitely don't want to have that kind of effect on the people I interact with.

You might very well have the same experience when you read this book. Some of the descriptions might strike a chord within you. If this happens, don't worry about it; instead, think of it as an opportunity to refine your personality. That's not a bad thing, is it?

This book contains a list of the different types I consider to be the greatest thieves of energy, lust for life, and overall motivation—yours as well as mine. This doesn't mean that there aren't further variations worthy of mention in this rather depressing area, but the following types are the ones I've chosen to focus on in this book.

In the sections discussing some of the more serious issues in the book, I've taken the liberty of inserting some humor in order to lighten things up a little. This isn't an attempt to make light of the problems themselves, but rather to make the text more enjoyable to read and make your way through. I hope you won't mind.

Join me on an exciting journey through a series of everyday situations I'm sure you'll be very familiar with. Keep a notebook handy, or make notes right here in the book. Consider this official permission to do so.

2

The Perfectionist,
an Annoyingly Common Variety

Perfectionists are sticklers for the rules, who can't abide even the slightest deviation from whatever they hold to be 100 percent correct. They are controlling individuals, who use instructions and manuals to bend others to their will. People who belong to this type can display some very abnormal behavior when they have to improvise or don't know the answer to something. These are usually hardworking individuals, who spend a lot of time on precisely the wrong things, in the hope that they will gain recognition for a pedantic streak that seems incomprehensible to most other people. To top it all off, they're often masterful when it comes to concealing their emotions.

This is a fairly common energy vampire. The common variety, though, is a simple, yet simultaneously complex, individual. Can you imagine how frustrating it must be to have to handle a hardworking, extremely diligent individual who does everything right?

THE PERFECTIONIST

Manipulation	Extroversion	Charm	Energy drain
7%	50%	2%	73%

There's really only one sensible reaction to that: *Ewww!*

In the film *Two Weeks Notice,* Hugh Grant's character says the following to Sandra Bullock's: *No one wants to live with a saint. Saints are boring.* Sandra Bullock's character was exactly this type. She did everything right, she never forgot anything, she had every last detail under control, she worked harder than everybody else, and she also made sure nobody else ever overlooked anything. Furthermore, she did it all out of the goodness of her heart, because she was working to protect groups she had labeled "the little people." And everybody hated her for it.

The reason for this was very simple: Bullock's character was a classic example of too much of a good thing. In the mind of a control freak, nothing is ever good enough. Being 100 percent finished with a task just isn't a thing for them. No mistake is too small to be highlighted or have a huge argument over.

This, my friend, is Blue behavior on steroids.

Perfectionists wage a never-ending war on nature, by striving at every level to prevent and eliminate anything they can't predict. Anything unplanned must be swayed, and the slightest diversion from absolute perfection must be corrected. And if hard work isn't enough, there's always harder work. And work they do.

Indeed, nobody works harder and with more discipline than a perfectionist. They simply can't get enough of it.

Besides hard work, their main weapon is an almost pathological ability to adhere to rules, a morbid sense of detail, and an uncanny knack many other people would love to learn: the ability to postpone reward. They're able to leave those until their next life, if necessary. They can stare at the prize and want it more than anything else, but if they don't feel fully deserving yet, because they could have made more effort, they leave it be. It's almost like a kind of masochism.

If they weren't around, entire societies would collapse and absolute chaos would ensue. These are the people who force difficult personalities, narcissists, and bullies to deliver results. The world would be a very different place without them.

However, this doesn't mean that they are entirely unproblematic to interact with.

DANIEL: A CASE STUDY

Daniel always gets his tax returns done on time. He often utters phrases like *a place for everything and everything in its place*. His days always start out with the exact same routine. His alarm clock goes off at 5:30 a.m. He gets out of bed immediately, because that's what you're supposed to do.

He puts on the clothes he laid out in preparation the night before. Then he heads straight down to his coffeemaker and presses the button. He prepared the filter and coffee beans the night before.

He lets his dog out into the yard and waits for exactly four minutes. If he were to give the dog less time to do what it needs to, it might not have time to finish, and if he allowed it more time, it might come up with something else to do. So he calls his dog back inside after four minutes and fetches its food from the pantry.

When the dog has settled down, Daniel says, *Enjoy,* and the dog eats its food. It immediately lunges for its water bowl while Daniel takes the feeding bowl and washes it with the special dish brush he uses exclusively for this purpose. He would never even consider using the ordinary dish brush, because dogs and humans don't have the same bacterial flora. He can name at least three different afflictions that might spread from animal to human if proper dish brush hygiene is not observed.

His coffee is made, and he pours it into the same cup he uses every morning.

He makes his breakfast. Three eggs, all the same size, are boiled in the same saucepan, for exactly six minutes. He sets a timer and settles down to drink his coffee and keep an eye on his watch. He makes sure to make the coffee last for the entire time it takes to cook the eggs.

While he waits for the eggs, he notes with a frown that somebody has left a used coffee cup on the countertop. He washes it—with the ordinary dish brush—and then places it in the dishwasher.

The eggs are finished. Daniel rinses them under cold water for exactly three minutes and then leaves them in the pan for another three. He eats his eggs from the same eggcup as usual, sitting in the same chair he always sits in.

Now he pours a cup of coffee for his wife. Before leaving the kitchen, he takes a quick look around to make sure nothing is wrong. All the chairs are neatly pushed up to the table, and all the surfaces are wiped. *Excellent*. He does all this even if he happens to be running late for work. He simply can't stop himself.

He walks upstairs to the bathroom and knocks on the door, because that's what you're supposed to do, even if you happen to have been married for fourteen years. When his wife responds with a sigh, he enters and places the cup on her end of the vanity.

While his wife gets ready, he meticulously makes the bed. Daniel stretches the sheets out diligently and notes to himself that they seem to have gone wrinkly sooner than usual this time. He makes a note on his phone to remind him to examine the iron tonight. Now he fetches a rag from the bathroom and dusts his nightstand. He does this every morning. However, he doesn't touch his wife's nightstand, for two simple reasons: mainly, because watching him dust it *again* makes her angry, but secondly, it's because her nightstand is littered with stuff.

When Daniel comes back down to the kitchen, his wife is reading the news on her phone. He wrinkles his nose. The reason for his annoyance is that both of his teenagers always used to sit around and stare at their phones all the time and it made them impossible to talk to. Daniel and his wife negotiated a solution to the problem two years ago. They were in absolute agreement. No cell phones at the dinner table. Daniel has never broken this agreement, but everybody else has on at least a few occasions.

He points this out to his wife: *I thought we agreed not to use our phones at the kitchen table?* She answers that this was a deal they made with the teenagers years ago. Daniel simply can't accept that—they had an agreement, and you only make agreements for one single reason: to honor them.

After all, after having pointed out to his wife how dirty her car was and having a long argument about the value of a clean car, he did promise to wash and clean out her car every Saturday morning, and he had done that ever since. Summer and winter alike—every Saturday morning, he washes her car, whether it's dirty or not. Agreements exist to be honored.

He simply can't let go of her using the phone at the table, and they end up having a loud argument. By the time they need to leave for work, they're both in an awful mood. Daniel dryly notes that this is their twelfth serious disagreement this year.

WHEN CONTROL FREAKS GO TOO FAR

Obsessive-compulsive disorder, or OCD, is a clinical diagnosis. An individual who suffers from this will feel compelled to think a certain way or do things in a particular way. Doing things any other way causes anxiety. The possible consequences are of secondary importance—they could involve real problems as well as imagined ones. It's more a matter of how creative the individual can be when it comes to imagining all the hellish things that might happen.

Of course, we all have thoughts and ideas we feel compelled to act on from time to time. For instance, we might go back and check that we locked the front door or make sure the stove is turned off. These are entirely reasonable behaviors. Personally, I always put my hand in my pocket to feel for my house keys before I shut the front door, even when I put them in the same pocket only fifteen seconds ago.

Why do I do that? Who knows? Perhaps I'm worried I might have failed to notice them falling to the floor through a hole in my pocket. Perhaps I'm afraid that the "Great Key Thief" might have struck again and brazenly teleported my keys from my pocket to the "Wasteland of Missing Keys." I really don't know.

However, if that compulsion had an excessive effect on my behavior, I might be suffering from OCD.

The symptoms of obsessive-compulsive disorder are often described as *obsessions* (thoughts) and *compulsions* (behaviors). Both of these are presumed to increase in intensity the *more* somebody worries or tries to *avoid* them.

Obsessions are unwanted thoughts or fantasies that come to mind. Examples of this could be anxiety over not having locked the door or not having turned the stove off. It's often a fear of unwittingly causing harm to someone. The thoughts could revolve around being worried about causing a terrible event of some sort.

But other examples could be germaphobia and fears of various diseases.

Compulsions are the behaviors people rely on to soothe their anxiety when their obsessions have been triggered. They involve feeling that a particular behavior must be carried out, in a particular way, to prevent the obsessive thoughts from being actualized. Perhaps the sufferer will wash their hands or shower for a very long time, to allay a fear of dirt or bacteria. Others might sort or count things in a very specific way until everything feels completely right.

Naturally, all these behaviors can get in the way of living a normal life.

However, and just as naturally, they don't always.

We're discussing the extremes here. Perfectionists don't have any sort of diagnosable condition, nor are tidy people or those who always double-check the lock on their door suffering from OCD. Perfectionists display distinctive, compulsive behaviors, but not to the extent where their lives would be disrupted or they would require any sort of treatment.

How to Spot a Compulsive Perfectionist

I've made a list of points to consider when trying to determine whether somebody might be a perfectionist. Since this isn't an exact science, your own opinions and personal preferences will be important considerations and it will be important to try to make the most unbiased judgments you can. If the person you're assessing has already become the object of some personal antipathy on your part, you might want to ask somebody else to give you their opinions before you come to a verdict. Unfortunately, we're all prone to judging people we don't like too harshly.

Here is a list of statements to label either true or false. One point for true, no points for false. Here we go! This person . . .

1. deems it necessary to point out every possible flaw
2. doesn't like to admit to their own mistakes
3. rarely displays emotion
4. has a hard time finishing tasks
5. keeps their promises

6. is a genuine workaholic
7. never takes time off
8. adheres to a strict ethical and moral code
9. micromanages others
10. takes longer to prepare for a task than to actually perform it

Well, well. How many points did you give them? If they scored more than five points, we can probably presume that this person is a bit of a control freak. We can probably call them a perfectionist if they scored eight points. If they scored even higher than that, don't expect anything you do to ever be good enough. Remember, though, this is just meant to give you an indication.

Perfection at All Costs

Imagine that you have to do something that's going to be absolutely critical for your future. A test at school, a presentation at work, a paper to hand in at university, or the most important job interview you'll ever have. This is the moment!

You prepare extremely well, in minute detail. You can feel your adrenaline kick in at the mere thought of messing it up. You simply can't afford to have this go wrong.

Can you imagine what it would be like to feel that way every single workday?

This is more or less how a habitual perfectionist approaches every single task in their life.

In studies of habitual perfectionists, an interesting pattern has emerged, and certain personality traits have been found to be more prominent than others. For example, these individuals are less indulgent than the rest of us when it comes to leisure activities. They don't enjoy spending a whole Saturday in front of the television. Regardless of how fascinating a new show might be, they prefer to spend their time on more important things. They don't rest, even when they've earned a break. If, on rare occasions, they make themselves stay in front of the television for some reason, their conscience will be gnawing at them.

I should be doing something else right now.

What is this "something else" they feel compelled to do? The answer is simple: work. Work is their passion in life, their only true joy in life, their only salvation from their own demons. Sometimes this attitude can actually border on the obsessive.

Their focus on work is simultaneously a gift and a curse. Working makes them feel safe, like they're successfully keeping chaos at bay. If you want to feel comfortable in their company and avoid feeling judged . . . the best approach is to work. Hard. For long hours.

It seems entirely plausible to me that the phrase *failing to see the forest for the trees* could have been coined by somebody who just had a confusing encounter with a habitual perfectionist. Their fevered attention to detail is the stuff of legend. People around them, whose attitude towards minor details is less rigid, have reported how fixated these energy vampires can actually get. They often skip from one detail to the next, turning everything inside out to uncover every last flaw. When people say that the Devil (or God) is in the details, they're not overstating the facts in this case. Perfectionists often display a shocking lack of ability to combine all these small things into a big picture.

Striving for Divine Perfection

Sometimes you can get the idea that achieving absolute perfection is somehow a divine virtue. However, this attitude can
cause problems, as nobody will ever satisfy the demands of
perfectionists. This includes the perfectionists themselves, by
the way. They tend to be every bit as hard on themselves as
they are on all the other sinners they encounter. If not harder.

This leads to the whole team having an endless list of
vaguely defined tasks that must be executed to perfection,
which causes a great deal of frustration. The team is frustrated by the demands for perfection, and the perfectionist is
frustrated by their failure to achieve it.

THE RELIABLE ENERGY VAMPIRE

Out of all the types of energy vampires, the perfectionist is
without a doubt the most reliable. They keep their promises.
Failing to do so would be a mortal sin, and they pursue their
moral and ethical agendas beyond all reason. But by George,
you can rely on them. Their word is practically as good as a
legally binding document. They're also very honest, even when
the truth they're delivering is a painful one. The reason for this
is that they don't really believe anything can ever be absolutely
perfect. There's no point trying to convince you or me to try to
achieve the unachievable. *As they see it, only the gods are perfect.*

They might as well speak out and tell it like it is.

It didn't work out.

You've probably heard the expression *anal retentive,* and
you may even have used it about somebody before. However,
like myself, you may have wondered where it comes from.

One of the founders of modern psychology, Sigmund Freud, stated that some people had been exposed to excessively strict potty training early on in their lives. As a result, they learned to subdue . . . let's say, their natural needs. In their adulthood, this need for control has spread to every area of their lives. Everything has to be controlled, all the way to the molecular level. It's their way of maintaining a grasp on reality. They want to use the you-know-what when they feel like it, not when their bodies tell them it's time.

What are the consequences, then? Habitual perfectionists seek to coerce themselves to suppress inappropriate behavior. They've made an art form out of not displaying anything at all. Like emotions, for instance.

Nothing can reach them on an emotional level anymore. What remains is an all-encompassing adherence to logic, efficient thinking, and a strict avoidance of mushy and sentimental displays.

Facts, rationality, perfection. Finally!

Control freaks give themselves quite a hard time, so we may actually have to be compassionate towards them. They suffer from this constant feeling that they've overlooked something, that something is about to go awry, and that they don't know quite what it is.

This induces a constant state of alertness that I can only presume must be exhausting to maintain. This is caused by the amygdala, a part of the brain that controls our *flight*, *fight*, and *freeze* reactions. Once, when we lived on the plains, it was necessary for our survival, but now it actually disturbs our inner peace. In most parts of the world, our survival no longer relies on these reactions.

However, habitual perfectionists haven't managed to shake off the effects of these primeval functions at all. To this very day, they remain constantly alert to risk, danger, and everything else that threatens to go wrong. Try to imagine having to stay sharp, always scanning the world for potential problems from morning to evening, constantly afraid of what might happen if you lower your defenses, even just a little. Add to this the feeling that you're the only person who is trying to plan for and avoid all these dangers, in order to protect everyone from them—only to be mocked for doing so.

Welcome to the everyday existence of a habitual perfectionist.

That's why they mutter, huff and puff, and roll their eyes when they witness others going through their oblivious existences, without maintaining any degree of alertness to unknown dangers.

Being Just a Little Pregnant

If you're not good, you're bad. That's the way it works, unfortunately.

There are only two ethical values: right and wrong.

For a habitual perfectionist, this is as logical as the answer to the question of whether somebody is pregnant. You can't be a *little bit* pregnant. Or 50 percent pregnant. Either you're pregnant or you aren't.

When somebody asks you if you've finished a task, this means, then, that there are only two acceptable responses: Either you've *finished* the task or you *haven't*. The same applies to all areas of moral ambiguity: Either a certain behavior is right or it's wrong. There's nothing in between. The people who witness this attitude tend to find it rather ignorant, and sometimes even intolerant.

And while these perfectionists struggle to bring order out of chaos, everybody else seems to them to be doing nothing but producing more chaos. Now, everyone has their specific set of basic values, regardless of whether they're fully aware of them or not. We all have concepts and beliefs that are so strongly rooted in our personalities that they aren't up for negotiation or reassessment.

There are a lot of these kinds of beliefs in circulation in our society today. Justice issues revolving around the concepts of gender, class, ethnicity, who's the victim of this or that. Not to mention anything to do with climate issues. Or what is or is not an appropriate subject for a joke. If you lean far enough in either direction on one of these questions, it's simply impossible to convince you otherwise.

Habitual perfectionists, in particular, are practically impossible to discuss these things with. Assurances that you meant no harm simply won't cut it in their world. If it's wrong, it's wrong, even if nobody else cares about it in the slightest.

Let me give you a simple example of this.

Whenever I got caught in a fight in school, my dad always used to tell me that violence is a sign that you've lost the argument. I could never keep my mouth shut, and this got me into trouble with alarming frequency. On top of that, I wasn't that good at fighting. As a result, I am opposed to all violence and firmly believe that conflicts should always be resolved through communication.

This is the origin of one of my own most important basic values: Violence is wrong. In essence, I think that everybody would agree with that.

But then, of course, there is the problematic question of self-defense. We all know, of course, that some situations can require extraordinary remedies.

What if somebody jumps you in the city and tries to steal your belongings? Then what should you do? The only way out of that situation is to put up some resistance.

Our habitual perfectionist friends also have basic values, which are often so strongly held that they can seem absolutely inflexible. This is where difficulties can arise. Once their minds are made up, that's it. No exceptions. But what are the consequences of that mindset?

If violence is always wrong, how could it possibly be right in some cases?

It's an immediate dead end.

One challenge habitual perfectionists struggle with is their strong sense of antipathy for anybody who fails to hold themselves to the same exacting moral standards that they do. Their ideals are very demanding, and failing to live up to them will immediately bring them to pass judgment on you and your unacceptable weakness.

In fact, practically *everybody* else is deserving of nothing but scorn in their eyes: We don't work as hard as they do to achieve the same degree of perfection, we're less ethical and moral, and we live our lives the wrong way.

Habitual perfectionists, however, tend to try to deceive themselves about this fact, because they realize that contempt for others is actually an immoral and negative mindset.

Nonetheless, it's the mindset they have, and you can bet that it will make itself known in some rather horrendous ways. You'll feel it when it happens.

Dissatisfaction.

Hostility.

Contempt.

You're just not good enough.

This is more than just discouraging; it also robs people of energy, time, and actual resources. A quick look at Daniel's behavior will reveal how an entire organization can suffer the effects of this behavior:

> *When Daniel comes to work and sees how chaotic everything is, his pain is obvious. Papers, pens, electrical cords, Post-it notes, different digital accessories like chargers, headphones, and other stuff are piled up on all the desks. Worse, perhaps, are the flagrant transgressions against the most recent workplace policy: family pictures.*
>
> *Not everybody in the workplace has a family, you know. Pictures of partners, wives, husbands, and children could cause others to feel inadequate, and Daniel doesn't want that. Some people can't even have children, after all. Now, it's not as though he's ever heard anybody actually complain about this, but he still decides, then and there, to clarify the policy for everyone by bringing up two points.*
>
> *Once he reaches his own desk, he pens a lengthy email that offers detailed recommendations as to how a workplace should actually look. He places particular emphasis on photos of family members, and the injustice of*

displaying them. Daniel is very aware of the fact that he's walking a moral tightrope here, but he can't help it. This is the compulsive part of his personality.

The kitchen. The dishes in the sink. The crumbs on the seats. There are no fewer than seven notices posted in the kitchen, all written by Daniel himself, providing guidelines as to what behavior is or isn't acceptable in that space.

He tidies up the kitchen to his satisfaction and then returns to his seat. The fact that his performing these tasks is an incredible waste of corporate resources, considering his hourly rate, is of no consequence to him.

At half past eight, everybody seems to have arrived.

Daniel notes that his email appears to have been particularly unappreciated. He sees angry faces over the desks. Somebody sends out an email with instructions on how to sit down on a chair without stirring up too much dust and contaminating the communal air supply. There are captivating, detailed descriptions of how best to shift one's weight from the feet to the behind. All in all, it's a very funny read. However, like most habitual perfectionists, Daniel has a hard time laughing at himself.

Instead, he writes a new email to the sender, admonishing them for wasting valuable work time on frivolous activities.

His first meeting is with Linda, who wants to discuss the preparations for the launch of a new project. She has a draft of a plan printed and ready to go. It shouldn't take more than an hour to finish the plan itself, but discussing it takes twice that, because Daniel can't resist turning every single sentence of Linda's document inside out.

He knows what he's doing is wrong, again. He's read all the books. He's taken the class; he was in the seminar. Hell, he's even been coached by an external consultant on how to overcome his perfectionism. However, he just can't help himself.

Linda allows him to correct her typos and syntax and make some other edits. She also accepts his expansion of the number of stages in the plan from seven to twelve. By the time lunchtime comes around, Daniel has worked himself into a sweat, but he hasn't accomplished as much all morning as he ought to be able to do in ten minutes.

An ethos I've always made a point of promoting is the one that getting anywhere in life will take some work. After all, the world owes you absolutely nothing and the people who put in the effort are the ones who end up finding success. This is true whether you're a nurse whose ambition is to give every patient the best possible care or an entrepreneur with ten thousand people working for you. Regardless of your own definition of success, you're going to have to roll your sleeves up to achieve it. (Naturally, this isn't the case if you think of success as lying around on the couch watching television. That particular ambition won't require as much effort.)

This is a truth that bullies, narcissists, melodramatic individuals, and passive-aggressive types would rather stay ignorant of. These people would much rather reap the rewards of life without having to work for them. However, perfectionists, or control freaks, have actually got this part right. They're fully prepared to work hard and take on any challenge. Nobody can take that away from them.

Adopting a somewhat perfectionist attitude to life in general and paying lots of attention to the details could very well be a useful approach.

The question is just how much is too much. This is an excellent question that perfectionists themselves are utterly unable to answer. Unlike many others, they actually have the right mindset for taking on work tasks they don't find enjoyable at all. They feel it makes sense to ignore their own lack of motivation, and they pass ruthless judgment on anybody who can't live up to these demands.

But where does it end? When have you worked too hard or become . . . too excellent?

I wonder if there's really a good answer to that. The line between Blue conscientiousness and habitual perfectionism must be drawn somewhere, of course, but nobody has yet managed to discover the exact right place.

There are some clues, however.

One of the more important ones is realizing the difference between *what* you're doing and *how* you're doing it.

WHY PEOPLE BECOME PERFECTIONISTS

A natural and interesting question at this point is what motivates this kind of behavior? Why do control freaks go to all this trouble? What is it that makes them unable to take life less seriously and approach it with the more reasonable attitude most of us hold?

The answer may have to do with their drives. Our drives, or motivational factors, provide the fuel we need in order to keep going when things get tough. Drives can be positive—e.g., a desire to be rich and famous and live to a dreadfully old age—or negative, as is the case with these individuals.

Perfectionists are motivated by fear.

Fear of making mistakes. Fear of failure. Fear of being exposed as fully normal people, with pathetic flaws and weaknesses. Fear of being found to hold anything but the highest and finest of moral and ethical ideals.

If they make the smallest of mistakes, their whole ambitiously structured universe can crumble in an instant, and all kinds of horrors might sneak in through the cracks. They try to overcome the things they know they have hidden deep inside. Of course, they're well aware that they're not really perfect and that they have a long list of flaws and weaknesses just like everybody else. They just don't like acknowledging that fact.

Perfectionists want to be the best at everything. They want to be the ones who always get it right and who have the best work ethic of any of us. But the best work ethic isn't always enough for them; some of them also go for the even bigger target of living the most perfect and morally impeccable life any human being could ever live. Basically, they want to be a cut above everybody else and, annoyingly (for everyone else), they're prepared to work to earn that distinction.

They champion the causes of the weakest members of society and paint people as victims who can't manage on their own. Perhaps they do charity work or vigilantly promote some social issue or other. Of course, not everybody who engages with important moral and ethical questions is a perfectionist and not all perfectionists are dedicated do-gooders. It could be any subject, really; the important thing is the obsession they develop for it once they've discovered their particular field.

How could anyone compete with that? Also, and most important, how do we handle these habitual perfectionists?

Feeling Sloppy

So what are the consequences of this behavior? The most common reaction in people who have been in contact with habitual perfectionists is a strong sense of *uncertainty*. Basically, they don't know if what they've done will be deemed acceptable. Or—and this is even worse—if they will be deemed acceptable themselves.

Will I avoid criticism? Am I doing this right? What if they give me that sullen, disappointed look in response to my efforts?

Their insecurity grows stronger, to the point where it could bring their entire system to a halt. Often, the result of this will be passivity. Nobody dares to make a move, for fear of getting their fingers slapped.

However, there is an even more diabolical consequence: Being under a watchful eye like that all the time doesn't just pacify people; it undermines their confidence, too. This causes a huge amount of wasted potential in people who are actually very capable. A lack of confidence can be highly problematic, as it isn't genuinely connected to actual competence.

I'm sure you've been in some situation where you've known exactly what to do but chose not to do it because you felt insecure. So you waited. And waited. For someone to guide you. But you really knew what to do all along.

This is the most obvious problem control freaks cause for the people around them. Besides common irritation, of course.

It makes people feel that they're worthless. It can be a blow to their self-esteem. If it happens in a workplace, people will eventually not want to work there. If it happens in a relationship, well, let's just say there are people out there who don't mind taking long detours on their way home. When you've come to expect nothing but criticism and negative comments, what's the point of even trying anymore?

It's not overly dramatic to say that it can cause psychological issues that require treatment before they go out of control.

Red, Yellow, Green, Blue—Let's Get Ready to Rumble!

Now, not everybody responds the same way to this behavior. The degree of insecurity it causes will vary somewhat, depending on your colors and other things. I'd like to go over this one color at a time and remind you before I begin that as I wrote earlier, most people's personalities actually combine two of the colors. This means that most of them will respond in a way that blends the standard reactions of different colors. On top of this, every situation is unique and you can never predict exactly how a certain person is going to react.

It's no wild guess that both Reds and Yellows will feel like they're getting hives whenever they're near a perfectionist. They already have serious trouble dealing with Blue behavior, and if it goes overboard, like in this case, lots of conflicts will result. The spontaneous and mercurial nature of an extrovert will inevitably collide with the perfectionist's absolute demand for rigid discipline. Red-Yellow or Yellow-Red doesn't make much of a difference in this case. It just doesn't work very well.

Purely Red individuals don't just dislike taking orders; they hate the very idea that someone else could have power over them. When the order seems absolutely nonsensical, they'll blow a fuse. They'll lose it and refuse to play along. Their egos can't handle being told what to do. Perfectionists are bound to be told in no uncertain terms how the Red feels about them, and it's possible they won't be able to work with each other at all.

Now, a Red person will certainly work like a maniac in their attempts to please the control freak, but once they realize that there's no point trying, they will cease all efforts and decide to spend their time on something else. Often, this insight will also trigger powerful fits of rage.

Purely Yellow individuals will be deeply frustrated. It's not so much that they mind taking orders, but more a matter of failing to carry out any instructions properly. They'll forget what's going on, to put it simply. Their attempts to keep the nine principles for tidying their room front of mind will fail ridiculously. Whenever the perfectionist is not around, the Yellow individuals will make the most imaginatively insulting comments about them. Because if there's one thing Yellow people are prone to do, it's talk about people behind their backs. It's not really gossiping per se; it's more a case of Yellows failing to keep their mouths shut. All that frustration will find a way out somehow, sooner or later. This will not facilitate further cooperation.

The Yellow will begin to fabricate fantastic excuses for why the results ended up this way or that. They're basically a terrible match with control freaks. Constant criticism is a huge drain on Yellows, who tend to have fairly bright and positive self-images. Excessive perfectionism stifles their creativity and will run the risk of making them feel mentally paralyzed and depressed.

If we head over to the introverted side, the reactions will differ mainly depending on whether somebody's personality is dominated by Blue or Green, i.e., whether they are task- or relationship-oriented.

Purely Green individuals are quite agreeable, but they also possess passive traits that will cause them to nod in agreement but then raise a silent protest by dragging their heels.

However, having a clear framework to work within can be good for Greens. They find it restful when someone else has already done all the thinking and all they need to focus on is the actual doing. It's not that Greens have fewer opinions or ideas about how the work should be done or how the trip should be planned, but they decidedly have less of a need to voice their views. In smaller groups where the Greens feel a lot of trust, however, they will make their feelings known before things get out of hand. However, there's no guarantee that the perfectionist will ever even notice. Depending on how intimidating the perfectionist is, the Green will tend to fold when conflict looms. They prefer to avoid that kind of thing and will go along with the most absurd instructions to keep the peace.

In the end, however, Blue individuals represent the greatest challenge a habitual perfectionist can face. These two types have many characteristics in common; there's no denying that. Both of them focus on the process rather than the goal. But while a Blue tends to appreciate details, facts, and quality, a perfectionist takes this attitude way too far. Although Blues will seem like perfectionists, particularly to Reds and Yellows, Blues can still be reasoned with. Facts and evidence can convince them what's right and what's wrong. It might take a while, but once they see the truth for what it is, the issue will be resolved. They'll get in line.

Perfectionists, on the other side, won't always be able to properly explain why things have to be a certain way. This challenge stems from their obsessive nature. They won't be able to provide solid evidence and will simply insist on their way *just because*. Blues will calmly and matter-of-factly explain at length why a certain course of action is worth pursuing. A perfectionist who doesn't officially hold power over a Blue might not make any headway with them at all. Blue individuals also have a knack for ignoring things they've decided are silly.

This isn't to say a Blue can't be forced to back down, just that factual arguments are the way to genuinely convince them. Habitual perfectionists simply can't let go of their ideas, because, well, they're obsessions.

This sets the scene for a truly epic struggle.

HOW PERFECTIONISTS CAN AWAKEN YOUR INNER TEENAGER

So what can we do about this? And how do we do it? This also makes for a great segue to one of the most important realizations you need to make about habitual perfectionists.

When people keep interfering with and commenting on everything you do, it's possible that this will make you feel like a sullen teenager. You'll be sure that you know best (while teenagers don't actually know best, this is more about the feeling, which I'm sure you recognize), and any attempts to inform you of things you find self-evident will do nothing but irritate you. Everybody else is wrong, actually. End of discussion.

But sometimes the person who is critiquing your efforts will actually have a point. There's almost nothing more frustrating than that. Most of us probably have a hibernating inner teen, who still longs for nothing more than an opportunity to rebel against everyone and everything.

A habitual perfectionist will often be the trigger for these negative and highly familiar emotions. Raging conflict will be in the air, waiting to be sparked by the slightest misstep.

I'm not going to say conflict is always unnecessary, but sometimes we do want to avoid it to save time or spare ourselves a headache. And in those situations, it can help to be aware of your own reactions. Instead of shouting at someone that they *just don't get it* and running off to your room and slamming the door, you'll simply have to remind yourself that you're an adult now and that people expect you to react accordingly.

It sucks. I know. But there's no getting around it.

Do All Roads Really Lead to Rome?

There's a famous idiom: *All roads lead to Rome*. This expression is usually used to express the thought that different methods or approaches to a task can all lead to the same results in the end. And if there's anything we all want, it's results, right?

Let's say a small team, just a few people, is about to take on a project. This team could exist in a work setting, but it could also be your family, or the neighbors on your street. Perhaps a soccer or chess club. The task could be a specific work project, but it could also just as well be something that needs doing in the home. You can let your imagination decide here; the principles will be the same, regardless. The task can be divided into two components:

1. *What* needs to be done.
2. And *how* we are going to do it.

Generally, what needs to be done isn't very complicated. We're setting up a new client database or expanding the back deck. We decide what needs to be done together. Everybody agrees. This is the desired outcome. In most situations, the individuals within the team with the most suitable skill set will be assigned the various tasks X, Y, and Z.

This is important to remember: *What* we're doing and *how* we're doing it aren't the same thing. One is related to the *desired outcome* for the work, and the other is related to the *process* that will take us there.

We *want* the new client database to be up and running and contain all the necessary data.

We *want* the new deck to be installed, measure twenty-five by thirty feet, and have a roof over it.

We *want* our new car to be washed and cleaned out before our vacation.

We *want* to organize our books in such a way that we can actually find the specific book we're looking for.

We *want* everyone to feel respected and acknowledged in the workplace.

What matters here is the result. The specific *method* used to achieve said result is secondary.

However, habitual perfectionists can't separate these two

things, and this means that it all gets jumbled into a long, never-ending list of miserable duties. For them, the question of *how* can actually seem more important than the question of *what*. Doing it the right way takes precedence over getting it done. If it won't get done right—i.e., in accordance with their own, superhuman expectations—it might not even be worth doing at all.

You're right! It does sound kind of backwards.

Asking them questions about the *what* can help them maintain their focus on the task. Constantly reminding them of the overall purpose can make things easier. What are we doing? The back deck. The client database. An organized book collection. A marketing campaign.

It can be difficult to keep habitual perfectionists away from the details. They'll try to interfere with everything related to the *how,* even when you know perfectly well what to do to get it done. This applies to a husband who interferes with your gardening, a manager who interferes with how you perform your work tasks—even if you are definitely the best at this specific task.

The key to handling them is simple:

Negotiate the terms first.

Once that's done, the rest of the journey will be much easier.

For example, consider a boss who keeps nagging you about the details until you just want to scream. As my own specialty is leadership, I do want to note: Sometimes a colleague will need instructions for how to best go about a specific task. This could be true of a new employee or when somebody is about to take on something new that they've never done before. In those situations, details about what, when, how, and with whom will be necessary in order for everyone to agree on what good execution of the task looks like.

The people involved will also need specific, hands-on feedback on their efforts. A lot of follow-up will be required. Instructing and giving feedback aren't the wrong ways to lead others. It comes down to how you do it, when you do it, and to whom you do it. Most of your colleagues have a pretty good grasp of how to get the job done.

However, habitual control freaks treat everybody as though they were absolute beginners.

In order to combat that, it's crucial to agree on what the final outcome should be, perhaps even in great detail, and then just get it done. Whenever a manager begins to gripe about the how, go back to the agreed target and tell them, *I'll be delivering what we agreed on, by the agreed date.*

This works pretty well, assuming you actually do what you're supposed to. If you let the quality slip, miss your deadlines, and start coming up with excuses, you'll end up in serious trouble.

All of this applies to habitual perfectionists who seem to think they're your boss, too. They could be your significant other, one of your parents, the coach of the soccer team, or the organizer of this weekend's fundraiser for child hunger. They might all succumb to the temptation to interfere with how you do something. Make sure to keep them out of your hair.

This attitude can also work well in a domestic setting.

Make sure to negotiate the terms first.

If your partner happens to exhibit some of these unflattering behaviors, you should make a point of negotiating *who* is to be responsible for the new deck, organizing *all* the bookshelves, or, for that matter, spring cleaning the car. This will make it more likely that you'll get to do your work in peace.

Unlike the other energy vampires in this book, this particular type has a strong inner sense of justice. They value playing by the rules, and if they've agreed to a certain set of terms they'll respect those terms.

The best approach, then, is to negotiate the terms before anybody so much as picks up a hammer. You need to reach an agreement on the "what"—leave the "how" out of it. The question of how shouldn't be in the contract at all, as long as you're reasonably competent when it comes to installing decking boards or washing cars.

Regardless of who you're dealing with, they're bound to try to interfere at some point. When this happens, simply remind them of your verbal contract. No system is absolutely perfect, but this will significantly improve your ability to work together.

When Negotiations Hit a Dead End

Sometimes, though, negotiating ahead of time won't be enough. Depending on how serious the control freak's issues are, they might very well turn up and get in your way anyway. If this happens, you'll need more tools in your kit.

To start with, I'd recommend not using the phrase "control freak" to describe them. They won't appreciate it, and it will only cause unnecessary friction.

The best way to handle a habitual perfectionist, in the end, is to focus on their positive traits. They do have them, after all, and that's more than you can say for some of the other varieties of energy vampires I'll discuss in this book. While narcissists are decidedly bad company and bullies can actually be dangerous to get too close to, perfectionists are really only irritating in the grand scheme of things. They're frustrating, but they can be handled.

The Double-Edged Nature of Praise

Most of us like to receive praise and positive feedback. For various reasons, many seek to deny this by saying things like, *I don't need recognition from others! I always do my best!*

While I'm not trying to deny that people who genuinely don't need affirmation might exist, I do believe they're incredibly rare. Feedback can be given in different ways, of course—while a Red individual wants to hear about the great results they've achieved, a Blue might prefer to hear about their world-class sense of excellence. A Yellow will like to focus on how what they've done has won appreciation from others, while a Green enjoys knowing they contribute to the team's stability and happiness.

However, habitual perfectionists often fail to seize opportunities to deliver supportive feedback. There are two reasons for this. On the one hand, they aren't that great at relationships. They don't understand the needs of others very well. They focus more on keeping an eye out for all the potential disasters that might occur.

On the other hand, they don't often see something they deem worthy of praise. Most people will eventually miss *something,* and when this happens it will only confirm the perfectionist's suspicions: *You don't know what you're doing. No praise for you!*

Negative feedback has more of an impact than positive feedback. It's been estimated that people need four or five positive comments for every negative one they receive in order to not feel discouraged. Regardless of whether that's actually correct, you shouldn't expect to receive any ovations, standing or otherwise, from a habitual perfectionist.

The thing to do, instead, is to ask for positive feedback. You'll simply have to swallow your pride and explain to them that it's important to you. It's a good idea to avoid emotive pleas like *You never say anything nice to me!* Instead, you should emphasize what you've both agreed to about achieving the outcome.

You might take some comfort from the fact that habitual perfectionists tend to be at least as critical of themselves as they are of others.

As I just mentioned, it's important to make sure all the terms are established before any actual work begins. To see this in action, let's return to Daniel, whose life revolves largely around trying to take control of just about everything and everyone. Take special note of the things he reacts to and how Linda handles him:

Daniel gets along with the various members of the team to varying degrees. For example, he and Anna are only barely on friendly terms.

Anna is seemingly unable to do anything on time. She doesn't listen to instructions or good, friendly advice. Worse still, she talks back.

When he wants a report on her latest sales meeting, she simply tells him nothing of note occurred. When he demands a report all the same, Anna loses her temper instantly. She can be quite disrespectful, often calling him a control freak or a hopeless micromanager. Now, Anna is a very good salesperson. But she is frustratingly disorganized.

She also has an unpleasant habit of making jokes at the expense of others, a behavior Daniel can't abide. It goes against office policy, and we can't have that.

Linda's sales performance is nothing like Anna's, but Linda is wise enough to observe the rules of the game. She allows her manager Daniel to go over every last thing in painstaking detail. Whenever he can't help interfering with the details, she gently reminds him about what they agreed upon. You see, she saves printed copies of all their communication, so it's very easy for her to go back and see what they discussed.

Linda always brings him her reports, in writing, before he's even asked for them. They're always five times longer than Anna's.

He asks everyone on the team questions about all sorts of things, and while Anna and several others tend to get emotional and gesture wildly, Linda always remains calm. Linda also has a knack for detecting when he's anxious that something is going to go wrong. Sometimes she'll even sit down with him and look for errors in her own materials.

Linda takes notes all the time. That's the only way she can remember things. He is very appreciative of the fact that Linda takes what he says and their agreements seriously.

Anna never writes anything down at all. All she does is tap her temple and claim she never forgets anything. But, of course, she always does forget, the moment she leaves the room.

However, the most important thing about Linda is the fact that she delivers. She never makes a promise she can't keep, and she always seems to work very hard. If only Anna would put in the same effort Linda does, there's no telling how far she could go.

Sometimes it actually makes Daniel angry that Anna sells so well despite being so all over the place. And, secretly, he wishes she would stick to the rules flawlessly even if it had a negative impact on her performance.
Rules exist to be followed, after all.

This is how you should handle somebody—whether they are your manager or not—who is a habitual perfectionist. Your job will be to accept them as they are. I'm not suggesting this will be easy, but the choice is always there.

You can let their stifling focus on insignificant details bother you, or you can humor them. You can hand in extremely comprehensive reports brimming with cross-references to everything under the sun, or you can hurl complaints at them for being control freaks.

You can tell your partner he's a big fool for being unable to settle for giving the house a quick tidying up before guests come over—you know, running the vacuum over the most exposed parts of the floor and wiping the faucet clean in the bathroom that you expect your visitors to use—rather than setting up an extensive schedule and involving the entire extended family in a three-day display of diligence that ensures every square inch of your home will be polished to a sparkle. Or you can also tell him that his approach is fine with you, as long as he lets you focus on your own priorities.

Always remember what the desired outcome is. *What*

needs to get done. That's the key. Don't lose yourself in minutiae in your eagerness to play along. If you have an agreement
in place with your partner that the house is to be presentable
when people come over, but not more than that—stick to the
agreement! Don't let him get away with cleaning the sink in
the laundry room with a toothbrush.

The good thing about these energy vampires, as I've
mentioned a couple of times but would like to emphasize
one last time, is that they're not out to get you. They're not
trying to hold you back on purpose, and that's more than
you can say about some of the types in this book. The fact
that they still do hold you back sometimes and give you
headaches, hives, and a terrible mood is the result of the
intensity they can't control.

They often truly believe that what they're doing is actually helping make your life better. And that's not too bad,
really.

3

Drama Queens Who Demand Red Carpets

The melodramatic energy vampire delights in causing mischief and disturbances and actually gains energy by acting out. Drama queens love to cause crises and catastrophes, as this makes them feel important and special, while also enabling them to avoid the genuine challenges life brings. More than anything, they thrive on attention, and they're prepared to go to great lengths to get it. If problems arise, all you really need is a big dose of motivation. That solves everything.

While drama queens also love attention, they aren't to be confused with narcissists. Narcissists are usually pursuing manipulative ends and feel entitled to special treatment, while drama queens simply can't help it—they have an internal need to feel seen and heard. They love attention, and many of them have what is sometimes known as a histrionic personality.

This phenomenon is far from new. The father of medicine, Hippocrates, who lived 2,500 years ago, called people who exhibited this trait hysterics, in reference to the uterus (*hystera*), as he believed the behavior to be uniquely female. Nowadays, his suggestions are dubious, as we know very well that men can also possess this attraction to melodrama.

But the origin of the term isn't the focus here.

Characteristic of histrionic personality disorder, or HPD, is the compulsive attention seeking that motivates the individual's behavior. They aren't content unless they're the center of everybody's attention. Their clothing, their liveliness, their dramatic flair, their flirtatiousness, and their overwhelming charm are all designed to attract attention.

THE DRAMA QUEEN

| 73% | 100% | 85% | 65% |
| Manipulation | Extroversion | Charm | Energy drain |

We've all seen reality shows on television that focus on human relationships. Drama queens act as though they're on a show like that all the time. They're constantly in performance mode. Being anywhere near a person like this involves being constantly showered with loudly delivered grandiose ideas and attempts at witticisms.

A genuine drama queen will do almost anything to ensure that nobody fails to notice that somebody incredibly interesting has just entered the room. They might wear imaginative clothing, in the most baffling combinations, to make themselves impossible to miss. I've seen people visit dinner parties in out-fits that were so deliberately off-kilter that they almost hurt my eyes. Color and pattern combinations that the most crazed designers in Paris could never even have dreamed of.

When a drama queen enters the room, they want us all to turn around and jealously gawk at their charisma and inten-sity, so they can lap up the admiration right from our big eyes.

TA-DAAA! Look at me!

They're prepared to do anything, if not more, to win not just acceptance, but love. They laugh, they joke around, they clown around, and they squirm. I doubt even they know how far they are prepared to go to knock our socks off with their mere presence.

This also tends to make them rather skilled conversational-ists. They've elevated small talk to a genuine art form. A drama queen can keep any conversation going and will use any means available to do so. They go to all this trouble rather than simply blurting out what they really mean: *Please like me!*

A drama queen will often beat other applicants and get the job. In fact, they're quite capable of climbing very high within an organization.

You might be wondering how this can be. It sounds crazy, after all. All that noise and hubbub! But the answer is a lot less farfetched than you might believe.

What do people look for when they interview job appli-cants? Skills and experience, of course. Plenty of applicants will have those. But how many of them will have the cosmic enthusiasm and drive that this personality type can so deftly display? The strength of dramatic individuals is that they radiate precisely what many managers are looking for: energy! They've definitely got that buzz about them, and they appear to be champing at the bit to get cracking and do some work.

Consider this: Training a new employee to do their job isn't really that much work. All you need to do as a manager is send them to a training course, and the internal educators will do that part of the work for you. What you want to see after that is motivation and positive energy. That's a lot harder to bring out in people, especially when the tasks you have to offer are some fairly dull work assignments that nobody really dreams of spending their life doing. And now along comes somebody who seems to really love filing papers. Or checking the biggest Excel spreadsheet in history for errors. Or performing the same task ten million times over.

The hangover will come, though, when the person who recruited this individual realizes that it was all superficial. Their motivation might have been genuine, but they don't actually *do* any of the things they were assigned. The situation escalates quickly. In order to handle this challenge, a recruiter will need to be incredibly alert and learn to detect the pattern quickly. References from past employers will be hugely important for anyone who's looking to avoid big mistakes.

Relying solely on your gut feeling is a surefire way to end up walking into this trap time and time again. You simply have to keep a level head when you're dealing with a drama queen.

Another problem with these individuals lies with the fact that if they end up being exposed as the great imposters they really are and it becomes clear to the company that they're all talk, they can make a full U-turn quicker than you can say "two-faced."

Now they become wounded victims, accusing everyone around them of being cynical predators. This change of mood, like everything else these people do, will be very dramatic. Not to mention the huge drain it will place on anyone who happens to be nearby.

PEACOCKS WHO SHOOT FROM THE HIP

In a way, this type is the direct opposite of the habitual perfectionist. Maybe you actually enjoy a little drama or action and can't quite see the issue here. I'll willingly confess that I've allowed myself to fall victim to the charms of people with this type of energy more than once in my life. Some of my best friends undoubtedly exhibit some aspects of this. In all secrecy and honesty, I think I could probably do with just a touch of it myself. Why? Well, because they seem to enjoy life so much.

Witnessing a drama queen from the sidelines can give you the impression that they're nothing but bundles of contradictions.

They hate conflict, but they excel at provoking it.

While they'll often be almost comically friendly, they can—especially when you question them in front of others—turn incredibly cruel at the drop of a hat.

They are notorious for breaking rules, but they're perfectly prepared to punish others severely for doing the same.

Doesn't that sound absolutely insane? It could drive you mad, surely?

Absolutely. Why do you think I've included them in my survey of energy vampires?

Why Think Before You Act?

Drama queens are at the extreme end of the extroversion scale. They're so extroverted that you couldn't get further away from the opposite—introversion—without moving off the scale. This serves as a helpful clue as to who will be the most provoked and drained by these particular individuals.

But what exactly is extroversion? It's partly a matter of energy and partly a matter of world view. The energy is sourced from outside the individual. An extrovert needs to get out there, into the world, and see and experience things. They find meeting lots of people, doing stuff, and staying active refreshing.

All those adverts for motor homes, boats, bicycles, trips to unusual destinations for people with "active lifestyles," were probably made by dramatic individuals. I suspect they simply use themselves as their target audience for the adverts. But, just between you and me: There are limits to how much activity anyone can actually endure.

Extroversion, however, is also a matter of how these individuals perceive the world. Everything happens external to themselves. Sitting down to think about something for hours on end is a typically introverted behavior. An introvert broods, goes over things in their mind, analyzes, and considers. The further you move along the extrovert scale, the more ridiculous that kind of behavior will seem:

Think before you act? No thank you! Action is all that matters.

They're actually right, to some degree. All the thoughts you have and all the plans you make in your mind won't have any significance if you don't act on them. In the end, you need to take some kind of action to realize any dreams you have.

However, refusing to think and plan seems like a rather

risky approach. Dramatic individuals shoot from the hip every time and let the chips fall as they may. That's hardly a viable strategy.

It's hardly a strategy at all, if we're being honest. Claiming that drama queens have a specific strategy would actually give these energy vampires more credit than they are due.

The interesting thing about the introversion-extroversion scale is that if you're somewhere in the middle you'll be able to shift in either direction as needed. Feel free to check out the section on ambiverts in chapter 9. A more moderately extroverted individual can move towards introversion in certain contexts, like when an outgoing executive attends active listening training in order to better understand their coworkers. Somebody who is reasonably introverted will also be able to shift towards extroversion, as exemplified by a brilliant, possibly genius-level, woman in tech who practices to prepare for a TED Talk about her latest breakthrough, which she'll be delivering in front of a thousand people. All of these things can be learned by anyone who understands what's required.

The motivations for wanting to do this can vary, of course. Usually, they will include a desire to adapt and learn more about cooperating efficiently with others. Extroverts who learn to listen to others and introverts who learn to socialize more smoothly will both be improving their social skills in excellent ways.

This is where things take a slightly comical turn for dramatic individuals. To them, the notion of adapting your behavior is an obscure, almost bizarre idea. They don't see the point, and they're not going to bother trying. They live so far out on the extroversion scale that they can't even grasp what lies at the other end.

Funnily enough, although this might seem to be a significant liability, it can actually benefit them initially. This is because our society currently favors extroversion over introversion. These days, we expect everybody to step forward and introduce themselves to the world. Schoolchildren are taught to speak out and represent themselves in ways that would have been out of the question just twenty or thirty years ago.

When I went to school, back in the seventies and eighties, my teachers told me to shut my mouth and carry on with multiplication tables. These days, even the most introverted children are encouraged to do group projects and give presentations. Both approaches have their flaws, as they both exclude large portions of the population.

However, as I write this, it's a fact that extroversion is generally promoted. Extroverts are deemed more likable and have an easier time appearing to have skills they might actually not possess. This is nowhere more apparent than in the world of business, where the emphasis on motivation and attitude is stronger than ever.

When business isn't going well, a variety of measures can be taken to change course, but an option that has grown increasingly popular over the last decades is to work on improving the motivation of the employees. Management—the members of which are not uncommonly dramatically inclined and may actually have earned their positions thanks to their enormous enthusiasm and unparalleled ability to find upsides to the bleakest of situations—likes to send their employees to motivational seminars. Just get an inspiring speaker in to give them their swagger back and all the problems will be as good as solved. Business will surely be booming again in no time.

Now, I want to be clear: I'm not saying all these exercises

are a waste of time. I've been present for more than one of these events, and I'd have to say I have usually found some utility in them. There are often inspiring nuggets of wisdom presented that I had forgotten, and I have nothing against positive thinking.

Heck, I've *held* exercises of this kind countless times. I'm fully convinced that I've inspired several thousand people in my time, and I usually enjoy the experience myself. However, just like everything else, it works beautifully some of the time and not at all some of the time.

Some people genuinely benefit from it, while others will, at best, enjoy themselves. Others still might find the whole thing annoying, but that's another story.

In any case, dramatic individuals win the Olympic Games of extroversion hands down, every time. Many of us actually also enjoy their company a great deal. Interacting with them tends to be fairly enjoyable and undemanding. As long as there aren't too many unforeseen incidents, it's usually quite pleasant to be around them.

However, the phrase "unforeseen incidents" is where the problem lies. If there's anything they excel at, it's behaving unpredictably. And that's exactly how they respond if they feel they aren't getting enough attention.

When Only a Standing Ovation Will Do

However, not all attention is desirable. Only positive interest will scratch their itch. If your intention is to criticize them, you'll soon end up on their wrong side. This is a rather interesting, although less than charming, characteristic.

They like you plenty, until they don't like you at all anymore. When this happens, they might just begin to loathe you. In mere minutes, they can go from being your biggest fan to evil incarnate. And they could actively be out to get you. Soon, all your mutual acquaintances and colleagues will hear about your betrayal.

No, nothing but positive acknowledgment will do. Drama queens need to be told how wonderful and amazing they are all the time. It doesn't really matter if they've actually done anything to deserve this praise; they demand applause anyway. And if they go uncelebrated, it'll bother them.

It's certainly naive, and a little childish. Also, we have to bear in mind that they're actually prepared to go quite far to live up to the expectations of others. If they see an opening to win a round of applause for themselves, they'll probably give it a go. Naturally, this will only apply if they can make this attempt without having to perform any boring, mundane tasks. Nothing kills a dramatic personality's enthusiasm quicker than that kind of thing.

If you were to criticize their efforts and point out details they overlooked, they would decide that you're just a whiny know-it-all and that you've made it your mission to ruin their lives. They don't want to hear about how they did sloppy work that lost the company an important contract. They would rather not be told about how they're incapable of following instructions. All that stuff is boring, and it's hardly the kind of information that will interest somebody who's expecting fanfare every time they enter the room.

No, life is supposed to be a song and dance. And don't you forget it!

One last detail on the topic of wanting praise they haven't earned: You might well encounter drama queens who seem to be quite hard on themselves and give the appearance of being very self-critical. They are fully prepared to bring their own low self-esteem to light for merciless scrutiny. You may even think this is an opening to give them an honest thought or two about how bizarrely self-centered they are.

But if you did that, it would be a grave mistake. If you want them to feel you're on their side, your job will actually be to talk them out of their slump, rather than amplify their own words. They're essentially asking you to convince them how wrong they are and that at this precise moment, as in every other moment ever, they are 100 percent fabulous, all the way through.

If they call themselves failures, that's just them being charmingly self-deprecating. If you call them failures, you're just being mean.

Their need for recognition is often also obvious from their physical appearance. They can present themselves in the most imaginative ways. You've probably seen people whose outfits are clearly designed to snag your attention—whether it's by being particularly colorful, unexpected, revealing, or creative.

But that's really not the point. Rather than assuming that the dramatic person's apparel is meant to be a countercultural statement or a suggestive invitation or a way of defying convention, we need to understand that *they* don't think of it that way. This is simply their way of showing themselves off, and do we really have the right to judge people by how they dress? These people crave attention.

These kinds of misconceptions have caused many unpleasant misunderstandings, particularly in workplaces.

We're talking about somebody who loves attention and is prepared to go to some questionable lengths to keep from being ignored.

My general advice when it comes to handling this kind of drama queen is to feel free to watch and enjoy the show but to ensure at any cost that you don't end up with a role in it.

Do you want an interesting and—most of all—unpredictable life? If so, you should join up with a dramatic individual. You'll never know what will be next, and no day will be the same as the one before.

A drama queen might not be onstage every hour of the day; they need to make their way through their lives, too, after all. But they can get up to almost anything, as they tend to follow their gut instincts.

The problem is that they rely on nothing *but* gut instinct. Thinking things through and weighing pros and cons just never occurs to them. And since they are so obviously extroverted, they simply let their impressions wash over them, like surfers on the beach looking for waves. Even they don't know which wave they will end up riding. They don't usually know which thought is going to decide their next step until they've already left their seat and headed off in one direction or other.

Living with somebody who acts on impulse like this all day long can be extremely tiresome. All I can promise you is that you won't be bored. That's something, I guess.

No plan is ever too important to be torn to pieces on a whim. It doesn't matter how long something has been in their calendar—they could still lose all interest in it the same morning it's supposed to happen. Something else could steal their focus at any moment. If you were to confront them about this, they'd accuse you of being insensitive and restricting their freedoms.

If their aversion to sticking to the plan causes stress—which is more or less inevitable—you can't predict what their reaction will be. They'll either overreact terribly and kick off some outrageous drama or other or simply deny that there's any problem at all. I'd say both options happen about as often.

You could think of the dramatic personality as a jumble of vague contradictions that have somehow been plastered over with a shiny, positive surface. On the outside, everything looks and sounds absolutely dreamy. But if you look underneath, you'll find something else. I can't tell you what exactly, because that will vary from individual to individual. If you want to get close to a dramatic individual, you'll just have to learn to be patient.

Sports Metaphors Always Work, Right?

Using vague messaging as a smokescreen is typical of dramatic individuals. Since they rarely bother to learn any actual facts, their conversation will often be rife with superficial platitudes and clichés.

We need to score a win here! This is just the kind of thing a dramatic middle manager might blurt out in a meeting. And yeah, that sounds good and everything, but what does it really mean? What game are we even playing?

Focus is essential! Certainly, but what should we be focusing on? Hard to say.

Work smart, not hard! That's another good idea. But how do we do that?

Naturally, it can help to spice up your language with powerful imagery, and sometimes a refreshing turn of phrase can be very useful. But when you rarely or never follow it up with any practical advice as to how something is supposed to happen, things can get very confusing for the recipients of all these imprecise messages.

They might even wonder why anybody would speak that way. But for drama queens, there's really no mystery. They want to look good. And sound good. And so they hurl out one cliché after another, completely unaware that most of what they're saying sounds like quotes from some movie where the new coach is trying to inspire his disheartened team.

There's no need to get into specifics, really. All you have to do is have the right attitude.

This all probably comes from writing letters to Santa or believing that motivational seminars will make all the difference.

I've already discussed details in the perfectionist chapter, and I'm the first to admit that you should avoid getting caught up in them. Trying to find the answer to every last detail and leaving no stone unturned can cause huge delays in any process.

However, that doesn't mean you should actively ignore the details. Dramatic individuals are unable to motivate themselves to pay serious attention to anything that they deem insignificant. A good way to extinguish any drive they might have is to make them sit through a recitation of the contents of an Excel spreadsheet.

They don't care why things are the way they are. Perhaps

that makes sense, seeing as they're still going to do whatever strikes their fancy, regardless of the facts of the situation.

HOW TO TELL IF YOUR FRIEND IS A DRAMA QUEEN IN DISGUISE

This checklist may not be a precise guide, but it can still offer you some guidance and perhaps help explain how to better understand your happy but pathologically mindless friend.

True or false. One point for each true, no points for a false. Let's go!

This person . . .

1. responds very unpredictably to stress
2. will feel absolutely betrayed if anybody talks about them behind their back
3. believes that having a positive attitude is everything
4. will lose their focus if the conversation turns to details
5. has a penchant for superlatives and exaggerations
6. is the kind of person who stands out in a crowd
7. doesn't appreciate criticism or negative feedback
8. tends to talk about others behind *their* backs
9. is prone to using sports metaphors, amusing clichés, or vacuous platitudes when asked to be more precise about something
10. treats most people, including rather loose acquaintances, as though they were the best of friends

How should we interpret the results? Being a drama queen may not earn somebody a psychiatric diagnosis (although genuine histrionic personality disorder *is* a diagnosis), so we'll simply have to use our imaginations a little. Without any doubts, I would say that many of these signs are cause for caution. Five points would indicate strong tendencies along these lines. If somebody scored eight points, they're sure to be a drama queen! Any score higher than that is a big warning sign.

When Drama Queens Go for Broke

Even without using this admittedly unscientific test, I'm quite convinced that you've already identified several drama queens in your life as you've read this chapter. They're definitely out there, but there's no need to go looking for them among the quieter types. There are plenty of varieties of draining behavior, but we're focusing on extroverts right now.

Details and facts will never be a dramatic individual's strong suit. They prefer to think they will succeed thanks to some kind of special magic nobody else can quite understand. Problems will simply go away if only we ignore them sufficiently. If we all stay positive enough and focus on being happy, everything will just work out. Living with an individual like that can be tiresome enough; having to work with one or more of them will soon become a problem. But let's take a look at a situation where you can't choose to ignore a dramatic individual: when they're your boss.

Many years ago, I worked for a man who I have since realized was a typical case of a dramatic personality or drama queen. At first, I was mostly confused and somewhat inspired by him. I adopted some of this individual's approaches without thinking critically about it, but now I think I can see why things never quite worked out for him.

This guy—let's call him Ronnie—could sell ice to penguins and sand to a camel. He could almost literally talk anybody into anything. I've personally witnessed him making deals worth millions without batting an eyelid, even though I knew he hadn't the faintest idea how he was going to hold up his end of the bargain.

Or did he? It's a little unclear to me actually, because once he had the client's signature on paper, the rest of us at the company would have to start trying to decipher all his notes and grand, ambitious plans. There were never any precise numbers, and he could seldom explain how it was all supposed to happen. We had to figure out most of the practicalities for ourselves.

Was this inspiring?

I'd have to say yes and no. It was exciting to be granted such freedom in taking over the big projects he handed us. I often felt that he was genuinely putting a lot of faith in us by asking us to shoulder his responsibilities. But at the same time, the fact that he could never give us any clear directions was quite frustrating. We never received any instruction, even when we genuinely had no idea what we were supposed to do.

A meeting with Ronnie could go something like this:

He steps into the room a little late. I say "steps," but honestly, "charges" would be more accurate. His hair is all over the place. His suit is a little too tight but very fashionable. His stubble is precisely the right length. His watch is a designer piece, the trendiest one available at the moment. (It's worth mentioning that he drove an Alfa Romeo, which was probably the worst-quality car you could imagine, but which always made people ask questions and gave him an opportunity to express his thoughts on the concept of individuality.*)*

Once he's inside the conference room, Ronnie tears his jacket off and tosses it over a chair. If it falls to the floor, he leaves it there for dramatic effect. He pulls his sleeves up frantically, to signal to everyone that the time has come to do some work: Let's do this!

The meeting begins. The subject could be anything at all. As usual, we haven't received an agenda. If a topic has been given for the meeting, it will be something along the lines of: THE FUTURE! *Or* GETTING AHEAD OF THE COMPETITION!

Ronnie gets right into it. He tells us it's time to get busy and take the company to the next level—the time is now, and this is when it's going to happen!

If anybody asks exactly what is going to happen or what, more precisely, the next level is, they will be rewarded with a torrent of exclamations like We're going to double our efforts!*,* We need to leave our comfort zone if we want to grow!*,* If you're still in full control of everything, that means you're not pushing hard enough!*, or even this old chestnut:* Being first is better than being best!

As the confusion mounts among the people attending the meeting, Ronnie decides to bring up an idea he's been considering for some time (I eventually figured out that this was code for I'm thinking out loud here*). He uses* *inventive metaphors to explain to us that* we're climbing a mountain *and that* we'll be leaving all the losers behind! Ha-ha!

I might raise my hand and ask something like, Well, that all sounds great, but how exactly is it supposed to happen? What's the plan?

If I get a response at all, rather than just an annoyed look, it would be some kind of play on words. Something to suggest that asking questions is the same as questioning and while we're on the subject of questioning we'd all do well to question our own attitudes towards change.

After the meeting, which has left us all in a strange no-man's-land, deep in the mists of confusion, Ronnie might take me aside and ask me about my motivation: How are you doing? You seem very negative lately.

Naturally, the only acceptable response is, I'm all fired up, and ready to go take it to the next level! *This needs to be accompanied by a smile. A really big smile.*

If I were to say I needed him to give me detailed instructions in order to know what I'm supposed to do differently tomorrow from the way I did it yesterday, I'd end up on his list of naysayers. And who knows how long it would take to make my way off it?

What can I say? While life with Ronnie was certainly exciting, it was also far from simple. Once, I actually asked his wife what he was like at home. She, who was a pragmatic and down-to-earth woman, gave me a dry response: *Exactly the same.*

WHEN PIE IN THE SKY CRASHES
TO THE GROUND

Interestingly, the main consequence of never getting any clear directions is very much the same as that of being exposed to excessive perfectionism: insecurity.

We all need frameworks and rules to relate to. Too much of that is no good, of course, but so is too little. We need to at least know what's expected of us. Imagine asking somebody to play a game with you. You tell them it's their move. But what happens next? What is the other person supposed to do?

A dramatic individual would simply tell them they could do anything they want. There are no rules.

But all this does is leave everyone bewildered and utterly confused.

This is fine for some folks—they don't really want to be told to do anything at all. Others might become passive, because they don't know what to do without direction.

It's usually quite easy to like a dramatic individual when you first get to know them. Their energy, charm, and naive faith that everything will work out is quite endearing. The constant smiles. They seem very . . . pleasant.

However, the hangover comes hard when their façade finally crumbles. Apart from the frustration of listening to their stream of hot air, all these clichés and empty statements don't really go anywhere. The same goes for a romantic partner who has entangled somebody with their ambitious plans, which turn out to be based on nothing at all.

Disappointment will follow.

What sounded so great turns out to be nothing but an

empty void. When you've been building someone up in your mind like that, have such strong feelings for them, and then have to face reality, it feels like a letdown. It's disillusioning. Was there really no substance to their claims? Was it all talk? What a disappointment!

So what happens when this disappointment replaces your glowing impression? It gives you a very negative perception of the person in question. When the illusion shatters and the proverbial honeymoon is over, you don't want anything to do with them anymore. This can cause a great rift between you and the dramatic individual. It's not guaranteed that this will be resolved. You've lost your patience with them, and in response, they have placed you firmly in the enemy category.

Green but Not Serene

As you've probably already noticed, the dramatic personality isn't too dissimilar to the profile of strictly Yellow people. They have their strong extroversion and the fact that they enjoy being the center of attention in common. However, just like control freaks, drama queens take perfectly ordinary traits to the insufferable extreme.

A Yellow person who doesn't exhibit the same aversion to facts and rationality as a dramatic individual can, of course, be reasoned with. While Yellows love to focus on and engage in fun activities and tend to try to evade any discussions related to actual problems, they're fully capable of having a normal discussion once you get them onboard with the conversation. A dramatic individual, however, will insist on shutting the whole thing down.

It's not uncommon that a Yellow would be the least likely to react to the antics of a drama queen. They will see the similarities in their own behavior and feel inspired by the positive energy they're being fed. However, even a Yellow might ask for an explanation from their happy friend, or colleague, or manager, or whoever it may be. When no explanation is forthcoming, the Yellow's response will be exactly the same as everybody else's: negative.

Despite this, we can't overlook the fact that a degree of competition will arise in this situation. The Yellow will be used to getting a lot of attention, and when the dramatic person resorts to their usual exaggerations to mop up all the energy in the room, the Yellow might feel rather sidelined. Depending on what their relationship is like, this could well kick off a struggle. The Yellow might also voice some rather critical opinions about the dramatic individual when they're not around.

The Red profile, too, contains elements of extroversion, although Reds are quick to lose their patience when a conversation gets too vague and incomprehensible. Since Reds are task-oriented, they will want to deal in facts, and while there's plenty that could be said about Reds and their behavior, they certainly don't appreciate prattle.

After I shared this chapter with some Red professional acquaintances of mine, most of them responded along these lines: *I'd listen for a while, but then I'd react just like I react to Yellow individuals: dismiss them with a wave of the hand, and proceed to do what I wanted to do anyway.*

In essence, dramatic individuals, despite all their shortcomings, are rather innocent souls—one might even call them naive. A Red is likely to view them as weak-willed chatterboxes and decide that they are best ignored.

If we move across the scale, to introversion, other problems will immediately emerge.

A Green individual who appreciates distinct, clear instructions (because they save the individual from having to come up with their own solutions) will be left entirely on their own in this case. A Green's knack for downtrodden displays will undoubtedly trigger the dramatic individual: *What a negative attitude! That's sooo booooring!*

When these types are supposed to cooperate in and out of the workplace, a forceful drama queen will soon form a poor opinion of a negative Green, and their collaboration might not get very far. Hanging your head and complaining about how things used to be better will immediately trigger conflict.

Greens are passive by nature, and they aren't necessarily going to try to find practical answers to any questions that might arise. If the relationship in question is between a manager and a subordinate, the Green will quite likely remain passive. And while it may seem like a contradiction, this can actually suit the Green fairly well. They're not too fond of running around all over the place, as you know. Is this good or bad? I suppose it depends. If it's a friendship we're talking about, both parties are likely to feel some friction. Both of them will also no doubt confide in their other friends how they actually feel about each other.

Now, what about Blue? A person with a purely Blue profile, like the Red, is likely to decide that a drama queen is an insufferable fool rather quickly. Being extroverted to that degree is simply undignified. Having such a poor grasp of the facts and details is unprofessional, and a Blue is likely to make a formal complaint about a colleague or manager who exhibits overly dramatic tendencies. If the relationship is a personal one, of course, things will be more complicated. I'm sure it's not a theoretical impossibility for a Blue to fall in love with and move in with a dramatic individual——love moves in mysterious ways, after all——but I think we can safely say it's a highly unlikely outcome. Friendship, then? It's not impossible. But again, it's less than probable. These two types are very different.

The dramatic individual is going to lose their temper in the face of the Blue's unrelenting questions. All these demands for facts and details are simply too tiresome to deal with. It's better, then, to spend time with somebody whose approach to life is just as easygoing as their own.

Shunned by the Herd

During some of those meetings with Ronnie that I mentioned earlier, it seemed to me that our whole group had fallen down one of those infamous rabbit holes. Suddenly, we had entered Wonderland. Nothing made any sense, and everything just seemed like a bunch of fake smiles. It sometimes baffled me that Ronnie could be making as much money as he was. However, I understand how it works now. They paid him for looking good and for making the company look even better. He gave them his energy, and for a short while everybody believed in the bright future he promised.

This is where dramatic individuals will excel. We know from experience, after all, that people won't always remember what we say or even how we said it. But they *will* remember *how we made them feel*. And Ronnie made people feel good. He also made us team members feel good, at least in the short term. When it came to leadership, he was obviously a bit of a failure, as leadership involves a thousand or so other skills beyond making people feel good. But Ronnie never saw it that way.

True leadership is something of a balancing act, as you know. A leader needs to be able to strike a balance between providing instruction and providing various forms of support. Leadership can be a purely informal thing, like when the neighborhood party organizer gets things done or when that passionate coworker manages to make things happen by getting everyone to do their part. However, skilled leaders usually need to be very clear and concrete in their expressions, while also having a good sense of when the best option is to shut up and listen to other people's ideas and suggestions. They need to win people over. While they do need to be good, strong role models, they also can't be afraid to be exposed as merely human. And a thousand other things. Leading others can be incredibly complicated.

Your team will need both desire (motivation) and competence (the ability to carry out tasks) in order to succeed at their jobs. The challenge for a true drama queen is that no matter how motivated their team members are, they still won't make any progress unless they know what to do.

It's somewhere in this area that the really strange things begin to happen. A dramatic executive will assume everybody thinks like they do, just to keep things simple. Because of this, they will convince themselves that anything is genuinely possible—even things that fly in the face of the established rules of the universe! What they don't know or can't do will be hidden away in some mental basement and forgotten.

Dramatic individuals actually see everything in very simple terms. Imagine a scale that goes from "good," through "better," then on to "outstanding" and "world-class" before continuing on to stratospheric levels that no human has ever reached.

Anything less than "good" is an absolute *disaster*.

This oversimplified view of the world that Ronnie relied on when he ran the company I worked for was quite harmful to some of my coworkers, and people were occasionally fired for reasons they never quite understood. It all basically boiled down to his very simple view of people. Some people belonged to what he deemed the positive crowd, which meant they were fairly secure. They showed motivation, they smiled frequently enough, and they delivered punchy anecdotes from meetings with clients where they performed brilliantly and made huge deals. That was the kind of stuff Ronnie liked to hear. But most important, they didn't demand any instructions or feedback. They were content to receive pep talks all week long.

I kept myself very busy just trying to stay on his right side. The danger that always loomed was ending up in the other category, with the team members he had decided had negative mindsets. This was a bottomless pit that offered no way out. People who ended up there usually didn't last very long.

I'm not trying to give you the impression I was somehow always getting it right; on the contrary, I found myself on the brink of disaster more than once. However, I've always been able to rely on my instinctive feel for what different kinds of individuals expect of me. I'm also able to make myself carry out the most incomprehensible work tasks, as long as I manage to keep the long-term benefits in mind.

Ronnie's body language was an important aspect of all this. He didn't hide how wonderful he felt some team members were or how terrible he felt others were. Anybody who criticized Ronnie would cease to be wonderful and become awful, especially if they did it in front of the team. Even though he didn't like conflict, he was causing it all the time. However, as he saw it, it was never his fault; the real reason why he lost his temper was the negative attitudes people would display.

HOPELESS BUT CHARMING

A boss is one thing, and a coworker is another. But what about having a dramatic brother or mother? If the dramatic individual were somebody you weren't close to, you'd respond in one way, but you'd respond quite differently if they were somebody you loved.

"Loved"? This word might give you pause. How could anybody love somebody that dreadful? If you're wondering that, you're not realizing how charming these people can be. You're also forgetting that they're not evil per se. They're neither narcissists nor psychopaths. They just happen to be incurably egocentric. And single-minded. And unpredictable. And rather hopeless. But can they be charming? You bet they can!

And this might actually be the gravest danger if you're in a relationship with one of them. It's easy to fall for their captivating façade. However, when things go wrong and the mask comes off, you'll be suffering doubly.

One of my own core ideas about how to make your way through this world is that rather than referring to people you don't immediately understand as idiots or worse, you should *try* to understand them. Perhaps there are things you could learn from them. Also, the more you try, the easier it will eventually be for you to reach whatever goal you set for yourself.

This applies equally to energy vampires. In this chapter, I'm discussing dramatic individuals, or drama queens. If you want to engage with them instead of simply turning your back on them—which can be challenging if they are, say, family members—you'll need to be able to see the world the way they do.

This applies to any situation, whether it be at work or in your personal sphere. The first thing you have to do is enter their world. The trick is just to do that without becoming an energy vampire yourself.

What you'll need to do is *try to put yourself in their shoes*.

Sometimes you'll have to do things the way they do them, although you should be doing them deliberately rather than the haphazard way dramatic individuals seem to do them. They just act, without giving the consequences a single thought. Try to avoid that trap.

The first important step is to make sure to refrain from judging them or their views of the work. What's right or wrong will have no significance. All that bringing that stuff up will achieve is making them defensive. The moment you begin to lecture them on how the world actually works, your cause will be lost.

In a relationship, the most pointless kind of conflict revolves around who's right and who's wrong. This will often cause your communication to break down. Even though I'm often sorely tempted to read the facts to these dreamers, I don't recommend that at all. I've coached a number of these individuals myself, and it took me years to realize they simply don't listen to that kind of thing. It didn't matter if I explained in detail why two equals two; if they don't want to see it, they will refuse to see it. End of story.

Your own view of the world isn't some undeniable, universal law. That's worth bearing in mind as you read on.

But surely, you may be thinking, they could just be sent to therapy, where some clever therapist could explain a few things to them? That is an option, of course, but we would then be faced by another challenge: A dramatic individual has no problems, as you know. Everybody else has the problems. Therefore, there's simply nothing to solve. On the other hand, they might enjoy an opportunity to talk about themselves, so they will probably show up for the first few sessions at least.

Appreciation and acknowledgment are more valuable than money in the mind of a dramatic individual. That's why they're always in performance mode and why they would never do anything that might risk bringing an end to their audience's applause. That's why your old friend never transitions from joking around to discussing something serious. Serious things are no fun—it's as simple as that.

It's also part of the reason why dramatic managers can struggle so badly when they need to make unpopular decisions that will cause discontent. This is the world that people like my old boss Ronnie live in.

Some viewed him as a classic bullshitter. Others felt that he lacked integrity. I viewed him as simply incompetent, at least when it came to his leadership.

Unfortunately, none of these attitudes did anything to make it easier for us to handle Ronnie.

I realized that what I needed to do was treat him the same way he treated people he seemed to admire. As he saw it, that was being respectful. Anybody else would call it sucking up.

Sucking Up for a Higher Purpose

One of my friends has a teenage son whose path through high school has involved some rather unusual experiences. One of his teachers appears to be a rather difficult case. He's never prepared for his lessons, he rarely sticks to the planned agenda, and he never stops talking about himself or involving his own personal projects in his teaching.

The teenager in question is one of those students who feel that their performance should speak for itself. Doing well on tests should result in good grades. However, in this case, he's sadly mistaken about how the system can work sometimes.

Students who sit at the front of class, waving their hands in the air during lessons and engaging with the teacher on various topics, might do a good job of inflating the teacher's ego even while failing to demonstrate the same level of knowledge other students in the class might have. They perform far worse on tests but still get significantly better grades.

They make sure the teacher feels important and shamelessly curry favor. He probably doesn't even realize this is happening. They make him feel good about himself, and he rewards them for it. The kids at the back of the room, who might work away in silence, are punished with lower grades for failing to boost the teacher's ego.

This is an example from real life, which I doubt is at all unique. It's also a complicated situation to resolve, as the students don't have any choice but to play along. They have to attend school, and they don't have any power over their situation. Changing schools is a lot more difficult than changing jobs.

When you're dealing with a drama queen, you simply have to play the game. Occasionally, this will mean having to suck up to them. Regardless of how you prefer to define it, sucking up can be a very valuable skill.

Please, don't overreact to this. I can understand if that sentence made your stomach turn, but if you'll indulge me for a moment, I think I can help you see how it can be a constructive thing to do at times.

Most people enjoy talking about themselves, but drama queens seem to live for this kind of attention. In this sense, they're quite similar to narcissists. They think it's only natural that everybody would be interested to hear them drone on about their fascinating lives. Anybody who interferes with this will be perceived as rude, while those who eagerly indulge them will be perceived as wonderful people.

Why does it work, though?

When you ask a dramatic individual questions, they will interpret this as evidence that you like and value them. It will make them regard you in a more positive light.

Dramatic managers make the same assumptions that dramatic teachers do: Anybody who shows an interest in them likes them, while people who don't want to talk to them are obviously hostile.

You could just refuse to do this, of course. You're fully entitled to decide for yourself. But if you want to have productive interactions with a dramatic individual, it's simply a sacrifice you'll have to make. You can always decide to sit at the back of the class, firm in your conviction that your soul is not for sale. However, you'll have to deal with the consequences of this approach. Only you can decide what your priority should be.

When listening to and engaging with this kind of person, you should make sure they can tell how attentive you're being. Speak like they do. Use the same expressions they do. If your friend has a catchphrase, use it! Draw attention to it! Tell them, *As you always say,* and then fill in the blank with their preferred nugget of wisdom.

Another approach that can work well is to explain to them what an inspiration they are to you and how much you learn from them by just being in their vicinity. It can even be true! They're bound to know a few things that are useful to you. However, this won't be enough. To win them over and convince them you're a great person, you need to tell them explicitly:

> *I've learned a lot from hearing you explain X.*
> *It's very inspiring to me to see how you approach Y.*
> *When I listen to you speak, it helps me realize how much I still have to learn about Z.*

If you boost the impact of this by doing it while others are around, dramatic individuals will love you for it. However, as you no doubt realize, other people will think of you as a bit of a bootlicker. If you can live with those reactions, you'll have a far easier time handling the dramatic person. If this feels like selling your dignity, you'll have to resort to other methods.

In any case, you need to stay *positive.* A drama queen doesn't want to hear a word about problems, risks, difficulties, dilemmas, conflicts, or limitations. They prefer to live in a neat, tidy

Technicolor world, where the sun always shines and everybody stays friends forever. The food is wonderful, everybody is smiling, and life is all one big comic opera.

This will involve having to smile back at them and raising your eyebrows a lot when you do so. If you leave the raised eyebrows out, you'll look more like the Joker, and that won't do your career prospects any good.

You should also use positive body language. Don't speak to them while facing away from them; give them your full attention. That means always turning fully towards the dramatic person and making an obvious point of how you're focusing exclusively on them.

Your language, naturally, should be very positive and include plenty of superlative statements. Apart from the obvious trick of giving them plenty of praise, you should also use a lot of words like "happy," "wonderful," "shiny," "cool," "wow," "world-class," "winner," "us," "the future," "victory," "success," "bottom line," and "trendy." Also, don't forget to insist that *anything is possible*!

Words you'll want to avoid include "problem," "difficult," "complicated," "don't know," "never," "don't want to," "negative," "conflict," "issues," "critical," "details," "statistics," "facts," and "control."

I know. It's all rather silly. But it still works a lot better than explaining to them how their egocentric attitude is impacting everyone around them.

Good luck! I'm sure you'll manage just fine.

4

The Bully,
an Unstoppable Tyrant

The adult bully is a type that feels empowered when bullying, threatening, or insulting other people. This is somebody who will stop at nothing to get their way, and who won't conform to any rules or social norms unless it suits them. These individuals are prepared to deceive, manipulate, lie, and possibly even assault others just for the fun of it. In many ways, they behave like alphas in a pack of hyenas. Adult bullies' blunt behavior can make them seem a lot like immature teenagers, and sometimes their displays are so appalling that it's hard to believe your ears: *Did that really happen?*

Just like teenagers, they sometimes revert to infantile behavior and act like overgrown toddlers. This is precisely what makes them so unpredictable. They are immature, but they don't realize it. They also assume that everybody else functions the same way they do. If somebody doesn't, that's tough for them.

THE BULLY

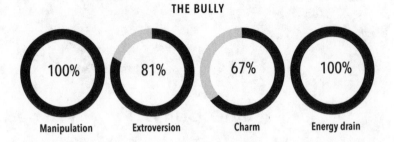

| Manipulation | Extroversion | Charm | Energy drain |
| 100% | 81% | 67% | 100% |

All these people want from life is to enjoy themselves and have fun. They want immediate gratification and demand to have their sudden whims and fancies immediately satisfied.

If they need your help to achieve that, they'll be charming, witty, and seductive in their interactions with you. However, if you get in their way, they can soon turn dangerous.

This is the type of energy vampire who is the most likely to commit crimes. There are a number of reasons for this, most of which are rather simple. Antisocial people want to have the things they want. And they want them now. If they see something they want to take from somebody else, they're going to do it. They are unable to consider the consequences of their actions or feel guilty about something they've done. They only did what was best for them, after all!

Immoral? Illegal? Who cares? They will make their way through life lying, cheating, and even stealing if it suits their purposes. What the rest of us think about it is no concern of theirs.

Of course, most of them don't end up as criminals. Most of them stay within the confines of the law, even if they feel fully entitled to break all the unwritten laws of how to behave that hold society together.

It's not uncommon for them to be blatant bullies. They seem to feel empowered and vitalized when they get to inflict misery on others. How many films have you seen where some schoolyard bully singles out a specific victim? In the movies, these poor people always turn out to have an alcoholic father or sickly mother at home. There's always some heartbreaking reason for their dreadful behavior.

But that's not the case in real life.

At least not when it comes to antisocial individuals. They aren't victims, with a difficult childhood to blame for their actions. Their fathers didn't beat them, and their mothers weren't self-centered addicts. They're simply acting in line with their nature.

To begin with, we have to examine the term itself: "antisocial." Unfortunately, there's some semantic sleight of hand at work here, which obscures its true meaning. Personally, I'm not a fan of the practice of shrouding unpleasant things in elegant, complex epithets that cloud the issue.

These individuals tend to be extroverts, and they're very comfortable rubbing shoulders with others. In this particular way, they're quite similar to narcissists and dramatic personalities. They love parties, especially unplanned ones. They are constantly bored and always want to be in the thick of things. In a crowded room full of people, they can bring out a convincing show of charm and wit. They will appear friendly, attractive, and highly motivated. That's not what the word "antisocial" brings to mind, is it?

There is a diagnosis classification called antisocial personality disorder with psychopathic traits. Presenting as a mere case of antisocial personality disorder would simply mean that you were in a precursive state to something rather more unpleasant: psychopathy. The way I see it, psychopathy is synonymous with pure evil.

However, while this type of energy vampire may exhibit some psychopathic behaviors, they aren't fully developed psychopaths or suffering from a diagnosable condition. Unfortunately, that's about all the good news you'll be getting here.

They can be manipulative and charming, especially to people who have something they want or are their superiors within some organization or other. In those situations, they tend to be on their best behavior. However, you shouldn't be fooled by this act—and you should know that it won't last long. Since they are professional bootlickers, their superiors tend not to see the problems they cause.

Imagine a regular individual, increase their energy level by 100 percent, and then boost their capacity to delight people by 200 percent. Then disconnect their ability to experience anxiety or stress. Doesn't that sound like a great hire? Or a great friend, for that matter?

NOT QUITE PSYCHOPATHS

One way of diagnosing psychopathy is to use a set of checklists, and it's quite likely that a bully would score some points on those tests. However, their scores wouldn't be high enough to qualify them as genuine psychopaths. If, for instance, the criteria for diagnosing psychopathy would be twenty-five points, these individuals would score less than that but still score high enough to merit warning the public to steer clear of them. The tendencies are clearly in place.

Here is a list of characteristics you can go through to check if you're dealing with an adult bully. The purpose isn't to offer a clinical diagnosis but rather to offer some clues.

The greater the number of traits in this list you feel apply to somebody, the greater the likelihood is that you'll encounter the behaviors I'll go over in this chapter. True or false. One point for each true, no points for a false. These individuals . . .

1. often break their promises
2. exploit others without remorse
3. can display incredible charm when it suits them
4. seem to think rules exist to be broken
5. occasionally seem to take risks just for the excitement of it
6. behave very differently to their superiors and subordinates in organizations
7. invariably blame others for their own mistakes
8. lie with surprising ease
9. can display incredibly dramatic mood shifts
10. seem to fascinate the people around them despite all this

How should we interpret this? Everyone would score at least a couple of points off of this list. You and I have definitely both lied more than once, and we both have some way of rationalizing our lies. But how many points would be a good indicator that, say, it's time to start looking for a new job?

My recommendation would be to do some serious thinking if somebody scores three to five points. That indicates an individual with behavioral issues. If you have accurately scored eight points for somebody and received some verification of this score from others, I would like to caution you to be watchful of the person in question.

At ten points, they have severe issues. Spending too long around this person could actually cause lasting harm to you. I'm not saying that lightly. An individual like that will do you serious injury if you don't take measures to distance yourself from them.

The Choice between a Ferrari and a Toyota

This is an example I've picked up from somewhere or other, but unfortunately, I've forgotten who I got it from. It's not mine, but I will take the liberty of using it here, as it is such an excellent illustration of a difficult dilemma that can arise in recruiting or dating.

What's a Ferrari? It's unique, beautiful, and extremely adept, a work of art and a powerful beast all at once. It's incredibly expensive and out of most people's reach. Sometimes the car spends as much time in the shop as it does on the streets. It's not really a great choice for an ordinary family. You can't fit many strollers into the trunk of this miraculous vehicle.

So what's a Toyota? It's a popular car for families. It's practical, comparatively cheap, easy to drive, and outstandingly reliable. It will never, or rarely, break down. But if we're being honest, it's not ranking high in terms of entertainment value.

On first impression, a bully will seem like a Ferrari. They will be highly skilled at deceiving the people they meet. A winning smile, a firm handshake, and the kind of confidence even highly successful people could kill for. A Ferrari in a world of Toyotas.

The problem here is quite obvious: Although you know a Toyota is what you *need*, a Ferrari is what you *want*. That's how I remember the quote, at least.

Navigating the Dating Jungle

If you're dating a bully, the first dates will offer you a taste of the good qualities of a Ferrari. They're exciting, attractive, and exotic. They respond to everything you do and all your requests. Their advanced onboard systems cater to your every whim.

This man seems to appreciate everything you do and everything you say. Nice restaurants, lovely gifts, and compliments all day long. He pulls out your chair for you, holds the door for you, never looks at other women—you have his complete attention. He can't get enough of you, he laughs at all the right moments, he listens to you, and he never questions your behavior. He's dying to know more about you and seems to disregard his own needs completely. He's handsome, fit, smart, and successful. To top it off, he tells you that you're his dream woman around date four or so. In fact, he thinks you must be soul mates.

You can hardly believe your luck.

It's almost too good to be true.

And that's precisely what it is: too good to be true.

Soon, you'll learn that what you thought were excellent standard-issue features are actually incredibly expensive add-ons.

After some time, his behavior will begin to change, gradually. He turns out to be rather unreliable. He spins yarns when there's really no need to. You'll catch him in lies. He's terrible at keeping times and promises. And, suddenly, he'll begin to display volatile moods. Soon, he'll want access to your wallet.

The Ferrari has begun to show its less attractive qualities.

Here's the problem: You can't have *one* without the *other*. They're basically two sides of the same coin.

A Recruiter's Headache

The same applies in a recruiting context. Antisocial individuals know how to play their cards to get the job, the salary, and the other benefits they want. For a while, everything will work out incredibly well.

After three months on the job, their first review will often mention their energy, independence and drive, good work pace, decisiveness, flexibility, ability to think outside the box, social skills, and the fact that they get along well with everybody. Good risk management is also commonly highlighted.

Hell, *I'd* hire that guy in a heartbeat, assuming this was the full story.

However, just as with the deceitful dater, there's a downside here. As always. After a year or so, the assessments might read very differently. Unreliable. Bad at taking instruction. Feels themselves to be above the rules that apply to everybody else. Terrible at routine tasks; takes shortcuts and seldom finishes what they start. Causes friction within the team. Seems to have difficulties managing their finances and sometimes smells of alcohol at work.

When you get one, you *automatically* get the other.

The strangest part is that these characters will often enjoy the special protection of the real decision-makers. The reason for this is simple: They are excellent bootlickers. They suck up to their superiors and treat their subordinates awfully.

Just like most bullies do.

Kenny: The Vicious Bulldozer

A year before I began work on this book, I experienced a fairly typical, but still rather startling, bully. This was at a medium-sized business that was owned and operated by a pair of passionate entrepreneurs and brothers. They had come very far in terms of thoughts and plans, but they didn't really have a close eye on what was happening in their actual business operations. One of them was the CEO, and the other was chairman of the board. However, neither of them really spent much time in the office. My assignment was to help them undergo a complete reorganization, and to get a better grasp of their business culture I tagged along to several meetings.

Kenny did decent work as a site manager for them. He had worked at the company for a year or so, hired by one of the brothers to help keep things afloat while they were out looking for new opportunities.

Kenny made sure to keep the owners happy by feeding them an endless supply of good news. This was also his approach to getting all the many benefits he had arranged for himself. He had two corporate cars, apartments, paid travel, and a salary fit for a king. I haven't even mentioned his biggest win—the bonus deal that guaranteed him a literal bonus in gold.

However, Kenny was soon exposed as a full-fledged bully. His successes all relied on his ability to shamelessly use and trample over everybody else in the organization.

He relished the excitement of having lots of things going on. Anything was better than having to sit through long, dull meetings. He hardly ever read his email, because it was either boring or just full of questions people kept asking him. Also, he knew that fear triggered reactions in people.

Like many antisocial individuals, Kenny was a bit of an addict.

Addictions can make you dependent on sex, pornography, alcohol, or various chemical substances. Dopamine, no matter where it's sourced from, is a fully natural brain chemical that also happens to be highly addictive.

Kenny's fix was bullying people. It fed him the dopamine dose he craved. His workers' fear was like blood in the water to a shark. It drew him in and made him lick his lips with anticipation over the prospects of stirring up even more of it.

I mean this very literally. Just like alcoholics always look for excuses to have a drink, bullies look for excuses to oppress and humiliate others. Kenny was a master of this art, and his efforts left him feeling terrific.

Occasionally, one comes across the advice that the correct way to handle bullies is to stand up to them. To not give way. Perhaps it is. But anyone who feels that is always good advice has obviously never met Kenny.

A management team meeting with him would go like this: Some people are sitting around a table. Everyone is well prepared, except for Kenny. He arrives late but doesn't offer any apologies. He looks around to see if anyone is exhibiting particular weakness today.

Let's say the last quarter's performance numbers don't live up to everybody's hopes. Development has hit a snag. Kenny loses his temper the moment the financial director reads the numbers out to the team. He needs a scapegoat. His immediate response is to accuse the financial director of being unable to count properly. The latter is Blue, of course, and accordingly argues that the numbers he's given are the right numbers, because he is able to count properly.

This pushes Kenny over the edge. He hits full throttle in an instant and is suddenly yelling at the financial director. He also yells at the sales manager, accusing the sales team of being useless for having failed to bring in better business. He shouts at the HR manager for recruiting a bunch of amateurs.

Everybody has come to expect all this by now.

Once everybody has had their turn at being verbally mauled and personally insulted, one of them might try to offer an explanation.

Kenny interrupts immediately. He's not interested in their pathetic excuses. He wants to see some results! Do they understand? Results! *Why is he surrounded by people who can't think for themselves?* They're all useless!

Somebody in the room, perhaps the sales manager, tries to move the meeting along. She clears her throat and explains that they're all very sorry about the unfortunate turn of events, but that she's confident they can all work out a plan to solve the problems together.

Unfortunately, this gets her nowhere. I personally witnessed the following scene, or variations of it, on several occasions:

The entire room falls silent for a few seconds. Everybody tries to catch their breath. Did she manage to turn the onslaught?

But then Kenny turns to her with a big smile on his face. Everybody knows what's about to happen. The sales manager is about to be executed, more or less.

Deceptively calm at first, he soon builds towards a diabolic eruption. He tells the team he's realized exactly what needs to happen now. Everybody needs to get their fingers out of their arses and take some damned responsibility. *He has no restraint when it comes to using curses and other offensive language in the management team meetings.*

He shouts at the sales manager to stop acting like a whiny *bleep* and do some real work for a change.

The sales manager reacts as though he had literally punched her in the face.

Why did the owners let this go on? The answer is every bit as simple as it is horrifying: they had no idea how he treated his colleagues. Kenny was always politeness incarnate when they were around. Also, he actually got results.

LIVE TO FIGHT ANOTHER DAY . . . IF YOU CAN

When I lecture on manipulation and psychopathy, I often encounter two rather different reactions in the audience. One of them is naivety. This comes from the people in the crowd who find it hard to imagine that anybody could actually behave this way.

The other reaction is more akin to pure horror. These are the individuals who know very well that these bullies are real, and may have actually encountered them in their own lives.

Most people who belong to the second category tend to experience some fear in their interactions with bullies. These predators feed on fear in particular, and they seek to elicit that exact reaction from others. The problems this can cause are extensive.

When I see how some people try to engender fear in others—even to the point of openly stating that they *want* people to be afraid—all I see is an ambitious manipulator. Somebody who wants to wreak havoc. Stir up chaos. People make poor decisions when they are afraid. That's often what causes the disasters that follow.

This is a very unfortunate mechanism in professional life. Carrying around genuine fear of your colleague, coworker, or—worst of all—boss can be devastating. An organization where people are motivated by fear will soon be struggling under the weight of a variety of problems. Everybody will be watching out for themselves and will be happy to push others under the bus to save themselves the worst of it.

Constant conflict will negatively impact efficiency and productivity. Stress levels will hit astronomic heights, and nobody will perform very well.

Why do people even stay in situations like that? It's a good question, and the answer is that this kind of work culture doesn't develop overnight. It sneaks up on you, so that you don't notice how things are gradually getting out of control.

Most commonly, though, these problems arise in organizations that suffer from weak leadership. When deviant behavior like this is left unchecked, you'll soon be on a slippery slope towards a myriad of problems.

In families, the suffering partners will often try to divert the bullies' attention away from their children by offering themselves up as targets. The bully is unlikely to be very lenient with them when this happens.

Intimate relationships where one partner fears the other will be dysfunctional from the get-go.

I can't tell you how many stories I've heard about women who tiptoe around their bullying, oppressive men, constantly fearing the next outburst. Physical abuse is by no means a necessary component (although it can occur, of course)—the psychological terror a bully subjects their victims to can be more than enough. Being subject to constant scolding, shouting, verbal abuse, humiliating treatment, and generally rude behavior is extremely emotionally fatiguing. A person who lives in a relationship like this will basically be broken apart, piece by piece.

Fear will become part of their everyday experience.

Insecurity. *What's going to happen next time?*

Passivity. *If I don't do anything at all, I might be spared the worst of the abuse.* However, the end result for anybody who's always on the chopping block like this will inevitably be burnout. Brain fatigue. Post-traumatic stress.

Spending too long around a person like this comes with a huge set of dangers.

SEEING RED OR TURNING YELLOW

This regime of bullying will break down individuals with the two relationship-oriented profiles first. Since both Yellows and Greens value relationships very highly, they can easily shatter in the face of repeated attacks. You see, they interpret this as evidence of a damaged relationship, which is the worst thing they can imagine. The bully will target their victim's most obvious weaknesses and seek to cause the most possible harm.

This is particularly obvious in the context of personal relationships. Having somebody behave like this at work is bad enough, but at least you get to leave work at the end of the day. But what if it's a close friend or even a member of your family?

A Green could be in danger of developing genuine psychological problems, and a Yellow, who is very sensitive to public criticism, will feel horrible. In both cases, having to take sick leave and suffering breakdowns are distinct possibilities. Yellows, who are less passive than Greens, will pack up their belongings and change jobs, social circles, or romantic partners if this goes on for too long. Greens, however, might actually stay. And, in the worst case, they could develop PTSD. This may be speculation on my part, but I honestly feel the dangers are quite obvious. According to psychologists I've spoken to, PTSD is not uncommonly caused by relationship issues.

I'm also not trying to suggest that Greens are somehow necessarily weaker; but this behavior does impact them particularly severely, because it involves constant conflict, which is the very thing that Greens fear the most. They are particularly vulnerable to this stuff.

People with the task-oriented profiles, Blue and Red, have a significantly different attitude to bullies. A Blue is unlikely to reward them with much in the way of external reactions. They're not particularly interested in pursuing that kind of relationship, anyway. If a Blue runs afoul of a bully at a party, they will probably just stare at the bully until the abuse ceases. Afterwards, they will simply avoid any party where this person might be present.

I'd like to remind you at this point that bullies are seeking to elicit a reaction. If this attempt succeeds, they'll move on. If it fails, they'll try to escalate. But the Blues won't reward them with any kind of reaction at all. They will simply turn into stone and make all their decisions internally. Stay or go? If they stay, they'll run the risk of being manipulated—and this is something that can happen to anyone.

If they go, they'll seek to rationalize what happened, to soothe their pain. This will lessen the danger of psychological harm.

Reds, depending on the situation, might retaliate when a bully has a go at them. If a Red feels attacked for no reason, this will naturally spark conflict. There's no avoiding it. The question is how it will end. Reds don't usually have a problem raising their voices and answering in kind. The probable outcome is a contest of wills, but who will win it is hard to say. We all have our weaknesses, as you know. If the Red deems the bully to be absolutely implacable, they will simply seek to leave the situation. They will either stop talking to their abusive neighbor or look for another job. They're not going to just take it.

However, if a bully sets out to break a Red entirely they might actually succeed. Reds are a bit like strong tree trunks in the wind, after all. They won't budge at all, but if the storm is strong enough they might just snap in half.

A Word of Warning

In my second book, *Surrounded by Psychopaths* (2020), in which I wrote about psychopathy and manipulative behavior, I offered the only advice that I genuinely believe to be good when it comes to handling a psychopath: *Walk away.* Psychopaths, to put it bluntly, are dangerous people, and there's no reason to remain in their vicinity, no matter how you may try to delude yourself into doing so. They will never change, and they will only wear you down more and more as time goes on.

But in this context, the people we're discussing are just bullies, or people with antisocial tendencies. These are individuals who display a number of psychopathic traits but nonetheless don't qualify as full psychopaths. This means that they are likely to be less dangerous than true psychopaths, but it doesn't mean they won't have the capacity to make you feel genuinely awful. Please remember, people make bad decisions when they're afraid.

The problem is that when you face a person like this you might react instinctively. And that means how you react will depend on who you are. It will depend on your colors, your motivations, your values, and, in fact, your current financial situation, if we're talking about a professional relationship.

You need to be clear on one thing: A bully like Kenny won't hesitate to remove anybody who displeases him from the company. If he doesn't literally fire them, he will keep piling the pressure on until they resign on their own. He knows a thing or two, and he presumes everybody else thinks more or less the same way he does. That's his inner world in a nutshell. He will show you no mercy.

I'm going to give you some advice now that might help you handle people like this if you choose to do so. However, if what you're about to read makes you feel bad, I want you to know that the best advice you could get might very well be to simply walk away.

SOME GOOD ADVICE FOR TAKING ON AN IMPOSSIBLE CHALLENGE

Maybe you'd like to slam your laptop into Kenny's skull. Or maybe you'd prefer to do the same to one of the company's owners. The problem with that approach is that it won't do any good.

What you need to do here is cut off the flow of negative energy.

Kenny doesn't mind conflict; on the contrary, he relishes it. He likes to see people fear him. That proves to him that he matters to them. He couldn't care less if they secretly hate him. He wants that high.

Somebody has to defuse the conflict itself. Put the safeties back on everybody's triggers.

But how do you do that?

One thing that often strikes me when I listen to people tell me about their workplaces is how many of them seem very unhappy there. The reasons may vary, but I always give them the same advice I'm going to give you now:

Sit down and think the situation through. Try to answer this question: *Why am I still here?*

Nobody deserves to be treated like filth. You know you deserve better than this. If you want to keep as much of your sanity as you can, you'll need to take certain things seriously.

If you're working for a bully or if you've noticed that somebody you socialize with frequently in your free time is a bully, you owe it to yourself to find solid, concrete reasons for why you're putting up with it.

Maybe the reason is money. On some level, we all sell

ourselves for money. Well, you can always ask for more pay. Some bosses, as it happens, are prepared to pay employees who never ask difficult questions rather handsomely.

It could be power, or attention, or popularity. Perhaps it's a hope to climb a rung on the social ladder or progress in your career. You alone can decide if it's truly worth it. That reason, whatever it is, is the thing that might keep you going when things get truly difficult. We all need a good reason to carry on the struggle, and you need to know what yours is.

Working with or socializing with a bully is like breathing toxic air. You get used to it a little at a time. As the dose increases, your senses will be dulled. In the end, you'll have become accustomed to the bully's methods and expect nothing else.

But it doesn't have to be that way. There are other things in life besides "job security" or the status that follows from being associated with the popular bully.

If you can't come up with a reason for why you stick around that makes genuine sense to you, there's only one solution. If the only thing keeping you there is fear of looking for a new job or finding new friends, it's time to move on.

Just as I wrote earlier, the best way to keep your sanity intact is probably to *just walk away*.

Time

Let's say you've decided to accept the challenge. Okay. If you were the sales manager in Kenny's organization, the best thing for you to do would be to take a deep breath. Do what I usually recommend to anybody who's feeling manipulated into giving a quick response to something they actually need to consider for longer: Ask for more time.

This is the obvious way for you to give yourself a chance to regain control of your thoughts and avoid stepping into any more traps. In this situation, Kenny senses blood in the water. He's quick on his feet and simply waiting for you to say something that he can use against you. If you were to simply say that you need more time, this can interrupt the flow of the conversation.

Kenny probably won't be expecting this, either. He may well simply continue shouting and hurling abuse at you.

You might have to repeat your request for more time when Kenny tries to drag you back into an argument with him. Once you've repeated it several times, however, he's likely to relent, as it's difficult to criticize you for taking him seriously.

Objective

You need to give some thought to what you want to achieve. Simply put, what do you stand to gain from resolving the situation? Rather than responding reflexively and seeking vengeance, you should consider what the outcome you need to bring about is.

What you want to do is disarm Kenny to the fullest extent possible. An effective way of putting an end to hostilities is to turn the bullying into an activity that will involve a lot of work for the bully—they don't like that.

In some cases, this could even boost the team's energy and help encourage them to pick up on your cues and begin looking for solutions themselves. Kenny may even leave the meeting in a hurry, with his horror at all the work he's in danger of having to do clear on his face.

Do workplaces like this exist? You bet they do.

On one occasion, the middle managers went to the owner brothers to voice complaints about Kenny. That was the most foolish move they could possibly have made. The owners didn't believe them, because Kenny had always made a point of keeping them happy. However, one of the brothers told Kenny about the complaints that had been raised, and the middle manager who had led the effort went on to endure the most hellish six months of his career before giving up and resigning. He spent ten months on sick leave for PTSD.

Taking Orders

The concept of self-leadership has come into vogue in recent years. It sounds a little strange to my ears, but I also find it somewhat appealing. I suppose the premise is that you don't really need a boss. Or a leader. And that actually sounds incredibly convenient. We can simply manage it all by ourselves.

How do most workplaces function? The boss gives an order, and the workers carry it out. However, there are plenty of people who have problems with taking orders. It's not necessarily because they have problems with authority figures; the fact is that being ordered to do something can be a little . . . hard to swallow. Many of us dislike being given direction even from people who actually have the authority to do so. Maybe that's the reason why? One way to handle bullying bosses can be to train yourself to *accept* having to take orders from them. They would happily give you the most appalling directions they could imagine, just to enjoy watching you lose your temper. Remember that seeing your frustration energizes them. You don't want to let them do that. Instead, you want to make them notice that you're *not* reacting. How do you do that? By carrying out a few chores for them, perhaps ones that aren't part of your regular duties.

This will help get you off the hook.

The same approach can work in social life. You might realize that there is a bully in your group of friends who is going after you or somebody else you care about. Since you don't appreciate this kind of behavior, you decide to tell everybody else in the same circles about it. However, it's far from certain that anybody will want to address it, or even believe you. You see, the bully will already have positioned themselves to look like the good guy. And if they think of you as a threat, you will already have been cast as the villain.

In other words, you shouldn't get involved in struggles about what's right or wrong. Rather, you should accept the occasional defeat in order to avoid drawing more fire.

Show Them You're Hearing Them

You will usually have no choice but to listen to your boss, but they will not always—or ever, if they see it that way—have to listen to you. How annoying is that? They can stand there, fiddling with their phone or looking at their watch, or interrupt you or just walk away. But you have to stay there. Listening. Train yourself to do just that. Listen. Make sure your bully of a boss sees you listening. Show them that they have your ear.

Nod. Smile and agree. Then go on with your life.

Laughing or Not Laughing Along with a Caveman in a Suit

The boss who tells jokes that aren't funny in the slightest is a classic trope. Nobody really gets it, but there's always someone in the room who will laugh uncontrollably, because they're too afraid to do anything else.

What did they get that the rest of us missed? When the boss makes a joke, it makes sense to laugh. Yes, I'm well aware that there are plenty of people reading this who are thinking I must have lost my mind.

In 2023? We don't laugh just to ingratiate ourselves with people. Forget it.

But this isn't somebody whose intellectual capacity is going to stun the world and bring us all into the future.

This is somebody whose primal instincts are more like those of a caveman. Suit or no suit.

Another thing to keep in mind, in case you decide to say something amusing yourself: Bullies won't hesitate to laugh at you. But they will never laugh at themselves.

The Art of Asking the Right Questions

One way of breaking this pattern is to try to help the bully arrive at the right solution of their own accord. In order to carry this off, you need to use a simple technique that you might not even have considered.

When somebody asks you a question, you want to respond. This is true almost regardless of who is asking. It happens automatically, sort of like the way you respond if somebody hands you a piece of paper: You'll accept it without a single thought.

In psychological terms, whoever is asking the questions will be exerting a kind of dominance over the person who's expected to answer them. The power over a situation rests with whoever holds the initiative, which in this case will be the person asking.

This offers an interesting opportunity to reclaim the initiative from a bully. You can control the communication. You can be the one asking the questions, because bullies are just like everyone else in the sense that they, too, answer questions when asked.

You can regain some of the control by using this against them. Say something along these lines: *I realize how serious this is. What do you think we should do to turn this around?*

Whatever the bully says now—and it might just be more insults and attempts at further bullying—you should treat it as a response to your question.

He might say coming up with a solution is your responsibility, because it's your incompetence and unreliability that caused the problem in the first place.

You could respond that you realize it's your responsibility, and that you're going to address the situation, but that you'd still like him to offer you some guidelines. What would he like to see happen next?

You're not starting an interrogation here. That would look more like a demand for information and a confession (which might be entirely appropriate when your teenager comes home three hours after curfew with a suspicious smell of beer on their breath, but it won't work in this situation).

The trick here is to massage the bully's ego while making sure to claim the initiative. You'll probably need to practice this to pull it off.

What follows is a fictional example. I've chosen a work situation here, in the interest of clarity, but the technique and the psychology will work in other situations, too:

We're in trouble, *says the bullying boss*. You'll have to write a report that explains that the market has changed.

You're fully aware that the problem is in no way caused by market conditions. Your boss might have some clue that his leadership style might be stifling the team's motivation, but he's not about to bring that up. He's also not going to offer that explanation to his own superiors.

But, *you begin,* nothing has changed noticeably in the market of late. It's really our own activity level that's dropped, isn't it?

The boss might reply: It's not my job to babysit all the lazy salespeople in this business. You'll have to explain that there's nothing we can do about the situation.

Your boss is refusing to accept that the issue is an internal one and have this relayed to his superiors, as this could affect his standing with them. He demands that you fabricate a report that clears him of all responsibility.

The question now is what you will do.

If you play along and falsify data to indicate that external factors are the explanation for the drop in performance, your boss will own your soul—and is there anything in this world we should fight more to keep than our souls?

Follow Your Moral Convictions

After working in the world of finance for a number of years, I can tell you I've come across a few people who made some very bad decisions. This sometimes triggered a sequence of events that might best be described as white-collar crime. Remember that bullies aren't too concerned with right and wrong or even the legality of their actions. If they can get you involved in unethical behavior, so much the better!

You need to decide what your own moral and ethical convictions are telling you to do. A fact is a fact. Numbers are numbers, especially when they are related to money and economics. Never let anybody bully you into coming up with data that's easy to expose as fabricated. If you do, your boss's demands on you will never stop.

Your first move is to ask for more time, as I outlined earlier. This will allow you to clear your head.

Another option is to play dumb. Go over all the figures again, find nothing out of the ordinary exactly as you said, explain this to the boss, and wait to see what happens. If he wants something other than the truth, make him ask for it explicitly.

The best approach is probably to be meticulous about it. Regardless of what data you have, make sure you know where it comes from. Study it in depth, and identify the true causes of the bad performance. Demand to be told how the numbers have been calculated and how those calculations were made. Ignore any temper tantrums or abuse you're subjected to. You have to just ignore that stuff. Remind yourself that in the long run your boss will have less of a hold on you if you refuse to play along and do anything that might be unethical or even illegal.

The simplest approach, however, is to just say no. Even if you're terrified of how they might react, you're fully entitled to refuse to do anything that conflicts with your own moral convictions. If, for example, he orders you to write a report that you can't write without lying or do any other task that seems morally wrong to you, ask for time to think. After thinking, explain that you're sorry, but you can't alter the truth.

This will require courage. It can cause sleepless nights, and I fully respect the fact that it's a lot easier for me to write this than it is for you to do in the real world. It might even require you to overcome your own instincts. And yes, if your boss is antisocial enough, he might fire you on the spot.

Think of it this way: If your boss can get away with firing you for refusing to commit obvious and serious ethical or legal transgressions, perhaps this isn't the right workplace for you. If this is what the organization's culture is like, you can expect people higher up in the hierarchy to be fully prepared to look away when somebody does something that can't stand the light of day. Remember that people like this also possess a strong instinct (and a lot of practice) that causes them to immediately deflect blame to somebody else and turn them into a scapegoat. If the lies and fudged data do come to light, your boss will make sure that you're the one who suffers the consequences.

I've never been in this situation myself, but I don't think I would chance it. This isn't the workplace for you. You need to protect yourself from serious energy loss.

Walk away.

5

Passive-Aggressive People: Fists in Pockets

Passive-aggressive behavior, among many other things, is a way to avoid ever having to apologize. This is the hallmark of people who constantly spend mental energy suppressing every urge to say what they really think. They clench their fists and gnash their teeth, while insisting that they're not upset in the slightest. These individuals might well be the least enterprising people you'll ever come across. They are absolutely unable to do anything they don't fancy doing and have turned inaction into an art form. They are essentially rocks in human form.

Passive-aggressive behavior is something you've almost certainly encountered and most likely found rather frustrating. This unfortunate phenomenon appears in every walk of life and tends to be characterized by passive hostility and evasive communication. It's an indirect form of resistance that prevents any genuine confrontation.

These individuals aren't just unaware of their own hostility; they actually believe that they're being incredibly nice to everyone. If, on the other hand, you were to show any signs of irritation, they'd soon brand you as a bully. This will cause them to revert to victimhood instantly—a role they're able to perform with an uncanny degree of believability.

The concept of passive aggression was first defined during the Second World War to describe soldiers who would neither get into line nor display overt unwillingness to obey. Instead, they communicated their feelings by whining and procrastinating. However, it's reasonable to assume that this odd behavior has been around since the dawn of humanity.

Passive aggression has occasionally been described as a kind of apathy. Apathy is derived from the Greek *apatheia,* which means something like "absence of emotion." In more concrete terms, this is a state of indifference and detachment. In psychology, apathy is a state in which an individual responds to emotional, physical, or social phenomena with indifference.

A passive-aggressive person responds to you with a great big *Is that so?*

A passive-aggressive individual isn't in the least bit excited about going to the big social event you've been invited to but will agree to join you all the same, after some nagging on your part. However, they will almost invariably spend so much time on various preparations that by the time they're ready to leave, the party might almost be over.

All of their behavior towards others is defined by their resistance to demands. *Well then,* you might be thinking, *what demands are we talking about?* How about . . . all of them?

THE PASSIVE AGGRESSIVE

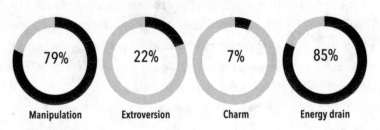

79%	22%	7%	85%
Manipulation	Extroversion	Charm	Energy drain

They adopt a passive attitude to entirely normal obligations that the rest of us simply have to put up with in life.

If a passive-aggressive individual has agreed, say, to wash their car before the end of the weekend, they'll wait until so late Sunday night that it'll be too dark for them to get the job done. When this happens, they will blame the sun for being so unhelpful as to set (as it always does), without mentioning at all that their own lack of planning might have contributed to the outcome.

But this was actually the plan all along. They intended to fail to wash the car.

Passive-aggressive people often exhibit a fear of being alone, and it's not uncommon for them to seem rather unconfident. In some cases, they struggle with a deep sense of melancholy and—to put it bluntly—bitterness. Bitterness is a complex emotion, which has proven challenging for researchers to define.

This is partially due to the fact that it includes a degree of disappointment. Disappointment, among other things, involves mournfulness. If you think about disappointment, you'll realize that anger can also be a component.

Bitter individuals often adopt a blaming and unempathic mindset. This is one of the reasons why they so often try to shift blame to others.

In their own eyes, they're as good as infallible. They also tend to avoid taking responsibility for their own actions. They want to avoid any guilt, even in situations where it seems ridiculous to even try. When something goes wrong, they'll immediately point at somebody else.

Do I need to explain how frustrating and draining this will be for absolutely everybody around them?

When people get irritated, they usually let others know what the problem is. Even if you try to be polite and keep quiet about it, you'll eventually have to say something. Most of us will make a comment to communicate our displeasure—occasionally, an unplanned and ill-conceived one.

That's not what a passive-aggressive person does. Oh no. They will keep it all inside and act like nothing's wrong. It's as though they hadn't even noticed a thing. They'll seem cool as cucumbers.

Inside, however, they might be in absolute turmoil. Their fury is blazing under the surface, and sometimes it might even make itself known through their cramped, suppressed body language. Many psychologists claim that passive-aggressive individuals are more or less constantly consumed by rage. However, they very seldom communicate this emotion, because they feel that it is an unacceptable one, for reasons we will soon get into.

They never unburden themselves, release the pressure, or blow off steam. Pick your own favorite metaphor. The consequences will be the same, regardless. In fact, they conceal their rage so well that many of the people around them will never even realize what's really going on. On the surface, they will seem warm and friendly, but deep down, they're actually jealous, bitter, and outraged.

Gradually, they transform themselves into living bombs, packed full of rage and contempt.

NONE OF IT WAS MY FAULT

Passive-aggressive people are experts when it comes to shifting blame. Nothing is ever their fault. They don't see their own role in any conflict or misunderstanding that arises. Their constant attempts to shift blame can only really be taken to mean that they believe that they are infallible. In their universe, there simply isn't any other possible explanation: It must be somebody else's fault.

They're happy to play the victim. They bear no guilt for anything that happens, even when they're the ones who are behaving badly. They will blurt out derogatory and spiteful comments while claiming that they would never have had to say what they're saying if only the other person had done what they wanted them to.

They "forget" agreed appointments, arrive late to meetings, and so on. We all forget things, after all. However, this is all a deliberate strategy, and they're actually only claiming to have forgotten. Actually, they simply didn't feel like coming. So they didn't bother. Claiming to have forgotten is an excuse they made up after the fact.

It's time for another checklist. What follows will give you some specific examples to keep an eye out for—the higher the score, the worse the problem is. This person . . .

1. tends to clench their jaw or fists but refuses to admit that they are frustrated
2. seldom offers any ideas or suggestions of their own
3. can keep quiet longer than anybody else you've ever met
4. has never admitted to a mistake for as long as you've known them
5. seldom or never takes responsibility when something goes wrong
6. claims to agree with what you're saying, despite clear body language to the contrary
7. blames others without hesitation whenever they receive the mildest of criticism
8. seldom performs boring tasks without being nagged to
9. is an individual who never openly displays their anger
10. can occasionally surprise you by saying the most terrible things behind people's backs

How I Tried to Figure It All Out

Once, in high school, I was about to take a math test that was scheduled to take five hours. Math had become an overwhelming subject for me. At this point, numbers had turned into letters and peculiar squiggles I couldn't read. There was simply no chance at all that I would pass this test without some drastic action.

If I had gone to my father, the engineer, he would probably have been able to explain most of it to me. I could also have overcome the challenge by studying harder or alerted my teacher to my struggles and asked for some extra help.

Any of those approaches might have gotten me back on track. I could even have talked to one of the girls in my class who were obviously on top of things. I was on good terms with most of the kids in my class. Somebody would probably have helped me.

Now, you might be wondering what I chose to do.

The answer is every bit as simple as it is embarrassing.

I did nothing. Absolutely nothing.

I didn't talk to anybody, and I didn't study at all. I just buried it all somewhere inside myself, as the menacing day of the test kept coming closer.

At 8:00 a.m., on the day of the test, I made my final decision: After carrying terrible anxiety around for four weeks, I decided not to take the test. I stayed at home. I skipped school that day.

Naturally, this decision was an idiotic one in every way.

However, I did find that for some mysterious reason, I actually felt better. At least I had made an *active decision*.

The procrastination I had engaged in led to my getting a failing grade in math. Not good. But as soon as I returned to being active, I felt better. Pretty good, even.

I'd be lying if I told you that I've never dodged a difficult task since then and that the experience of failing my math test taught me the value of taking responsibility for my actions and blah blah blah.

But I'd also be lying if I told you that I didn't learn *anything*. Apparently, getting back into the process and *doing* something made me feel better. In my case, what I did may have been wrong, but at least I had reclaimed my control of the situation.

A highly passive-aggressive person won't do that. They will just carry on being passive until the very end. The reasons for this behavior are shrouded in mystery. But whatever the reasons, it makes them feel worse than they need to in the long run.

Imagine a car that's about to race straight off the road. In the back seat are two people, with their hands tied behind their backs. They're screaming at the driver to do something, prevent a potential accident. Behind the wheel is a person who could easily regain control of the car. All they really need to do is press the brake pedal and grab the steering wheel. But for some reason known only to themselves, and sometimes not even to them, they have decided that they don't want to drive the car. They don't feel like it. So they leave things be.

Rather than taking responsibility and preventing a potential accident, they will allow the car and all its passengers, including themselves, to hit the ditch, consequences be damned!

Does this example seem exaggerated? Perhaps it does. However, this is what passive-aggressive behavior is all about. Being *aware* of how everything could go absolutely sideways but somehow *failing to* act to prevent disaster.

Somebody else should have addressed it, you see.

Why People Fail to Empty the Dishwasher

A few years ago, I coached a woman who was very obviously passive-aggressive. Everybody in the workplace except for her was painfully aware of her problems. She worked for an office that was part of a public agency.

Her manager sent her to me because she kept getting into disagreements with people. Everybody else felt that she was the bad guy in all those disturbances, too. However, I didn't accept this premise at all. Conflict, after all, might easily be a symptom of an underlying organizational problem. If the woman was being obstructive, this might simply be her way of making sure she wouldn't end up getting the short end of the stick.

In this case, however, I realized fairly quickly that the problem was indeed sitting across from me in that chair.

This woman, you see, had fairly normal work assignments. She wasn't limited to simple, repetitive tasks but had a fair share of reasonably advanced responsibility. But she never seemed to get the job done.

She kept coming back to the same two things. One of them was that she didn't always *feel like* doing her work. When she didn't feel like doing something, which could happen literally anytime, for any particular task, she wouldn't get anything done at all. Rather than working, she killed time by engaging in absolute nonsense.

The second part was a little more complex. This was about how much she genuinely hated being told what to do. It didn't matter if it was her boss—who was, generally, a well-meaning and fair leader—or a colleague asking her for help.

This woman was so severely provoked by the mere thought that somebody—*anybody*—would feel entitled to interfere with and impact her workday. She would simply short-circuit.

This also happens to be an important aspect of the passive-aggressive behavioral pattern.

These people really hate taking direction. For some strange reason, they feel that nobody has the right to tell them what to do.

I checked out her references. Each and every one of them confirmed that she was a dreadful pain to deal with. Delegating tasks to this woman was fine—she would rarely ask any questions and never really objected. However, with alarming frequency, she simply didn't carry out the task in question. Other times, she would do it but put in such a poor effort that nobody would ever ask her again. It was as though she had sworn to never do a good job of anything, even things she could manage just fine.

After a long, frustrating talk, one of her previous managers came out and said it: *She stalls on purpose, and then avoids everybody, and delivers bad results, so that she won't be asked to do anything at all ever again. If she does a bad enough job, we'll ask someone else next time.*

Of course, this was right.

This is an important clue for understanding the passive-aggressive mindset. I'm sure you've seen somebody who seemed to be unable to carry out the most basic of tasks. They manage to do everything the wrong way. It could be anything from closing an important project to emptying the dishwasher. How do they manage to fail?

The answer is right in front of you. If they can carry out the task poorly enough, you'll stop asking them. Their capacity to obstruct is far greater than your capacity to nag.

This woman had been leaving a trail of annoyed bosses and frustrated colleagues behind her for years. I confronted her about it all. Lots of people were bothered by her passive behavior, and I asked what she had to say for herself.

How did she respond? Apparently, people make unreasonable demands. She had nothing to do with any of those problems. It wasn't her fault. I should forget about it.

She wasn't going to give in to pressure.

In the strange world of a passive-aggressive individual, being coerced into obeying is the same thing as admitting defeat. They will habitually deny the legitimacy of the most common of instructions or demands from other people, and they obviously have problems dealing with authority, as they prefer to decide things for themselves. Intellectually, they do realize the need to fall into line from time to time. The thing is, they don't want to. I suspect that this is why they so often feel bitter.

This brings us to yet another rather bizarre paradox. These individuals would gladly put themselves in the epicenter of power, ideally as top dog, if only it weren't for one little detail: Getting there is simply too much work.

When I tried to speak to this woman about her inability to take instructions, her fists were clenched hard enough to turn her knuckles white much of the time. I could practically see the smoke billowing from her ears. However, her face was entirely peaceful. She denied being upset, too. Not her, oh no. Someone else, perhaps, but not her.

Fascinating enough, she kept describing herself as an incredibly friendly and agreeable person. Unfortunately, she was treated badly by people who asked things of her that were either ridiculous or absolutely impossible to achieve. To my ears, these supernatural efforts she was being asked to make sounded like perfectly normal work tasks, and it seemed that she just didn't feel like doing them.

THE ART OF SULKING

One very common passive-aggressive behavior is to withdraw and sulk rather than express your opinions and your needs. It shows in the body language, in the refusal to communicate, and in the mere act of withdrawing. Others who are nearby might have difficulty believing their eyes, as it seems like such a blatantly immature, or even childish, response. The passive-aggressive person might refuse to participate in meetings, for example. Take some extra sick leave. Convince themselves that it's not their fault.

They can also turn sarcastic and make comments that are intended to be humorous but are actually anything but. Rather than being straightforward about their differing opinion, they leak their sarcasm all over the place. The idea is that this is going to protect them from being confronted. They could always claim to have been joking.

These people are full-blooded energy vampires.

In romantic relationships, passive aggression can express itself in all kinds of ways. For instance, doing the dishes rather noisily. Slamming doors. Causing some ruckus without having to commit to actually having anything to say.

The use of deafening silence. Or leaving the room in mid-conversation. All of these techniques have been honed to perfection by passive-aggressive individuals.

Rather than talking out whatever needs to be resolved once and for all, they clench their fists in their pockets and sulk. When their partners ask them what the problem is, passive-aggressive individuals will, at best, tell them it's nothing.

Nothing in the world could compel a passive-aggressive individual to participate in a conversation they don't feel like having.

One woman I spoke to about this explained that for the last forty years her husband had consistently raised the newspaper to cover his face whenever a conversation got too sensitive for him to deal with.

Before you start thinking that this was just some colorful metaphor, let me explain: This man *literally* raised his newspaper and sat behind it, keeping silent until his wife either stopped trying to get him to respond or simply gave up and left the room.

I know. It sounds absolutely bonkers.

Passive-aggressive people, as I've mentioned, don't always express their feelings or thoughts. On the other hand, the messages they do express are often completely contradictory. Their partners will spend a lot of time wondering what's going on between them. It's very difficult to resolve a conflict with somebody who provides unclear and insufficient information. One of the people in the relationship will seldom mean what they say and seldom say what they mean.

The other person will try to understand but always risk being on the receiving end of some variation of that hiding-behind-the-newspaper ploy. The only way to truly know how a passive-aggressive person feels about something is to observe their actions. In this, they are just like everybody else: Their actions are the only thing you can really rely on.

The Innocence of Forgetfulness

Some people have bad memories, of course. However, somebody who systematically *forgets* about agreements they've made, times, places, and anniversaries is probably acting out of passive aggression. Forgetting things that matter to a significant other is a highly effective way of making that person confused, angry, worried, stressed, and off-balance in a variety of ways. They will feel as though they don't have much control over their own life, and their partner's "forgetfulness" can very well end up sabotaging their career and social life.

Forgetting an important anniversary can also be a powerful way of hurting your partner without being too obvious about it. It could be the punishment exacted for some imagined slight. It's difficult to address forgetfulness because it seems so innocent. We all forget things sometimes. How can you criticize anybody for that?

When somebody points out that a passive-aggressive person is behaving badly, everything will be turned against them. The innocent party will now be portrayed as the deranged lunatic of the situation. The passive-aggressive individual will attempt to justify their actions, shift the blame, and refuse to accept any responsibility or guilt. It could very well end with the innocent party apologizing for their own—perfectly reasonable—behavior.

If their partner responds with anger and causes a scene, a passive-aggressive person will simply stare at them and possibly say something along the lines of, *You're out of your mind*. Or, simply, *You've lost it*. Or both.

The Consequences of Drinking Brake Fluid

The passive-aggressive person won't let their partner get what they want deep down. They will act as though they would do anything for their partner, but they will never follow through on anything at all. The partner is left confused and frustrated.

The partner will feel as though they're asking for too much, and that's exactly what their passive-aggressive abuser wants them to feel.

A good example of this would be a couple that's hunting for a new home together. A passive-aggressive man might appear to be very eager to find the home they're going to share but won't contribute at all to the process. Checking out the market in neighborhood X, which was the task he took on during the last family meeting, never crossed his mind. Or, perhaps, he lost the contact details he needed. If, by chance, he does actually come up with some suggestions, he'll find some flaw with every property they look at. Nothing will be good enough.

Why? Well . . . Maybe he drank some brake fluid? Maybe his batteries ran out? Or, maybe, he just doesn't want to?

Is passive-aggressive behavior manipulative? That's actually a very good question. How much of this behavior is deliberate?

Passive aggression is, beyond any doubt, a kind of manipulation. In some cases, the objective will actually be to control others for personal benefit.

A person with a passive-aggressive nature will manipulate others in order to hide their own shortcomings and their own underlying anger. The purpose is to avoid confrontation and conflict. As I mentioned earlier, it won't work very well. More than anything, it actually makes people mad.

Psychological and verbal abuse is often a kind of underhanded assault, and it can occasionally manifest as passive-aggressive behavior. Passive-aggressive people tend to be masters of the art of abusing people while giving the appearance of being perfectly normal, helpful, and polite. In other words, passive-aggressive behavior can be both difficult to identify and difficult to address.

However, I would still call it manipulative, as it involves *getting* what you want without having to *express* or *take responsibility* for what you want.

An example: Rather than come out and say he doesn't want to tidy the house, the man will announce his intention to clean up and then avoid actually getting started on tidying. Rather than being honest about how he feels, he will procrastinate and do other things.

When his partner eventually loses her temper because he hasn't done what he *said he would do,* he'll give her a perplexed look. Once again, it's his partner who is being unstable, irritable, and irrational. This man will always have reasonable explanations for his behavior and will seek to shift blame rather than accept responsibility.

In the end, his partner might end up apologizing for having "gone off" at him. In this situation, then, psychological abuse has been perpetrated without the passive-aggressive man ever raising his voice. Instead, he remains calm, passive, and rational, while his partner is upset, angry, hurt, confused, and, eventually, apologetic about her own emotions.

If that's not manipulative, nothing is.

HOW DID THINGS END UP LIKE THIS?

Passive aggression is a kind of rage, hostility, and frustration that an individual—for whatever reason—isn't comfortable expressing directly. Instead, the anger will come out in vague, indirect ways. Behind this behavior, there is a sad, unhappy individual, and it's important to remember this. There's no doubt that there's some kind of message hidden away in the depths of any passive-aggressive behavior. The question is just what that message is.

Many seem to believe that the reason for this absolutely unreasonable behavior is a combination of nature and nurture. Self-esteem, childhood experiences, family dynamics, and partially learned behaviors can all play a part.

But why is this unreasonable passivity the chosen response? How did things end up like this? Disproportionate discipline in childhood? Possibly. The effects of their parents' overtly aggressive behavior? It can't be ruled out. Witnessing constant arguments and listening to loud voices might lead somebody to assume that openly displaying your anger is a bad thing.

Dad was always screaming; I don't want to end up like him. I'd rather just keep it inside.

Okay. Now, if that were the case, it would revolve around not wanting to scream and shout to get your way. To refuse to show open aggression. That kind of angry response looks and sounds bad—*I'll pass.*

However, that still doesn't explain their total unwillingness to take responsibility for anything. Their constant evasiveness. If aggressive outbursts traumatized you as a child, wouldn't you rather be likely to develop an excessive drive to be *appeasing*? Doesn't it seem reasonable to assume you'd be more likely to be a bit of a doormat, who always ends up tidying up other people's messes? The kind of person who's prepared to do practically anything to *avoid* angering others?

Passive-aggressive people, after all, do little else than annoy others.

They feel put upon constantly, and the more reasonable or factual explanations you offer them, the stronger their perceived victimhood will grow.

When Passivity Gets Going

How do people like this affect the rest of us, then? That's a good question, but one that defies simple answers. Usually, it will depend on who you are to some extent. But when one party in a romantic couple, for instance, constantly shifts blame for everything, the person on the receiving end will feel increasingly troubled, perhaps to the point where they experience depression or even physical symptoms, while the passive-aggressive party shields themselves from any kind of self-awareness. By definition, a passive-aggressive individual utilizes a very common defense mechanism: suppression.

As a consequence, the other person has to keep track of everything. Literally.

Bearing all the responsibility for a relationship on your own is extremely fatiguing and can consume a great deal of energy. Even if you happen to be a very responsible individual and don't mind picking up some slack for others, you'll eventually get worn down if you never get to relax.

Imagine that you're packing to go on a trip. You're running around, getting things from inside the house, carrying them down to the car, loading them inside, redistributing stuff when there's not enough room, suddenly remembering something else you've missed, tearing it all out again, repacking everything, and having to do lots of rational thinking. It's all on you. Meanwhile, your partner is leaning against the car, asking you, *Aren't we supposed to be leaving soon?*

You'll be exhausted. You'll also be feeling rather fed up. In interviews I've done with people, these questions often seem to pop up: *Why won't they help? Why do they make me do everything? Can't they see how exhausted doing everything myself is making me? Can't they see it all just makes me want to cry?*

And then another, perhaps worse, question comes to mind: *Do they not love me anymore?* When one person in the relationship doesn't seem particularly dedicated to any part of their shared life but rather comes along when it suits them and stays home when it doesn't, friction is sure to follow. Perhaps you'll choose to raise your voice and demand some more involvement and responsibility, or perhaps you're one of those people who's so worn down by this kind of thing that you'll turn passive, too. Regardless, you'll end up on a dangerous, slippery slope.

Divorce could easily follow if both parties can't agree to address the real issues.

Of course, the dynamics will be different in the workplace, but energy drain happens just as quickly there. One member of the team just sits on their ass all day, watching everyone else scrambling around just to keep up. And somehow, there don't seem to be any repercussions. The boss lost their patience ages ago and has decided to make things easier by always giving the important tasks to other members of the team. The passive-aggressive individual is, on the whole, quite content with this arrangement. However, you and I most certainly won't be.

It's depressing, exhausting, and kills your faith in the notion that hard work pays off: *If they don't need to make even the slightest effort, why on earth should I have to do all this work?* Passivity can easily spread in this situation and cause the most dreadful consequences. To some degree, this will depend on the particulars of the organizational culture involved and how passionate people are about their work—but no workplace is completely immune to the danger of everyone beginning to drag their feet.

Soon, results will begin to suffer, which can cause serious financial difficulties that might cost people their jobs.

This Gives Reds and Yellows Hives

Passive-aggressive behavior is most closely aligned with the Green profile, but this is a near-pathological case of refusing to commit to anything at all. Green individuals aren't anything like that, despite tending to be more passive than active. They still have thoughts on stuff, and opinions, like everybody else. In the right circumstances, Greens can be reasoned with without any serious difficulty. What they're the most resistant to is *rapid* change. The trick, generally, is not to push them too hard and to give them plenty of time to consider how they feel about things. Besides, Greens want to please people, which is something passive-aggressive individuals have no intention at all of doing. They are the polar opposite of helpful; nothing like Greens, who are prepared to work themselves into the ground to prevent arguments.

Greens will tend to be quite lenient towards passive-aggressive individuals, because they will recognize parts of themselves in them. Also, Greens don't tend to pressure others into doing stuff in the first place. They're very perceptive when it comes to subtle signals. And they genuinely want the best for everyone. Upsetting people is the last thing Greens want to do, because of their aversion to conflict. This means that Greens will tend to cope quite well when dealing with passive-aggressive people. Generally speaking, Greens will take care of all the things the other person doesn't want to get involved in.

Will they feel used? Yes.

Will they do anything about it? Not necessarily.

While I was writing this book, I performed an informal survey among my friends. My sample size was too small to provide any definite evidence, but it still allowed me to make some interesting observations.

People whose profiles were dominated by Red, including fully Red, Red-Yellow, and Red-Blue individuals (Red-Green is a highly unusual combination), singled out this variety of energy vampires as the most frustrating kind in the entire book. Some people lost their temper just reading about passive-aggressive behavior. Everybody had a story to tell, and they all felt very strongly about not wanting to have anything to do with this energy vampire, ever.

You'll find many of their reactions in the section on how

Reds respond to Greens—only here the reactions are turned up to eleven. Here are some excerpts from the survey responses:

If they would at least say something, there would be something to address.

Simply refusing is immature and irresponsible—I'd never let somebody like that work for my business.

If they would just be prepared to discuss things, we could make some kind of progress!

If my partner behaved like that, I'd have to really love them—because just thinking about it makes my skin crawl!

Yes, one woman actually wrote that.

What about Yellows, then? Just like their Red friends, they will be terribly provoked by the inactivity. Although Yellows do talk more than Reds, they are also relationship-oriented, and highly active, in general. When somebody just sits there and refuses to participate, it makes Yellows see red, too. Unlike Greens, they won't always keep their feelings hidden away inside, either. Yellows have an easy time finding the right words, including the right harsh words. Being told off by a Yellow is actually an unpleasant experience, considering how well they express themselves. They can verbally execute people in the most creative ways.

How about Blues? Well, they keep calm and carry on. It's safe to say that Blues are, generally speaking, the best at handling energy vampires. They never get worked up over anything. If it's Blue combined with Red, the reactions may be more severe, and if it's Blue combined with Green, they might get slightly more emotional. However, they're unlikely to lose it entirely.

HOW TO KEEP FROM BECOMING
A NERVOUS WRECK

As you've no doubt realized, this behavior isn't very easy to address. If you have no choice but to interact with a person like this, the best approach is not to let their destructive moods drag you down.

If you have enough influence over the situation, it can be a good idea to encourage an individual like this to get some help. An experienced therapist might be able to provide them with strategies that can defuse their anger and frustration.

They prefer to do things their own way, and they don't want to feel any pressure or obligation. If they never finish something, it won't bother them. It'll be your problem: You're the one who gave them an unreasonable deadline, after all. It's all your fault.

Naturally, this will have a huge impact on their work performance. It can also impact the ability of their team to get the job done. If, for instance, their manager asks them to finish a report for the next day, it isn't just that it won't be done in time—they won't even try to explain why. They'll simply allow time to pass until they *feel like doing it*.

In some cases, they might come up with a fabricated explanation or bend the truth to get out of the situation. However, if they're not motivated—which they very seldom are—they just won't bother to do it. They'll keep messing up like this, even when they know that it might have dire consequences.

Confusing? Indeed.

Basically, you're going to need some effective methods for how to deal with them.

To begin with, you need to understand that they're not actually lying. They're not fully aware of the fact that they're angry with you and keep pushing back on what you've asked them to do. Nothing you can say to them will change this. If you were to explain to them how their behavior seems to you, they probably wouldn't understand what you were talking about.

You'd be unlikely to ever convince them of anything that conflicts with their *own self-image*.

It's like trying to untie a double fisherman's knot. The harder you pull, the more difficult it will be to untie it. You'll have to find another approach.

The most important thing is not to reward their behavior—if you do, it will probably continue. I'd also strongly advise against repaying them in kind. Don't try to fight them with their own favorite weapons; you won't stand a chance if you do. These people are as stubborn as they come.

It won't help to be openly aggressive, either—i.e., lose your temper, raise your voice, and use harsh language. Remember: While these people are absolutely oblivious to their own inherent aggression, they also happen to be hypersensitive to other people's aggression.

Nobody wants to be lectured to about right and wrong, however well-intentioned the message might be. Most people hate it. This is a little contradictory, because what often motivates us to do the most boring of chores is our desire to *spare ourselves* precisely that kind of lecture. Let's just agree that motivation psychology is a complicated subject and that people can be different.

Because of this, you should set aside any thoughts you have about their *attitudes*. Don't comment on that at all.

Passive-aggressive people have learned their hopeless habits because their behavior has helped them avoid discomfort in the past, without triggering any guilt. You can't do anything about their snorts, rolled eyes, and demonstratively loud stomps. Just leave it be.

Punishment—a Last Resort, to Be Used Only When You Feel Up to It

Opinions differ on this, but punishment is very unlikely to affect anybody's attitude, although it can induce behavioral changes by making people seek to avoid further punishment.

You should also never go down this path if you don't feel prepared to commit to seeing it through to the bitter end. This applies to all kinds of punishment, for all kinds of passive-aggressive people.

If you're bluffing or don't really mean it, expect them to call your hand. And refuse to change their ways. You'll be in even bigger trouble if this happens. They'll be demonstrating to themselves, as well as to everybody else, that your antics are pointless. You'll be completely disarmed. They won't take your threats seriously ever again.

You might consider indulging in some passive aggression of your own, as a way of overcoming their unhelpful behavior.

Think again.

These people already didn't care what you would do, and trying to defeat them by going silent and withdrawing will only give them more space to do absolutely nothing in. They won't care at all if you go off to a corner to sulk. (However, don't be surprised if they accuse you of being passive-aggressive!)

Now, punishment can actually work, as long as it involves having to do more work. Ostracism or groundings won't have any effect. The passive-aggressive person's goal was to not have to do anything, remember? However, making them work in the garden or help a coworker with some tedious task might be effective, because it involves having to work. Before you start handing out punishments for behavior you find unacceptable, you should think things through.

Managers often ask me if they should just try to make somebody's work miserable enough that it will convince them to quit their jobs. The problem is, passive-aggressive people won't quit. How do I know this? Well, it's right there in the first half of the term "passive-aggressive."

You have to make your mind up. Trying to ignore reality is *not* the answer.

That was an example of what you shouldn't do. Now let's move on to what you should do.

A Perfect Cocktail of Clarity, Nagging, and Praise

Try to identify the things they actually do right. These people enjoy positive affirmation and recognition. Unfortunately, that's not the whole story. Ideally, they want recognition and positive affirmation for *an absolute minimum of effort*.

You'll simply have to go looking for things they do well and acknowledge these achievements until your face turns blue. If they get something right, praise them.

There's a question here: How much praise is the right amount? As these individuals tend to feel rather unappreciated, expect to have to give a great deal of it. How much recognition and positive affirmation would you like to receive? Give them *twice that amount*. This will at least reduce the chances of failure.

You can't change their attitudes. They've been set in stone for years and years. Focus entirely on the things they do and don't do. Overlook their annoyed expression, and find out if they did the task or not.

Skip the whole part about telling them how their bad moods affect you. Moods are a matter of attitude. Let it go. Comment *exclusively* on their behavior. Unless you're dealing with a sulky teenager, your goal here shouldn't be to improve this person. What you're looking to achieve is to have things get done the right way, in time. This approach is the right one both at home and at work.

Accept the fact that these individuals will try to get away with putting in the very minimum of effort every time they complete a task. If possible, you should make it more difficult for them to cheat by monitoring their work and forcing them to actually do what you agreed on.

This is true of everyone to some extent, but I repeat: Passive-aggressive individuals will never put in more effort than they have to. So you shouldn't simply tell them to *do the dishes*. All that means is something involving the dishes needs to get done. They might decide all that's required is for them to get half the dishes out of the dishwasher. That means they've done some dishes, doesn't it?

When you remark on what a poor job they've done, they'll simply point out that *you never said they had to do* all *the dishes*. You'll both know what's really going on, but you shouldn't leave them any outs.

If you want the kitchen tidied, you'll have to explain that the job isn't done until:

a) *the dishwasher is completely emptied,*
b) *the dish rack is clear of frying pans and other things,*
c) *all the dirty dishes are in the dishwasher, and*
d) *the countertop has been wiped.*

If you think there's a chance the dirty dishes will more or less fill the dishwasher again and that it would be a good idea to have the dishwasher started again, you'll have to add this:

e) *If the dishwasher is full, start it.*

Seems simple, huh?

Now, I get it. You're wondering if they honestly can't think for themselves. They can. But their default mode is simply to try to get away with doing as little work as possible.

Be clear. Be specific. Be absolutely *unambiguous*.

However, you should realize that not even this approach is guaranteed to work. You might still come home to an emptied dishwasher, in a kitchen where none of your other ridiculously specific instructions have been carried out.

When you point out that the dishwasher is empty and the countertop is full of dirty dishes, they might well give you a response along the lines of, *Well, I did it that way once before, and you didn't have a problem with it then.*

The implicit question here is why you're causing a fuss about it this time. Pretty exhausting, eh?

Passive-aggressive individuals, as I've discussed, commonly carry around a great deal of anger and resentment. The strange thing about them, I suppose, is that they're only vaguely aware of this—at best! In normal situations, there's not much point in asking somebody who's enraged to talk about how enraged they are. All that does is intensify their rage.

But when it comes to passive-aggressive people, this doesn't quite apply. It's as though it actually helps them to let it all out.

Convincing them to speak their minds can actually defuse some of their pent-up hostility. However, you can't go about it any old way, for the very reason that they're not generally aware of how angry they are. A more indirect approach is called for.

Try to ask the question sideways by getting them to tell you what everybody else is so annoyed or upset about. When they are free to dress up their own frustrations as the opinions of others, they will readily share them with you. There's no danger in it.

This approach can reap huge rewards. When you give them an opportunity to voice their resentment, albeit indirectly, this will make them less likely to act on it. And maybe, just maybe, things will go a lot smoother afterwards.

Nagging can actually work, because *negative reinforcement can encourage avoidance*. In practical terms, this means that you threaten somebody with something irritating in order to encourage them to choose to change their behavior to avoid the discomfort.

Everybody hates nagging. Nobody wants to be on the receiving end of it. This way, nagging itself becomes the punishment. However, if you nag with sufficient intensity, you might get a passive-aggressive person to actually do what you're asking them to, just to get rid of you. Naturally, when this happens, you *stop nagging immediately*. That part is key: You cease immediately.

Note: This is the *only* way it will work. This removes the negative reinforcement, which is what the other person wants. If you continue going on about how they *never do so-and-so* after they've actually done so-and-so, it won't work. Doing it didn't shut you up, so what's the point of doing as you ask? Next time, they'll ignore your nagging completely.

Instead, you should combine their reception of the negative reinforcement with a positive reinforcement—by starting to praise them the very moment things begin to happen. In an instant, their discomfort will give way to contentment.

Suppose you have a colleague who's always late for meetings. The solution is to make them in charge of taking minutes. Does the individual do a sloppy job on purpose? Give them more of the work to do to *help them learn*.

Let me make one thing clear here: This behavior on your part is essentially manipulative in nature.

The thing is, it works. Only you can decide if you're prepared to go this far to correct a behavior that causes you a great deal of frustration.

Getting Your Energy Back

My goodness, you might be thinking. *That all sounds like a huge load of trouble. Am I seriously supposed to be keeping track of all that stuff? That's going to take a huge amount of time and involvement. Where am I going to find the energy for all this?*

Well, I'd have to refer you to the title of this book.

Think of it like this: If you can achieve a 50 percent change in this person, that will make you a winner. You will have succeeded at something many others have failed at. Congratulate yourself for that.

However, if you don't have the time or the energy, you're faced with a choice: Act like a Red and tough it out or run away. You don't have to do anything at all. You can continue tiptoeing around this individual. It's entirely up to you.

6

The Eternal Victim Who Demands Constant Attention

The eternal victim, or martyr, is a person who generally feels that they have suffered such terribly unfortunate circumstances and hard knocks in life that everybody else is obliged to listen to their complaining. This is somebody who actually *gains* energy by imposing their endless martyrdom on everybody around them. An individual whose belief in their own innocence with regard to every misfortune they suffer in life is so genuine that nothing seems able to shake it. A miserable wretch, basically.

These energy vampires are all over the place, and they seem to all wear the same constant look of anticipation. *Anticipation of what?* one might ask. That a safe is about to drop from the clear blue sky on top of their head, proving decisively that they were right all along: Life *is* deeply unfair. No matter how they try to get out of their situation, the world, fate, the universe, or chance always seems to drag them back down into abject misery. They are entirely innocent victims of horrible circumstances.

They're also very keen to inform others of all the potential disasters they see looming ahead, and they seem to feel a great need to tell as many people as possible about their misfortunes. This is why they use visual signals to such great effect. Their faces will tend to have tormented expressions, with deeper furrows than most, the origins of which they don't hesitate to explain. Their posture will be strained or resigned. Any kind of motion or activity will become significantly more difficult when performed in the presence of others. If you didn't know better, you might think they really were carrying the weight of the world on their innocent shoulders.

THE MARTYR

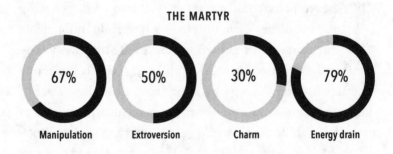

Manipulation	Extroversion	Charm	Energy drain
67%	50%	30%	79%

You will often hear martyrs say things like the following: *I had the best of intentions; It was only to be expected; Not everything suits everybody; I've had my fair share of suffering, but you won't hear me complain about it; Don't worry what I think, nobody else does; What would I know? I've only worked here for thirty-five years; I'm such an idiot!;* and similar variations on the theme.

The purpose of these lines is to demonstrate that the person in question really *is* badly victimized by life, by their surroundings, or by you or me, but that despite their terrible luck, they stoically accept their lot in life: constantly having to face new troubles. Another purpose is to convince you, me, and anybody else nearby to immediately rush to their rescue.

Note: There are some people who suggest that they are the victims of this or that injustice for manipulative purposes, in order to attract attention and benefit somehow. These individuals aren't martyrs, however, but rather narcissists or psychopaths. Everything they do is performance to manipulate others. These people actually think of themselves as natural-born winners. I'd like to refer you to the chapter on narcissists for more about them. However, it's not always easy to tell the difference. In order to do so, you have to look at specific patterns over an extended period of time.

True martyrs really do feel that life has treated them unfairly. They genuinely *feel* like victims, which is actually their whole problem in a nutshell. Their behavior isn't necessarily intended to deceive or manipulate others; they truly think of the world as a place where most people are seeking to treat them unfairly.

Naturally, it's quite obvious that this can be used for personal benefit. They gain a great deal of attention and compassion, which is better than being ignored. At least it means they're being seen.

Even when something good happens to them, martyrs will manage to find some troubling concern that will allow them to continue engaging in their negative, toxic thinking. They can't, and won't, find any pleasure in anything. This becomes a vicious circle, which prevents them from ever overcoming the feeling that they're missing something.

When a martyr speaks, it'll often be with a slightly melancholy tone of voice that implies that they're dealing with great difficulties. They might mention things like how they've called so-and-so at least eleven times, while so-and-so has only called them back three times at most. *Not that they're keeping score.*

If you should dare to point out that they might need a change of attitude or expectations, you'll be rewarded with a lengthy complaint in which they seek to convince you that they are saintly Good Samaritans, constantly seeking to do good in a cold, cruel world.

Their motive for "helping" is to be told they've done a good deed rather than to actually help. If you don't acknowledge their efforts appropriately, or fail to mention them to everybody you know, they will immediately revert to victimhood. Worse, you'll have given them further ammunition to add to their expanding arsenal of weapons of self-victimization.

Martyrs often end up waiting for somebody else to resolve their issues. Which is only natural, really. After all, they convinced themselves a long time ago that there's nothing they can do to get out of their situation on their own.

They can't resolve the issues by themselves. They don't have it in them, they don't know how to do it, it's just the way they are, okay?

Any serious attempt at understanding this behavior will yield some interesting observations. In motivation theory, there is a concept of drive. This is the motivation we have to do a certain thing or actively refrain from doing it.

There are many different drives. One of the most common drives is the social drive, which involves being driven to help others and avoid conflict. People who have this drive simply feel very good about doing things for other people, regardless of whether they are deserving or not.

A large portion of people on this planet are helpers, believe it or not. I'd say around a quarter of all the people you'll come across would help somebody else without giving it too much thought. (The sad news, of course, is that a large portion of the world's population would protest making the smallest effort even if you asked them to.) Naturally, there are many parameters to consider here, including the extent of the help needed, the problem involved, the expected time involved, and the helpers' ability to actually solve the specific problem.

Looking closer at the factors that influence our choice to help reveals a critical coefficient: the relationship between the person in need and the potential helper. Even somebody who might lack this social drive would help a relative, for example, if only to maintain a sense of basic decency. When a child displays the behavior of a martyr, their parents tend to respond with more time and effort than they would if it was the neighbors' child who behaved that way. That's only natural. If a parent is an eternal victim, their adult children won't be able to ignore the problem as easily as they would if it were a distant aunt who lived thousands of miles away. This relationship proximity factor probably explains why the majority of the population wouldn't help you or me out even if we needed it. They don't know us. We simply have to rely on the existing relationships we do have.

However, an experienced victimhood vampire will know exactly how to behave to instill the desire to help in others, even in those who don't possess this instinct.

Martyrs will often talk about situations in which they were treated poorly and the negative impact these have had on their lives. This could be an old relationship, a broken marriage, a mean boss, or just general adult bullying. Their histories are full of missteps and injustices. You've just been tasked with doing something about it.

CLINGING TO VICTIMHOOD WHEN THE WIND IS IN THEIR SAILS

Eternal victims like to sprinkle some health problems over their never-ending martyrdoms.

They will often be the first to contract any new, rampant contagion, whether it be COVID-19 or something else. Martyrs are always keeping their eyes peeled for anything they might fall victim to. Often, they will be on the lookout for opportunities to take sick leave for this illness or that disease.

Is there a strange new bug in the newspapers that the scientists are still trying to figure out? The victim will almost instantly contract a serious case of whatever it is.

Is virus X running rampant? Guess who will be first in line to get tested!

Various side effects from taking different medication? Interesting allergies most people don't know about? Exotic reactions to certain popular medications? All of the above.

And why not? It's confirmation that the martyr always gets the short end of the stick, of course. Many people might say that anybody who fakes being sick to take a day off is a lazy jerk who doesn't pull their weight. Now, while I wouldn't want to suggest that no one has ever faked a sick day, it's a good idea to remind yourself that this view is a serious oversimplification.

These martyr types actually feel sick. It's also not necessarily a case of hypochondria. Rather, it's a case of being excessively sensitive to anything that might affirm their status as victims: *Check this out! Now I'm sick, too, on top of everything else!* It wouldn't surprise me if many of them get genuinely disappointed if they *don't* catch the big new bug: *Life is so unfair.* This is plainly paradoxical, as you can see.

Note that I'm not talking about posting about your latest cold on social media or bringing it up at family gatherings. There's plenty of people who do that as well, but they could just as well be attention-hungry narcissists.

Remember that martyr types have worked hard for their victimhood and that they're hardly going to give up this self-image for nothing. If they're unable to go on thinking of themselves as eternal victims, their entire internal balance will be disturbed. That would make them just like everybody else, i.e., responsible for their own fates. Which is bad news if you're someone who's protective of their victimhood. Apart from the obvious fact that this would be better for everyone, it would mean that they could no longer shirk responsibility. They would have to take charge of their lives. Take action. Go to all kinds of trouble they'd rather avoid.

No, far better to lean into their martyrdom and remain victims. It's a lot easier to keep saying *Poor me* than it is to dust yourself off and start taking some grown-up responsibility.

An eternal victim would have set off on a brilliant career and possibly had power, glory, and fame—if only it wasn't for their current boss. Or their next boss. Or their first boss, from twenty-five years ago. He totally killed their drive. What a jerk.

It could also have been that in-house developmental coach

who gave them negative feedback the last time around. The economy that took a turn and let them down. A partner who got in their way and held them back.

You get the idea. It could be anything really. If only it hadn't been for that something or other. Now it's too late for them to do anything but drag themselves to work for another bleak day at this soul-destroying workplace where all they can hope to do is tread water. The only light at the end of the tunnel is the fact that at least they only have twenty years left until retirement.

Now, you might be thinking that this sounds like nothing but a long stream of common—but meaningless—excuses and complaints. People are always blaming their personal failures and character flaws on these kinds of things.

Again, this is something far more complicated than walking around with their blinders on and pretending they can't do anything about it. These are individuals who genuinely and sincerely feel that they are victims of circumstances beyond their control. That's why they hold on to this idea so fiercely.

This is their place, their role in life.

This is their *identity*.

Spotting a Martyr

We're going to need a checklist for this category, too. Take a look at the following list of questions, and see if you can use them to identify an eternal victim. This person . . .

1. finds it difficult to express happiness, even when they get good news
2. looks for the negative side to any news
3. sometimes does self-destructive things
4. reacts begrudgingly to other people's success

5. displays despondent body language
6. often blames what happens to them on others
7. thinks that other people are actively out to get them
8. sighs a lot but explains it away as *just the way I am*
9. actively looks for reasons to single themselves out as the victims of unfortunate circumstances
10. doesn't like to be questioned

This list only presents a few indicators of this behavior, which can be very draining on anybody who has to deal with the person in question for extended periods of time. Remember that we're all somewhat prone to complaining about life's injustices and that doing so doesn't necessarily make you a martyr in this sense. However, the more points an individual scores and the more frequently they display these traits, the more difficult the problem is likely to be.

The example I'm about to give you is 99 percent authentic. Out of respect for the real-life martyr involved, I have chosen to alter some of the basic facts to protect the identities of the people in the story. However, the structure of this narrative, its contents, and the consequences are all true, although I've found it necessary to abridge it somewhat, as the whole truth would simply be too much to take in:

A woman, let's call her Jessica, has a complicated relationship with her mother, to put it very mildly. Let's call her mother Vera.

Vera met a man many years prior to this, and they had a single child—Jessica.

The marriage was obviously an unhappy one from the very start. When Jessica was nine years old her parents divorced, and eventually Vera found a new man. Jessica's father found a new wife, too. The two couples, however, continued to socialize regularly. My interpretation of this is that although the father may not have been Vera's perfect mate, he must have been decent enough for her to want to spend time with him after the divorce.

The interesting thing is what happened after Jessica became an adult. At this point, Vera explained that she'd always suffered greatly when she was with Jessica's father. He had been cruel to her and physically abusive, and in some peculiar way Vera managed to lay blame on Jessica for the way her father had acted.

If Vera has decided she's a real victim, there has to be a perpetrator. Since her ex-husband was neither available nor interested in hearing about Vera's misfortunes, that really only left her one outlet—her daughter, Jessica.

Note that I'm not speculating on what Jessica's father may or may not have done to her mother. The one thing we know for sure is that Jessica wasn't the guilty party.

Vera asks Jessica for help getting an apartment. When Jessica asks why, Vera explains that she really shouldn't be asking her that, what with everything she's gone through. She had to put up with Jessica's dad, after all. And her home is such a miserable place—cramped and depressing.

Jessica feels sorry for her mother. She moves to another town, and Vera moves there, too. Jessica begins to make money of her own and is able to buy some things for herself, some nice jewelry and whatnot. Vera announces that she never had any nice jewelry like that. She's prac-

tically walking around in sackcloth and ashes, and all her jewelry is fake.

After hearing this lecture about her mother's poverty enough times, Jessica buys Vera a gorgeous bracelet.

Jessica moves again. Starts a family. Has a daughter of her own. Buys a house. Vera moves to the same neighborhood and finds a rental that overlooks a sad, dingy backyard—an appalling view. She arranged it all by herself.

She goes to Jessica to complain about how awfully everything ended up. Is Jessica really going to let her mother live in this kind of squalor? In a small, dark apartment?

In the end, Jessica takes out a mortgage for the down payment on a house that she helps Vera buy. The house is right next door to Jessica and her family. Vera ends up needing more money, so she offers to help out around Jessica's house. When Jessica tries to say no, she's told that her mother is going through a hard time at the moment.

Note: When martyrs apologize, they seldom do so sincerely. They're such effective manipulators that they can always find a way to justify their behavior and make themselves look like the good guys.

Vera misses no opportunity to inform her daughter about her terrible suffering, and Jessica feels constantly guilty over the things her dad did to Vera. She also blames herself for Vera's poor health, which led to her disability retirement.

In the end, Jessica suffers burnout, falls into a deep depression, and ends up going through a painful divorce. When this happens, Vera loses her sway over her daughter. Jessica knows what real suffering is like now, and so she turns off the money tap. She does this mainly because she's out of funds but also because she realizes that even if she had the means to put Vera up in a luxurious palace, Vera would still be feeling sorry for herself, and feel entitled to a better life, despite making no effort to give herself one.

Vera decides to move. Her argument is that she doesn't want to be a burden to Jessica in her old age. (She's sixty-nine years old at the time, but she's not suffering any obvious ailments.) Her plan is probably to act the victim and be asked to stay.

Jessica's daughters, Vera's grandchildren, ask their grandmother not to move, but since Jessica is no longer playing along, Vera still ends up moving. She demands that Jessica buy the house from her. Jessica, however, has no money left. Instead, she gives her half of the house to her mother. She never sees a penny of the down payment she paid for. The net profit from the sale is quite large, but Vera shows no signs of wanting to share it.

Once she's moved to another part of the country, Vera begins to frequently contact her young grandchildren to explain to them how difficult and troublesome her life is, because of how awfully she's been treated by her daughter, Jessica. There's nothing these young girls can do about it, but they become increasingly troubled over their grandma Vera spending so much time crying about her misfortunes on the phone.

This tragic story is still unfolding. How it will end is anybody's guess.

Turning Weakness into Strength

Eternal victims genuinely believe that they're at the mercy of the world's whims and that their suffering is mainly caused by other people. However, rather than taking responsibility for their lives, they engage in constant blame shifting, manipulation, and emotional blackmail. Their dysfunctional behavior isn't exclusively caused by their low self-esteem, although this is a fairly common contributing factor.

It's also rather unclear what exactly they hope to gain from all this. In any case, they see themselves as the victims of tragic circumstances, which they respond to in one of two ways: If they're extroverted, they will seek attention, and if they're introverted, they will spend huge amounts of time on soul-destroying emotional self-flagellation. They simply don't know any other way. I'd have to guess this pattern is something they got caught up in a long time ago and now they don't know what to do to escape it.

They also tend to surround themselves with people who are unable to see through their façade and seem willing to accept everything they say, for whatever reason. Perhaps these individuals suffer from an even poorer self-esteem? There are other eternal victims out there, who seriously expect to be struck by lightning at any moment.

I suspect that this group, too, develops an internal hierarchy of sorts, in which somebody eventually takes on the role of the alpha. This individual is, by consensus, the greatest sufferer of all and by some perverse logic enjoys an elevated status by virtue of that. The alpha is now free to dominate all the other miserable martyrs. Perhaps, paradoxically, this individual is stronger than the others in some ways. The others are even weaker and simply accept all the blame that comes their way.

Who Wants to Be a Victim, Though?

Well, that's actually a pretty good question. Since their problem may originally have been caused by a lack of love and recognition when they were children, a martyr might feel essentially unworthy and unacceptable. Their approach to resolving this pain is to seek sympathy from you, by getting you to feel guilty about their predicament.

This is all rather complicated, especially considering how the general trend in recent years has focused so strongly on helping people improve their self-esteem. While I'm firmly supportive of the idea of helping people who need support, I feel this situation is more complex.

Anybody who's grown up in a dysfunctional family, where they were belittled by their parents rather than being built up by them, certainly deserves to be freed from the burdens such a childhood can leave you with. In my own social circles, there are a number of people who would certainly benefit from spending time addressing the things they went through between, say, the ages of two and fifteen. However, none of them make a particularly big deal out of it. They've accepted their childhoods as facts they can't change, however badly they might wish they could. Some of them have sought help from therapists to resolve specific issues, while others haven't done anything in particular.

I'm not in any way attempting to make light of a painful childhood, and I think that those memories are far from insignificant or exaggerated. A person's experiences of and feelings about any given situation are always genuine, even when the rest of us feel that they are exaggerated or irrational. However, some individuals tend to just shrug these things off once they reach adulthood, accepting their personal histories, while others suffer more.

Why do people react so differently? Is it a matter of personality? The extent of the suffering? Something to do with their own drive?

Also, some people elect—whether deliberately or not—to wallow in and amplify their unfortunate backgrounds and cultivate their role as victims of a difficult childhood in various ways. They choose to adopt an attitude that does nothing to help them move on.

I even suspect that some individuals would prefer never to be "cured" of this state. They'd rather continue thinking and speaking of themselves as victims of all the injustices in the world. As I mentioned earlier, in these cases the situation will often have progressed to the point where it has become part of their identity. It's what they've become.

This is a somewhat depressing thought, as nobody is actually born a victim and if they knew how wonderful their lives could be if they could only let go of this cherished victimhood I doubt they would hesitate for a moment.

You've almost certainly heard the story of the two brothers whose father was a dreadful drunk. The brief version is that one of them grows up to be a carbon copy of his father, while the other becomes a hardworking, upstanding citizen. When asked why they turned out the way they did, they both answer the same way: *What else could I do, with a father like that?*

You get the point. We cannot choose our circumstances,

but we can and do choose our responses and our attitudes. Of course, it's a lot easier for me to write about this than it is for somebody to actually do it in real life.

However, I'm firmly convinced that people who are stuck in this paralyzing victim's mentality could stop behaving and feeling the way they do if they were able to distance themselves a little from their situation. There's help to be had.

Many of these martyrs, however, persist in their "poor me" mentalities. The world is against them, and that's the cause of their misfortunes. Now, here comes the interesting part: When you suggest a possible solution to their problems, they say, *Yes, but* . . . and then give you a long series of explanations why all is lost and there's no point in trying.

The challenge here, of course, is to separate these individuals from the ones who actually have suffered serious setbacks. As I've mentioned previously, you need to pay attention and look for patterns. The same words don't necessarily mean the same thing. If you know that somebody is genuinely suffering, you'll naturally have to respond compassionately. However, if what you're dealing with seems more likely to be an attention-seeking monster, you'll have to consider your approach.

What do you do about it all? Is there anything you can do to address the underlying issues?

Well, the first step is probably to figure out what the underlying issues *are*.

Victim Extraordinaire

An initial thought here is that this behavior probably causes more harm to the person exhibiting it than to anybody else. I can imagine that it's not particularly uplifting to walk around constantly feeling like everything you do is going to go wrong or that nobody wants the best for you. However, this doesn't mean the rest of us are out of harm's way, particularly as the eternal victim's assumptions about the world happen to be wrong. Most people we meet won't be at all interested in whatever it is we're doing. They'll be focusing on themselves.

Being in the vicinity of an eternal victim is draining, for the simple reason that they tend to be so negative. We need to strike a balance between the positives and the negatives in our lives. Very few of us, probably only the dramatic individuals, actually expect everything to be great all the time and that their lives will be peaches and cream all day long. We actually need a bit of each to balance out the other. So when we see somebody turn almost everything into a negative, this can cause a peculiar dissonance. We can tell that something is wrong, and it wears us out.

Initially, we feel the urge to explain to the martyr that life is actually amazing, that there is so much magic to experience if you can just keep an open mind. However, this motivation eventually wilts in the face of their onslaught of explanations about how unfair everything is.

Perhaps you know the metaphor about the rotten tomato. You have a packet of ten tomatoes, and one of them is rotten. This presents you with a choice: either eliminate the bad tomato and save the rest or seal the packet up and hope the problem will have disappeared the next time you take a look. Perhaps the rotten tomato will allow its fresh peers to influence it, and somehow get better.

This isn't what happens, though. What happens is that you end up with three bad tomatoes.

I have a relative, a happy and positive-minded guy who used to enjoy talking to everybody he met, who spent several years living with an advanced-level martyr. Her negative mindset—she would have scored very high on the checklist we went over earlier—had a dramatic effect on his outlook. He would side with her, because he assumed she was right: Lots of people really were trying to deliberately ruin her life.

After twenty years with her, he was almost impossible to speak to. Everything was doom and gloom. Eventually, they split up—she felt he wasn't supportive enough of her—and after a couple of years happiness mysteriously returned to his life. Everybody noticed it. *He's himself again.*

This may well be the most serious consequence of this self-victimizing behavior: It's contagious. It's like breathing slightly toxic air. You can't help but be affected. In the end, it makes you just want to give up.

Listening, Arguing, Covering Your Ears: The Different Strategies of Different Colors

What are the effects, then? Yellows and Greens tend to let eternal victims carry on for quite a long time. They'll show more understanding if they feel that the victim is genuinely struggling inside. Greens, who are good listeners, will give them all the rope they need to get well and truly tangled in their martyrdom. Greens are probably too polite to be of any use here—assuming the objective is to free these individuals from their own mental prisons. It's obvious that it was the Green aspects of the man in my example in the last section that got him into trouble. He was far too tolerant; he took too much of it in, didn't question enough things—he was very nice, basically. But that was also the part that got him caught up in the whole situation to begin with.

Yellows, of course, are nowhere near as good listeners. Their general attitudes to relationships will allow them to stick around for a while, perhaps offering some solutions along the way, but they're bound to lose interest quite soon if things get too negative. After this, they will simply withdraw from further contact. It gets too depressing for them, essentially. None of this is necessarily deliberate on their part, but negativity is quite toxic for Yellows, and they instinctively save themselves by calling somebody else in the future.

Blues and Reds tend to suggest different ways for the victim to, well, stop being a victim. A Red might be prepared to get into an argument with the martyr but will soon discover that they're not receptive to that kind of message and leave them to their miserable fates.

If there's an important relationship to protect here, things will get more complicated, of course. But Reds won't be able to hold back on delivering their opinions. This will cause conflict to erupt with incredible frequency. If nothing happens to improve the situation or if the bond between them isn't strong enough, the Red will simply leave the martyr. Resignation, divorce, relocation—whatever it takes!

What about a Blue? I'm not sure a Blue would do anything at all, really. If they're not impacted by the victim's behavior, I suspect they would just cover their ears. Being around somebody who is feeling miserable won't necessarily bother a Blue too much. It's a shame, of course, but it sounds like a personal problem. Besides, they already suggested the number of a good therapist. That's all anybody could ask, really.

You can't solve a problem unless you're prepared to accept that it is a problem.

And you can't find a solution to a problem until you've agreed on exactly what that problem is.

Let me give you an example: A woman has an aging father, who seems to be losing much of his vitality. The father is a widower of many years, who lives alone. He's always been strong and taken care of himself. But now something has happened. The daughter has noticed that he seems weary and never seems to get up to anything anymore.

After a brief interrogation, she finds out that her father isn't eating properly. Aha! It's simple! In the daughter's mind, the problem is that he's not eating.

That could be correct. However, her father feels that the problem lies elsewhere. He feels as though food has lost all taste these days, and he finds it boring to eat alone. He has nobody to talk to in the evenings. So, as a result, he skips far too many meals.

Two people, two different problems. Before they've agreed on what the problem really is, they won't be able to find any lasting solutions. My own conclusion is completely different from both of theirs, perhaps because I have the benefit of seeing the situation from the outside. I would guess that the father is simply depressed. It wouldn't be strange at all if he was, and it wouldn't be unsolvable.

However, as I said, until the two of them have managed to agree on how to define the problem, they will never arrive at a solution that will last. Whatever they try to do, the real problem might remain unsolved.

And as a result, this corrosive victimhood might even

spread. Every day, we can read some story about how some-body *fell victim* to something or other. Or *suffered* some set-back or other, or *ended up in* some difficult situation.

We seem to be obsessed with finding victims of this and that—to the point where I'd guess that this exact behavior creates a fair number of victims! When we encounter obstacles in life, I'd like to see more of us respond to this with questions along the lines of *How can you change your response to this situation?* and *What part did you play in what happened?*

HOW TO NUDGE SOMEBODY OUT OF THEIR COMFORT ZONE

I don't want to seem absolutely heartless, but it needs to be said that some people take on the role of a victim intentionally. When they do, it falls on you and me to see through their deceptions.

Many eternal victims probably realize that they are stuck in a negative, destructive pattern of behavior. However, things have gone so far that it's all they know how to do. This is their world and their life now, so what options do they really have?

If you've spent years developing a specific pattern of behavior, it can be very hard to break it. How do you change your habitual, self-destructive trajectory?

The problem tends to be that you know what you have but not what you're going to get. You're going to have to leave your comfort zone. Inside it, you feel safe and warm.

Everything looks the same way it always does. But there is *no progress there*. Anybody who wants to grow will have to take some big steps outside of their comfort zone. Sometimes they might even need a push.

It can be exhausting to interact with people who always think of themselves as victims. I'll willingly admit that I personally find this behavior particularly draining. Perhaps they refuse to accept responsibility for their mistakes, and blame others when things go wrong. In this sense, they can be quite similar to passive-aggressive individuals. You should bear in mind that many people who live with this mindset have faced difficult or painful setbacks in life. However, this doesn't mean you're obligated to take responsibility for them or accept blame and accusations from them. All it means is you should try to put yourself in their shoes.

Generally speaking, labels aren't particularly useful. Terms like "eternal victim" or "martyr" are loaded, and using them to define people probably isn't going to do much to help them. It's best to avoid referring to people as victims or telling them that they're behaving like victims. It might be challenging at times.

Remember, you can't solve a problem you don't know you have. What you should do, then, is point the problem out to the martyr, in the clearest terms you can find. You need to alert them to the fact that what they're doing isn't working. However, don't just say, *You seem to have decided to make an eternal victim of yourself, and you keep acting as though the whole world were against you. How are you going to fix this?*

This blunt approach will meet stiff resistance, and the martyr will explain to you that you've got it all wrong. Their life really is this miserable, and who are you to criticize them?

Imagine having your entire self-image put into question

like that. There's no way you would buy it just like that. Look at the checklist from before. Discuss specific behaviors or emotions you've detected.

But this won't be enough on its own. They might well tell you, *That's right, but you know why, right? It's because blah blah blah . . .*

You'll also have to explain that what they're doing to themselves is a problem. But you need to frame it as a problem for them, not a problem for you. That's the challenging part. You need to get them to realize that they're moving in a dangerous direction and help them accept that they need to break their habits.

This is classic coaching stuff. Make sure they realize they have a problem. Then make them part of the solution. My own thinking on situations like this is that *if you do what you've always done, you'll get what you've always gotten.*

Ergo: When you behave the way you're behaving now, you'll only be reinforcing your negative mindset. Is that really what you want?

What you need is to get confirmation that they actually understand what you're telling them and feel prepared to say, *Yes, you're actually right.* Ideally, they should go on to say, *You're right; I don't want to go on like this.*

Only then will there be an opportunity for change.

Try to listen and really understand how this person is feeling. If they tell you they're feeling troubled, you'll both have acknowledged that there is a problem. If, however, they insist that things are just fine, that would be very confusing—but I very much doubt that will happen.

Ask them how they would like things to be instead and how they would feel if that were the case. Give them examples:

If you hadn't felt like this, what would your life be like, do you think? What could you do, what could you spend your time on? Would you be happier and have a more positive outlook? What would that mean for you?

If you can both agree that (a) this person is stuck in a victimhood mindset and (b) they don't want to stay in it, you'll have a foundation to build on!

An experienced therapist would probably listen and try to figure out what made them choose the role of a martyr. However, if you don't have that kind of training, I can't really recommend it, as it has the potential to open doors you won't be qualified to go through. You could very well end up over your head.

Ask what this person could do to take a step in the right direction to change their situation. Remember that any step, however small, is better than no step at all.

You'll need to be quite persistent here, as it's likely that they will try to be evasive or understate their ability to change things.

Ask if they need any help or support in taking this next step and what you can do to offer it. One option is to offer help, without simply fixing it all for them. This is done in three stages:

1. Acknowledge their feeling that they can't do anything to improve the situation. Make it clear to them that you understand that this is their viewpoint. Don't argue, don't tell them they're wrong, and so on. All that will do is spark a conflict.
2. Ask them what they would do if they had the en-

ergy to do something about it. Do this by saying things like the following: *I know you don't really believe this or even have the right words to explain what progress would be, but if you did have faith in a solution, and if you did have the energy, what would you do?*

3. Next, help them brainstorm different ways they might try to reach that target. Invest some time into listing different possible solutions. But for God's sake, make sure that you're not the one making all the suggestions! If you do that, they win. You'll have taken all the responsibility, and your martyr friend/partner/other will get away with doing nothing.

You might be wondering why that matters. A good idea is a good idea, regardless of who came up with it, right?

Well. In psychological terms, it makes a huge difference if the suggestion is yours or your friend's. When you give them an idea that then turns out not to work, it will all be your fault, again. No responsibility will fall on the person who actually needs the change.

For example: *I know that it seems to you that nobody wants to hire you. That must be really frustrating. But what would your ideal job be?*

Depending on their response, you can encourage them to broaden or narrow their job hunt, consider various businesses to approach, or explore other fields. Rather than giving direct advice, giving specific suggestions, or solving the problem for them, you'll be helping them realize that they actually have the tools to solve it on their own. Basically, you need to move responsibility for their lives back to where it belongs—with them.

Ask them to summarize what you've agreed on and plan their next step.

When some time has passed, reconnect with them and ask how they're getting on with the plan. It all hinges on your having the energy to involve yourself in this process. Your empathy and encouragement may not bring about immediate change, but they can still make a difference.

How to Help People Get Over Their Self-Imposed Victimhood

This is what you need to do to keep yourself from being dragged down by somebody who would rather go on suffering than take charge of their life.

We all have to take ultimate responsibility for our own lives. Personally, I'm convinced most of us are more capable than we believe. We can do a lot more than we sometimes imagine we could. I also believe that we all deserve to find success in our lives.

That doesn't mean that you should refrain from offering your help when you think you could have a positive impact, but simply that in the grand scheme of things, nobody should put their life in somebody else's hands. Doing so is an effective way of perpetuating your status as a suffering victim, and it's hard for me to imagine how this could help anyone— least of all the martyrs themselves!

Never accept anybody's self-imposed victimhood. Don't affirm this attitude. Rather, tell them that you think they have what it takes to escape the misery they're experiencing.

This is such an important point that I'd like to emphasize it: It's bad to speak to people as if they were victims. Why?

Because if you do it often enough, they will begin to act and feel like victims, and that'll be the end for them.

What many people do when they hear somebody complain about their pitiful situations is try to get them to change their mindset:

Yes, but what if you looked at it this way? Have you considered this, then? There are lots of people who like you/admire your skills/would like to work with you, et cetera.

The problem with this approach is that it presupposes that you're dealing with a rational agent—and I think we've already established that you simply aren't. What you need to do is go back to the underlying problem—without wallowing in it or any other past injustices—and try to change the way the victim views whatever it was that happened.

Let's suppose that you've genuinely done all you can do. You've spoken to them, listened to them, reasoned with them, had the occasional outburst of frustration, and had to apologize. Their situation may even have improved for brief periods of time, but you've noticed a recurring pattern: Eventually, the martyr always returns to their usual attitude: *Woe is me.* You're beginning to suffer, too. You're getting the bucket of ick emptied on you, time and time again. It's all starting to wear you down.

You need to make a decision: Is this relationship worth all this? The danger here, as I've already discussed, is that you'll begin to behave like a martyr yourself. After all, this person has had a rather bad influence on you. Before you know it, you could be suffering as much as they are. If you can't beat them, I guess you'll have to join them.

That way lies disaster.

So what to do? Naturally, it will depend to some extent on the kind of relationship you have to the other party.

If it's a distant relative who keeps texting you every hour of the day to send depressing, soul-destroying updates about their personal tragedies, block them or stop answering. It's not your job to be constantly available to offer sympathy for situations you're not even remotely involved in. If it's weighing you down, ignore it.

I'm absolutely serious about this: If you've genuinely tried and given it the best you have and this person is still refusing to play along—maybe you've even dragged them to a therapist who specializes in challenges of this kind, but nothing seemed to help, or they stopped going—you're going to have to prioritize self-preservation eventually.

Shut it out. You'll feel so much better.

I'm not suggesting you simply erase this person from your list of contacts without giving any advance warning, but distance yourself from the drama.

If it's somebody you work with, perhaps you'll find it easier to avoid getting emotionally involved. Sympathize with your coworker and tell them, *I'm going to continue believing that things will work out for the best*. Next, add, *I hope you understand that I have a deadline to meet and I have to get back to work*. Body language that signals that this isn't the time, like crossed arms or broken eye contact, can help you maintain a healthy distance from their constant lamentations.

If it's a friend, you might want to help, but know that even a friend's stories of woe can eventually become overwhelming. Set some friendly, but nonnegotiable, boundaries. Listen to your friend (or relative) for a short period of time, but then tell them, *I want you to know that I really appreciate you, but unless you're willing to discuss solutions, I can only listen to you for a few minutes.*

Married to a Martyr?

If you're dealing with a significant other, the problem can be quite serious. If you knew about this person's behavior before you got together, you can't feign surprise. However, this pattern might have appeared over time. It could have started when your partner got fired without justification, which triggered a downward spiral into a negative mindset. However, you shouldn't follow the martyr along the trajectory they've plotted out.

If you're facing a situation where your partner genuinely displays far too many of the traits I've discussed here, it's decision time for you:

Do you stick around and fight to help your partner? It's a beautiful thought, and naturally, it would be my initial advice in most situations. But all the same, you can't let them avoid their own responsibility.

What's it worth? How much are you willing to have it cost you? How much are you prepared to sacrifice for somebody who keeps burdening you with all their problems and blames you for things you have nothing to do with? How much suffering will you undergo to save somebody who doesn't want to be saved?

The romantic response, of course, is that you should stop at nothing to help the person you love. It *is* a beautiful thought.

However, if we were to approach this all a little more realistically, we'd see that we need to reflect over the costs involved.

To put it bluntly: If your partner loses a hand in a workplace accident, that would be a terrible turn of events. But how would it help them if you chopped off your own hand in response?

Setting Boundaries

Part of the stigma that surrounds this kind of self-imposed victimhood is attached to the way it makes people blame others for their problems and fail to see their own role in things not working out as they had hoped.

You might feel constantly accused, like you're walking on eggshells, or feel the need to apologize for situations that you feel you're both responsible for.

If they seem judgmental or accusatory towards you and others, it can help to set some boundaries. Remember this: Being stuck in a victim's mindset is no excuse for bad behavior.

However, you can help clarify the problem by explaining that you won't be sticking around if they refuse to do anything about it.

You are *not* joining the martyr cult.

7

Narcissists: The Greatest, the Best, and the Most Beautiful

Narcissists are people who have unrealistic, inflated self-images. They're self-centered and never talk about anything but themselves. These are individuals who genuinely view themselves as entirely unique and very special. They're often highly critical of the rest of us but entirely blind to their own shortcomings. If they don't receive constant affirmation, they will often lash out. They feel entitled to the best of everything life has to offer. They imagine they are deeply appreciated, even if the opposite happens to be the case.

Narcissists are somewhere in between dramatic and antisocial individuals. While drama queens seek constant attention and want everything to be enjoyable and simple for them, and bullies are constantly seeking excitement and relief from boredom, narcissists seek recognition and praise for being the most talented, attractive, and intelligent people who have ever walked the earth. They want every

possible advantage, and they don't care who they have to push aside to get it.

Narcissists go through their lives with the strange misconception that they somehow deserve a better life than everyone else. For some unclear reason, they feel entitled to the best table, the nicest car, the biggest salary, and the loudest praise they can imagine. Not because they've earned these things through hard work or great success, but because they happen to be who they are.

That pretty much sums up their world view. For some reason, they see themselves as divine beings and feel they should be treated accordingly:

I've arrived! See me! Obey me! Worship me!

The rest of us are just a lowly band of followers, who would do best to play along in this peculiar game. If we don't show them the right degree of respect, they're prone to erupt in violent rages.

The interesting thing about narcissists is their innate conviction of their own inherent superiority; it's simultaneously horrific and fascinating.

There are very few clinical narcissists out there in society.

Depending on who you ask, you tend to get a figure somewhere between 1 and 2 percent. They can't help having this personality disorder, and no feedback or therapy can change their inner workings. That would be like asking a cat to stop chasing mice.

Actually, the nature of a narcissist is quite similar to that of a cat. They act sweet and endearing when it suits their purposes.

They are picky about where they sleep and what food they eat. They have that look of unfiltered contempt that says *If I could eat you right now, I would.*

However, the moment subtle insinuations aren't enough, their claws will come out. Just like cats, narcissists can be absolutely relentless in their attempts to crush their enemies.

A cat is also likely to leave the household if something doesn't meet its requirements and maybe move in with another, more generous family that's wise enough to appreciate its divine presence. Only to return, suddenly, six months later and be found on the steps, unflinchingly meeting the surprised looks of the family. Then the cat will simply stride right back into the kitchen, settle down by its bowl, and look at you as if to say, *You're getting one last chance. But you'd better get it right this time.*

There are countless stories showing that narcissists can behave exactly like that. They come and go as they please in relationships.

Despite this, plenty of people are very fond of cats. They enjoy that somewhat unpredictable part of cats' personalities. They find that absolute self-control fascinating.

It's the same with narcissists.

Imagine playing golf or tennis, or working in your garden, or going on a quiz show on television. You're doing really well, too. You succeed at everything you try to do! You feel completely amazing, absolutely wonderful, every single second. But at the same time, you're terribly afraid you might lose everything you've worked so hard for.

Imagine the pressure you'd be under if everything you did was the act that would decide if you were *just like everybody else* or a *very special person*.

The greatest fear of a narcissist is being the same as the rest of us. They expect to be extraordinary in every known human domain, regardless of whether they've ever even practiced it in the slightest.

Their mental wall between a state of absolute confidence and the abject terror of being absolutely average is as thin as a sheet of wet tissue paper.

Perhaps you would pity them, if you hadn't witnessed the horrible lengths they will go to in order to maintain this illusion of superiority.

Narcissists can be quite smart. You might believe people who are this smart and well educated would have learned the value of being considerate to others. Dream on! That's the last thing they would do.

It's likely that every discipline that anyone can compete in was invented by a narcissist. And here I don't just mean sports, or business, or whatever else comes to mind. I also mean art, literature, music, architecture, anything at all: As long as there is the potential for an *oooh* and an *aaah*, narcissists will flock there to cash in.

Even being good-hearted—they compete in that, too! Just

look at social media today: Whoever can present themselves as having the biggest heart is the winner. You might have seen all those videos where people give money or a big meal to a homeless person while shoving a camera in their face. It's simply not good enough for the Good Samaritan to be a good person. They have to demonstrate their goodness to everybody else, so we can all exclaim, *Wow! What an amazing person you are!*

And then there's cancel culture, which is largely fueled by individuals looking to show everybody that they're better, more righteous, and more good-natured than the likes of you and me. The fact that their methods—which involve absolutely destroying people and maybe ruining their lives—are brutal is neither here nor there. These individuals' goal is to win—and appear to be the best—at everything.

They wouldn't hesitate to be cruel towards one group in order to supposedly relieve the sufferings of another group. They wouldn't flinch at brutally silencing somebody to promote freedom of speech. They wouldn't lose a second of sleep over committing the most immoral acts imaginable, as long as it served to demonstrate the excellence of their morals. Causing somebody to lose their job fills them with glee. The fact that they made sure somebody who had an opinion they deemed unsuitable is now no longer able to put food on the table for their children is no concern of theirs.

They'll resort to literally anything to present themselves to the world as they want us to see them: as the best, basically. But all along, they're also the most efficient, dedicated haters out there.

That's narcissism in its purest form.

TOP OF THE PODIUM WITHOUT
ANY REAL PRIZE

When I've described the various kinds of energy vampires in this book to different people, I've made a rather unexpected discovery: Narcissists are, without a doubt, the most hated of the bunch. Much of the stuff you'll read about narcissists relates to personal and mental abuse. Many actually portray narcissists as absolute monsters.

Why is this?

I think it's because narcissists use other people as means to their own ends in such blatant, shameless ways.

While dramatic individuals are mostly just a pain, passive-aggressive people just refuse to participate, and bullies openly berate and bully people, narcissists attempt to present themselves as wonderful, highly ethical people despite being nothing of the sort. They do this out in the open, without ever apologizing for any of their occasionally detestable behavior. I suspect that this explicit sense of entitlement to the best of the best of everything bothers the rest of us and makes us want to judge them harshly, like the mob has done, cheering as they tore down the aristocracy in various revolutions.

At the same time, however, we want to love narcissists for daring, for showing courage and ambition, for having the guts to present themselves the same way the rest of us might only dream of doing. Who wouldn't want a never-ending supply of that kind of confidence?

What's really going on here?

Let's take a more in-depth look at how they actually function. While you read the following section, feel free to ask yourself this question: *Is this a person I'd like to keep close, or will they end up draining me of so much energy that I might fall and never get back up? Or—horror of all horrors—do I have any of these traits?*

A narcissist's self-image is in no way rooted in reality. They are people who, regardless of their personalities and behavior, think of themselves as God's gift to humanity.

They walk into the room with the expectation that they will be appreciated and praised simply for being the people they are. And if anybody doesn't realize how wonderful they are, that's just their loss.

They can get into discussions about topics they know nothing about but sound confident enough to make the most informed people doubt themselves.

They apply for—and get—jobs they have no qualifications for whatsoever. Just like bullies, narcissists will quite often display precisely the kind of obvious confidence that many employers are looking for.

It also works in nightclubs. A narcissist will make a move on an intended partner who, according to every available social code and unwritten rule, is simply out of the narcissist's league. But it works. Both men and women find confidence and audacity attractive.

We all know how annoying we find it when people start every single sentence with the word "I." We don't always identify what's bothering us, but bother us it does.

When we're spending time with narcissists, we simply have no choice but to get used to it. They speak about themselves incessantly. Any subject is likely to morph into a story about themselves:

Did you have bad weather on your trip? Well, let me tell you about my *vacation a few years ago.*

Busy at work? You should see my *to-do list!*

In the end, you'll find yourself just wanting to scream. If you do, the narcissist will look surprised. What's the problem? How could you not want to learn more about the most interesting person who ever lived?

SELF-OBSESSION DELUXE

Since a narcissist is already the best ever at practically everything and will happily share this fact with anyone they come across, they will, of course, also recognize that everybody else must, by definition, be their inferiors. They don't mind sharing this fact, either, and they tend to do it in a rather judgmental way. Narcissists quite often enjoy belittling others, since it makes them feel more important. The little people aren't really worthy of a narcissist's attention, anyway.

Although narcissists can be quick to criticize, they're extremely sensitive to the opinions that others hold of them, particularly if they happen to be even slightly negative. Criticism can be interpreted many different ways. On the one hand, it could be genuine criticism, i.e., a negative assessment of the narcissist's performance, say. But it could also be the fact that somebody failed to cheer sufficiently in celebration of the narcissist's amazing work.

Since they will always take any criticism as a sign that the world around them doesn't sufficiently appreciate their greatness, they'll respond immediately, often with intense, sudden rage. Along with this reaction, they'll feel a thirst for vengeance. Their vengeance can be brutal, too.

The rules and regulations that the rest of us have agreed to simply don't apply to narcissists. Speed limits, social norms, responsibilities at work.

They operate beyond the usual rules of society. Narcissists can make an effort to be nice or behave in a polite and welcoming fashion, but as they feel no genuine compulsion to obey these norms, they can drop the pretense with startling speed if provoked.

This is one of the reasons why other people seldom genuinely like them. Their lack of respect for the rules makes them exhausting to interact with in the long run. Their relationships are a lot more superficial than they might realize.

Narcissists strive for a kind of fictional perfection, to have the very best of everything. Just like little children do, they imagine that they can get away with doing whatever they like, because they feel entitled to it.

Apart from this, it's also part of their fundamental birthright to live in the most expensive house in the best neighborhood, drive the flashiest car, and only ever be seen in the finest designer clothing. Ideally, they should get all that without having to work for it.

This also happens to be the reason why they can treat their fellow human beings so terribly. It's their birthright. They can do anything they want to you or me.

In a narcissist's mind, power and fame are highly desirable qualities. Attention matters to them. Funnily enough, they won't insist that the attention they're getting is positive. Negative attention is better than no attention at all. In this respect, narcissists are just like little children.

As a consequence, narcissists, much like bullies, find themselves drawn to any place where power and attention tend to concentrate. However, problems will soon arise if people fail to acknowledge the narcissist's great importance. Some narcissists can even show signs of suffering mild depression if they don't get the attention they crave.

Narcissists are quick to spot other people's weaknesses. They will shamelessly exploit these weaknesses to scam anyone they can for whatever they want. Exploiting others comes naturally to them. They're essentially indifferent to other people's emotions and experiences, which makes them very well equipped for manipulation. They're also fairly indifferent to the dangers of being exposed for what they are. This is why they sometimes take strange risks and it can often be hard to believe how deceitful they really are.

Identifying a Narcissist

It's time to look at another checklist. Usually, this isn't something that can be used to make a psychiatric diagnosis but is more of an aid to help you spot patterns you might otherwise overlook. This person . . .

1. loves competition but is a sore loser
2. fantasizes about amazing achievements and becoming famous and expects to be treated as though these fantasies have already been realized
3. is very uninterested in hearing what others think or feel—unless they happen to need something from them
4. will often name-drop
5. doesn't mind exploiting others to reach their goals
6. doesn't think the rules apply to them and accordingly doesn't mind breaking them
7. interprets criticism as an expression of envy

8. suffers from an innate inability to see their own mistakes
9. will get their smartphone out in the middle of a conversation with somebody, without apologizing
10. complains a lot about being mistreated and misunderstood

Remember what I said earlier: We'd all probably score a few points on a list like this. If somebody scores five points I'd say they're displaying narcissistic tendencies, and at seven or eight points I'd have to say it's a clear case. Ten out of ten? That means it's a good idea to tread very lightly.

SHARPENING A SHARK'S TEETH

Narcissism is commonly misconstrued as being wholly related to self-esteem. However, that's simply incorrect. A narcissist doesn't think like that at all. They already know they're the best, the most attractive, the most popular, and so on. Self-esteem is almost a nonissue for them. They don't need a concept like that to explain to them that they're the most amazing creature who ever lived, just as you and I don't need a concept of oxygen to be able to breathe the air.

Some people argue that a narcissist's constant need for affirmation stems from excessively poor self-esteem and that if we could only bolster their self-esteem their behavior would improve. If we could only teach them to appreciate themselves more, they would accept themselves, and this would stop them from acting like such jerks.

Oh boy, what a mistake that would be! It would be like

sharpening a shark's teeth and telling it that now that it has such sharp teeth it has no reason to attack anything.

Don't do it.

Loving a Narcissist

Are narcissists similar to dramatic individuals in romantic relationships? Irritating, frustrating, but tolerable? Well, not really. Narcissists go to much greater lengths to get the adulation they feel they need, which means they're more likely to harm others in order to achieve their goals.

Falling victim to a narcissist is a lot more like falling victim to a psychopath. At first, being around their glamour can be quite inspiring, but you'll soon realize that you're just a pawn on their chessboard.

As a consequence, you'll end up feeling used. You'll realize that it's always you that's expected to give, help out, and be there for them. The narcissist will ask you for favors all the time, but if you ask them to do something for you, conflict will soon arise. How long will you be prepared to accept their terms? The problem is that once you acquire the habit of accommodating somebody like that, it can be pretty hard to break. This is particularly true if the other party is using every trick they can to convince you to keep it up. You'll be unable to quit, basically. You'll keep on feeling used.

This will, in turn, lead to insecurity, and you'll question whether you actually deserve better than this. In a personal relationship, this can be particularly problematic, as the person in question could very well be somebody you love. You might not *like* her—but you *do* love her. Emotions are complicated, and this really can happen. The next thought to enter your mind could be that you must be the problem. She did say that, after all. And she sounded credible at the time. You're the one who got yourself into this difficult situation. Essentially, you're a bad person who doesn't deserve any better. Now your self-esteem will be dropping off the chart, and soon you'll feel awful—through no fault of your own. You will be plagued by self-doubt.

However, just as the old theory says—if you throw enough dirt at somebody, some of it will stick—you'll find that the things the narcissist says and the way she treats you will have an effect on you. Constantly being told that you're only any good if you do exactly what she says can cause a great deal of stress. Just like with bullies, this will vary somewhat depending on the particulars of the relationship, but PTSD is just one of the consequences you're at risk of experiencing. We know that PTSD is common in survivors of dysfunctional relationships. And any relationship with a narcissist is going to be dysfunctional in some way or other.

There is also a great risk of experiencing trouble concentrating. You might find that your memory is impaired. You might start losing sleep and worrying about your reduced capacity to perform under time pressure. Brain fatigue could be the reason behind it, and it's a common consequence of staying in a bad relationship for too long.

Yellow Enters the Battle for Attention

You'd be amazed if you knew how often I've met people who tell me that they are somehow "immune" to manipulation. It's a naive mindset, to put it mildly. It's also wrong; nobody is immune to manipulation. A skilled manipulator is actively looking for openings. If they want to con you, in the end they will.

It's a lot easier to con somebody than it is to convince them they've been conned, too.

Usually, people with the task-oriented profiles will get irritated when big egos consume all the oxygen in the room. Blues and Reds find it annoying when people keep talking about themselves all the time. A Red might take it into their head to sabotage a particularly insufferable narcissist, and this could have rather severe consequences. Narcissists, like psychopaths, can hold some serious grudges.

While a Red will attack head-on—hard but essentially honestly—the narcissist will go behind their back instead. There the narcissist will try to turn everyone against the Red. This can end with the Red getting into some rather serious trouble. However, it also means the Red will exclude the narcissist from their circles as soon as the opportunity presents itself.

A Blue will, usually, stay pretty calm but register absolutely everything. They will deem the narcissist to be essentially untrustworthy. Blues tend to have very good memories. When a narcissist who's seeking to gain an advantage from the Blue makes one promise after another, the Blue will remember this. They'll also pick up on the manipulative qualities of this pattern quicker than anyone else on the palette. Blues remember things. However, they don't always reveal all the information they possess. They can solve the mystery in silence.

The difference between a Blue and a Red is that a Blue is unlikely to say anything. Once they've figured the puzzle out, the game is over for them. They'll simply withdraw from the narcissist if that's at all possible.

Somebody whose profile is dominated by Green—Green-

Yellow especially; it's less marked for Green-Blue—will be an excellent target for narcissists. Their somewhat evasive and deferential demeanor is perfect for a narcissist who doesn't think twice about using other people. Greens are also more tolerant when it comes to having to be there for others. How things will end is a matter of speculation, but narcissists do cause harm to other people. There's no room for doubt here.

In close relationships, Greens will go to extreme lengths to accommodate all of the narcissist's peculiar whims. When they can't do it, the response will be harsh and brutal. Leaving an intimate relationship will be difficult. Greens are a little passive by nature, and they won't always have the forcefulness to break things off themselves. The end of the world might be nigh in this situation, metaphorically speaking.

What do Yellows do around narcissists? This one's a bit tricky, because just as with the dramatic individuals, Yellows actually have some aspects in common with narcissists. They like to begin sentences with "I," and they do spend a lot of time thinking about themselves. However, Yellows are actually genuinely interested in other people, which narcissists really aren't. They see the rest of us as resources to be exploited. A Yellow is prepared to do a lot to win admiration, but they won't become mean and manipulative, like narcissists will. This dynamic can trigger an epic competition for attention. If the narcissist's behavior is too excessive, the Yellow will respond much like a Red or Blue and try to ignore them.

If this approach displeases the narcissist, they might start to *malign* the Yellow behind their back. This will have a huge impact on the Yellow's ego. Being slandered and being ostracized are two of the worst things a Yellow can imagine. They need their groups. Without them, the Yellow feels like nothing. They'll definitely begin to hate the narcissist, but they won't always know how to handle him.

And I suppose this is where the true challenge for narcissists lies: Nobody really likes them.

The most common response to narcissistic behavior is a strange blend of fascination and disgust. This reminds me of the reaction many have when they're around some of the most charming psychopaths. You see what you see, and you often like it, and admire their almost outrageous confidence, but at the same time you can instinctively sense that what seems too good to be true most likely is.

However, not everybody responds by distancing themselves from the person in question. Some of us actually try to get closer, because it can be quite exciting to be near these people. Call it a buzz of excitement, if you will. At first a narcissist can make you feel divine. For a moment, at least. Right before they spring their trap.

Does that sound dramatic? Well, if it does, that's because it *is* dramatic.

HOW TO PLAY THE GAME

Naturally, you could do what the title of this section suggests and play along. Just like with everything else, there are different levels of hell, to borrow a worn but apt metaphor. The narcissist may only display a limited number of irritating behaviors. If this is the case, it might be appropriate to give them a little extra space.

Basically, give them space to talk more about themselves. Let them express themselves. If they happen to be a good friend, you could let them boast for a while, and show them that you're appropriately impressed. If you exclaim *oooh* and *aaah* at the right intervals, your relationship will function a lot better.

Ask a lot of questions. Ask them to tell you more and to talk freely. If your friend has been on vacation ask to hear all about it, and if you feel that they're exaggerating don't call them out on it. Don't tell them you find it hard to believe that they actually wrestled an alligator. Instead, ask them how they weren't terrified.

Now, it might not be easy to play along when you know that what you're listening to is just one long sequence of embellishments and total lies. I realize that.

But ask yourself this: *Does it really matter?*

When your friend tells you that they were at the same party as Prince Harry and Meghan Markle, does it really cause you any harm? Does this obvious lie actually impact you in any way?

When they explain that the apartment they made a down payment on downtown couldn't be sold for some made-up reason, is it really any skin off your nose?

When your colleague brags about the Mercedes they're planning on buying, which you know there's no way they can afford—will you be able to congratulate them without thinking about how they're likely to turn up in the same old Ford as usual?

What does it really matter?

In a workplace, a narcissist might well attempt to take credit for the things other people have done, to make themself look better. They also might break the rules. If you're their manager and you witness this, put a stop to it immediately.

Don't put up with it, even once. You should make it plain, right away, that you noticed what happened and that you're not okay with it. Act like a slightly indignant parent and tell them, *Fredric, you know that you're better than this. I don't want to see this happen again.*

What will matter, however, is if this potential narcissist tries to use you and treat you badly. Or treat others badly in obvious ways. You can't accept *that*. This situation requires a great deal of vigilance.

The same applies to personal relationships. When the behavior goes from being generally annoying and a little childish to manipulative and harmful for people in the vicinity, it's time for you to follow your gut instinct. It's right a lot more often than we can really explain.

A general reflection, and an admittedly personal opinion of mine, is that if a relationship *feels* wrong it *is* wrong.

All you need to do is think about how you feel deep inside. What would your ideal relationship be like? How would you like to feel when you walk into the office? How would you really like to live your life?

Compare these insights with the reality of your relationship with this individual.

What's missing for you? What are you putting up with that you'd prefer to be rid of?

Is your gut instinct right? What if you're wrong?

Sometimes we can't quite be sure if we're dealing with a real narcissist or just somebody who's going through a few really bad days. It can be difficult to tell if somebody is behaving badly because they don't know any better—i.e., because they're just an ordinary jerk—or if they are a narcissist who is planning to manipulate you and use you any way they can. There are certainly ways to test the waters and find out how bad things are.

What follows are some hands-on ideas you can try.

Actively look for patterns. Ask yourself: *Are these random occurrences, or does this person act this way routinely?* As I just mentioned, anybody could have a bad day, but few people have several bad weeks in a row. Find out if these negative emotions you're experiencing have genuinely been caused by your partner/manager/colleague/friend.

The simplest way to do this is to compare what they say with what they do. Narcissists will say almost anything to either make themselves appear better than they are or achieve something they want. It could be service, sex, money, power, attention, or anything at all.

This is an effective way of isolating the problem, as long as you know what to look for.

When they promise to do X, double-check whether X really got done. If they did X plus something else, that might be okay. If they did X minus some detail, that might also be okay—you'll have to judge this on a case-by-case basis. Nobody's perfect, after all, and you don't want to come across as a habitual perfectionist. You might have to accept some degree of flexibility.

However, if instead of X, what they did was a big case of Y . . . or even number 4 instead of X, you have a problem on your hands. This means that what you're dealing with is somebody who doesn't take their own word seriously.

Don't accept excuses like this: *You're just imagining that stuff*; *I never said that*; *You've always been hysterical*; *You're the problem, really, not me*; *I don't understand what I see in you*; and so on.

None of that has anything to do with the real world. All that matters is whether this person's words match their deeds to an acceptable extent.

Simple, no?

Take notes. Sound strange? Maybe it is. However, a motivated narcissist will become an expert at twisting people's minds. Taking notes of the things somebody says to you might seem extreme, but you shouldn't rely on your memory too much. Also, making it very obvious that you're actually taking those notes is a good way to discourage future attempts at manipulation.

Imagine that your narcissistic partner tells you he's going to the pub with John, and possibly Eric, this weekend. However, from experience, you can tell there is something else going on. In order to keep from being manipulated, you should say the following out loud, as if you were speaking to yourself: *I'm terrible at names. I'm just making a note on my calendar that you're going out with John and Eric on Saturday.* This will make it a lot more difficult for your partner to lie when it turns out that neither Eric nor John saw him the weekend in question. Sometimes liars are opportunists. If he's planning on going out and meeting women in bars and then claims never to have told you he would be meeting Christian, whose number you don't have, instead of Eric, things will get a lot more complicated for him. Also, you'll be able to notice this pattern of lies much more quickly. When your manipulator can see you taking note of things, he'll know that path is a dead end.

This might all sound rather odd, and honestly, if you feel that you need to write down the things your partner tells you, it's very possible that your relationship is less than ideal.

Another thing to pay good attention to is favors and returned favors. A narcissist will be very open to receiving favors from you and will be masterful at making you think there's no way they could manage without your help. They might tell you they need you to give them something: your time so you can help them finish their work, your money so they can afford things, or your ears so you can listen to the narcissist's problems.

All of those things could be perfectly fine in a functional relationship. If you have a partner, or a coworker, or a good friend you care about, you'll naturally be there for them. However, eventually, the delicate situation where you're the one needing help will arise. I'm not suggesting you trade favors back and forth; that's more of a transaction than genuinely helping each other. But always being the one to give can eventually bring about a harsh realization.

That's what you'll discover about narcissists. When you're the one who needs time, advice, attention, or whatever it may be, they will always be busy. They'll give you a reason that might not sound very plausible, but the true reason for their unwillingness to do whatever it is you're asking for will always be the same: They're not interested in you the same way they're interested in themselves.

This, too, will probably be a pattern that might take some time to discover.

Naturally, this means you'll have to get more vigilant and observant. You need to become more aware, basically. As I mentioned earlier, you need to compare their words to their deeds. Although many people make promises they have no intention of ever keeping, narcissists do it so often that unfulfilled commitments linger around them like a bad smell.

When confronted with this, a "normal" person who's just a little selfish will say something along the lines of, *Whoops, I'm sorry, I didn't mean to hurt your feelings! I never thought of it that way before, and I'm going to make more of an effort now.*

Now you'll be able to have an adult conversation about honesty and respect, and this may very well trigger new, positive development in the relationship.

As is the case with bullies or full-on psychopaths, there are some obvious risks involved in being too close to a narcissist for too long: It can be harmful, particularly mentally.

A woman I met described her thirty-year marriage to a narcissist like this: *It was as though my whole life had been a lie.*

A narcissist will never change.

Walk away.

It sounds dramatic, but that's only because it really *is* dramatic.

Even if you think you love this person, you shouldn't spend another minute in their presence.

Even if it's your dream job, you shouldn't stay and tough it out. Things aren't going to improve.

Walk away.

Even if they are the only "friend" you ever had, you shouldn't let them continue to walk all over you. Don't drink poison just because you're thirsty—not even in small doses. Eventually, you'll have filled your system with so much misery that you're never going to break free.

You deserve better than to be used and then tossed aside by a narcissist. I'm giving you my permission:

Walk away.

Be strong.

Walk away.

A Personal Reflection

This is one of the most difficult energy vampires to deal with, and as you've realized by now, I'm suggesting that it might be best for you not to try. If you've fallen victim to a narcissist who would check off a lot of boxes on the list earlier in the chapter, you're bound to have felt some of this. PTSD is a common side effect, which you should take very seriously.

If this applies to you, I'd like to suggest that you seek help at the first opportunity. You can heal, but it's going to be difficult to manage on your own. There are plenty of competent psychologists and therapists who specialize in this particular situation, and although it can cost some money, I'd suggest that it's worth it. After all, this is the rest of your life we're talking about.

8

A Few Less Serious but Nonetheless Annoying Types

L et's take a look at some behavior patterns that might seem like subcategories of some of the types I've already discussed. In reality, these are people whose bad habits have led them to adopt some harmful patterns.

Sometimes that's all there is to it, of course. We all run the risk of falling into an unflattering habit and behaving in ways that might cause headaches for other people. If I experience too much stress in my everyday life, I tend to come home from work and lose my temper over the tiniest things.

If my back aches, I might get grouchy over nothing, and if I'm very worried about what the doctor might have to tell me, I can become impossible to deal with.

Maybe I'm the kind of person who isn't very tolerant of bad news. I have a way of going on about things that frustrate me without really noticing.

Most of these things can be solved with a good conversation and perhaps some therapy. But they're far removed from anything that would merit a proper diagnosis. Despite this, my behavior on my worst days is enough to drain my partner, my colleagues, or my children of their energy.

Let's take a look at some common energy vampires you can probably learn to handle just fine on your own.

THE WHINER

As the label suggests, this is somebody who always finds something to whine or complain about. They seem to be constantly on the lookout for flaws and will soon chew the ears off of anybody who will listen. Whatever happens, they will always find some reason to voice their discontent. Another suitable label for the whiner would be "incurable pessimist."

Deep down, the whiner is just like you or me but has simply ended up in a downward spiral of general dissatisfaction. These dedicated complainers have trained themselves to presume that something is going to go wrong and that problems will be coming back to bite them.

The whiners, however, shouldn't be conflated with the martyrs, who are more consumed with their own personal misfortunes. Whiners, on the other hand, simply possess a natural knack for finding external things to be unhappy about.

When you go to dinner with a whiner, you can expect trouble before you've even reached the restaurant. If you're driving, they won't like your parking spot. It's too narrow. If your companion is driving, what if somebody opens their door too hard and hits your companion's car? However, they won't move the car; they just leave it there. A perfectionist would have kept looking for a better spot, but whiners are really only looking for a chance to voice some displeasure. This is simply their way of communicating.

Once you've parked, the walk to the restaurant is too long and they're wearing the wrong shoes. Besides, somebody stole their gloves and now their fingers are cold. They might be too cold to even hold a fork and knife.

When you enter the restaurant, they'll look around, and when you exclaim that it looks lovely, they'll tell you they've seen better.

Their inner pessimist will assume that things are about to take a turn for the worse. They vividly remember a past restaurant dinner, a lukewarm piece of fish and lumpy sauce, or some cut of meat that wasn't properly cooked.

Oh well. You sit down to eat and you try to keep your spirits high, but the complaints keep coming. Their chair isn't very comfortable. Their boss is an idiot, and they hate their job. Not that they're going to look for a new one. That would leave them with nothing to whine about.

When the food arrives, they forget to thank the waitress, who is already starting to look annoyed.

You're having misgivings about this dinner before it's really started, and you're wondering how you could be naive enough to believe the whiner would have changed since your previous dutiful dinner last year. This is the same miserable sourpuss you take out for their birthday dinner every year. Had you really forgotten?

Oh well. The wine list is too short, too long, or too expensive. When the whiner decides to order a bottle of the house red, it's too warm, too tasteless, or too dry. You point out that they're free to choose another, better wine, but this is where the interesting psychology of the incessant complainer kicks in:

They *don't want* to order a better wine.

They *want* to have something to complain about.

What makes somebody a whiner who's never happy about anything? The core causes are very difficult to identify, but somewhere along the line you can be certain that this person has adopted an unfortunate habit of actively looking for problems.

Just like many of the other energy vampires, these people aren't fully aware of their own behavior. What we have here is a person who's probably healthy and completely normal but who suffers from poor self-awareness and is, for all intents and purposes, stuck in this behavior.

The Effects of Hanging Up the Phone

Being around somebody who whines constantly can be exhausting. This is the opposite of positive thinking. It would certainly be satisfying to adopt a dramatic outlook on life for a while. The advantage of positive thinking, after all, is that it's precisely that: positive. Personally, I reckon that even if positive thinking won't solve all problems, or even close to all, it still works out better than negative thinking most of the time. Although a negative focus can help us avoid problems, it can be extremely draining for everyone else to listen to all the various things that might go wrong. When we focus exclusively on problems and ignore all the opportunities that come our way, we essentially lose our focus. Nobody wants to wander around in that negative goo. It will eventually crumble any hope for a brighter future and leave us with no reason to carry on. Maybe it's time we simply gave up?

You can reason with them, certainly, and you could plausibly voice what's going on, but it'll wear on your mood. Do you want this individual, whom you *do* care about, after all—it could be your parent, partner, good friend, or colleague—to snap out of it? Or would you rather just rid yourself of them and move on with your own sunny, happy life?

The latter option is the simplest, of course. You call the whiner and explain that their constant complaining is taking too much of a toll on you and if you're going to be staying in touch they'd better shape up right now. *Or else* . . .

Hang up. Now, it's all up to them.

Seem harsh? Maybe it is. But in the end, you can't take responsibility for somebody else's attitude. Your own attitude, however, is your own responsibility, and I know plenty of people who have severed relations with people who kept draining them of energy through their tiresome, whiny behavior. You're entitled to feel that way. There's no need to be rude about it, but you're not responsible for the way this person behaves.

But suppose it's a close relationship, one that you don't want to ruin. If you have a parent who's grouchy and negative and keeps ruining the mood all day long and you still live at home, then what options do you really have? Or suppose you have a friend whom you've noticed a change in recently, somebody who isn't usually that negative but is going through some kind of phase. In those situations, you might want to help and support them.

That would be noble of you.

Here are some simple steps for you to follow:

1. Confront them. Explain that their constant whining and complaining is harming and/or ruining your relationship.
2. Explain to them that you'd like to continue spending time with them but that some changes will be necessary if it's not going to be too costly to you in terms of energy.
3. Explain exactly which behaviors are problematic for you and how. For example, tell them, *When you keep complaining about how boring work is, it makes me lose my focus, which impacts my performance. Do you really want that?* (Note the importance of this question. Without it, *you* would be a whiner, wouldn't you?)
4. Help them by giving them some good advice. Explain that rather than complain about X or Y, they should do something to improve their situation. If their job is boring, they should get a different job or ask their boss for a change of assignment.
5. Ask them to comment on what you've just said.

Now, usually, it's unlikely to be this simple. You may have to repeat these steps many times before the person in question manages to break their whiny habits.

But there is hope. Be aware that whining and complaining is usually only done by people who believe that things could be better. Complaining about your partner is a common pastime, as you know. Sometimes there is good reason for the complaint. But the complaints reflect a belief that there could be someone better out there. If their partner was the last person on earth, it seems doubtful that the complaints would be as intense.

Also—and I'm not sure if I should actually recommend this or not—perhaps you could ask somebody who's whining about their partner this question: *Are you absolutely sure that you're perfect yourself?*

THE WALKING DISASTER

Somebody who keeps running into problems, often rather unusual ones. The kind of person who seems to keep wandering into trouble through no fault of their own. An individual who doesn't shift blame—instead, they accept responsibility for everything that happens or doesn't happen. Essentially, a good-hearted person. A helpful soul who gives their own energy until it runs out.

The innocent energy vampires are basically only energy vampires to the people who are closest to them. They help others freely, but at the same time they seem to keep suffering constant mishaps for some reason.

They say yes to any request, without considering for a second if perhaps it would have been wiser to say something else. "No," for instance. They'll help others before they help themselves.

Occasionally they're helpless individuals, who actually need help themselves, and other times they're good friends who place too much trust in you. They have a fundamentally positive outlook on everything and everyone, and they have a hard time imagining that there might be evil people in the world.

They lend others their tools and never get them back.

They answer the question about their weaknesses completely honestly in job interviews. While everybody else has learned from clever consultants to dress up a strength as a "weakness" to make themselves look good, they honestly and sincerely own up to getting anxious when their workload gets too intense.

They promise to help their neighbor build a fence without finding out if it's fifteen or fifteen hundred feet long first.

They will confide in a colleague about how they intend to apply for an open position and then proceed to be outmaneuvered for it by the very same colleague.

When a good friend asks for some help hosting a party, they end up spending the entire night working in the kitchen.

Their basic naivety makes them very easy targets for anybody who's prepared to use subterfuge to exploit them. They have no capacity for self-interest. In some bizarre way, they manage to think the best of everybody, and suffer one setback after another as a result. Naive? Could be.

It's easy to think of these people as genuine victims (I went over the opposite of this in the chapter on eternal victims), and although I'm not very fond of the idea of labeling people as victims, I wonder if it might be appropriate in this case.

But at the same time, it seems reasonable to ask: Victims of *what*, exactly? A cruel world in which callous people actively exploit one another? Or their own all-too-naive attitudes to these people?

When I've discussed this with psychologists and psychotherapists and listened to their explanations, a slightly different picture has emerged. Walking disasters are, basically, very appealing targets for people who improve their lives by exploiting others, whether they do it intentionally or not.

So what exactly are we dealing with here, and how is this type of person an energy vampire? I mean, what could be better than a person who is so happy and willing to sacrifice themself for somebody else? Isn't this a good thing? Isn't it noble and worthy of admiration?

Well, it's not quite that simple.

When I write each of my books, I test my thoughts and ideas on a group of people I trust completely, to see which ones are useful and which ones might be based on misunderstandings on my part. I do this before I write a single word.

When I discussed the concept of the walking disaster with the people who made up my test panel, the topic of good and bad luck came up. Somebody suggested that we might have to accept that some people are simply less fortunate than others and that there's nothing else to it.

However, it's not really about bad luck or being in the wrong place at the wrong time; it's actually about the fact that there are a number of individuals out there who have a knack for sniffing these people out and exploiting them shamelessly. In the long run, this will impact those who are closest to them the most. That could be you or me.

Good versus Bad Luck

Let's explore this in more detail. If you believe in *bad luck,* that would imply that you also believe in *good luck.*

It's certainly an exciting thought: the vague idea that the universe, chance, or karma strikes more in some people's lives than in others. However, that would also mean that good luck happens, well, completely randomly. But that's not the case. There is no proof of this, basically.

Most people who have been successful at anything will, at some point, be told that they've been lucky.

The tech billionaire who started out with a million he inherited from his family—what a lucky break he had! But honestly, if your mother left you a million, would you really manage to turn it into a billion?

The athlete who wins every race—how lucky she is to have been born with that talent. Well, whether she's talented or not, she's almost certainly put in more time training than her competitors. We're all born with talents in various disciplines, but very few of us make the decision to nurture that talent to the best of our ability.

One of my favorite examples is a quote widely attributed to Ray Kroc, the man who purchased McDonald's in the sixties and turned it into the global franchise that it is today: *Luck is a dividend of sweat. The more you sweat, the luckier you get*. Kroc, undoubtedly, did pretty well for himself. What you think of Ray Kroc or McDonald's has nothing to do with the idea of good luck.

Back to the walking disaster. You might be thinking that this is still just somebody who happens to suffer more misfortunes than others. They keep getting hurt; they keep losing their luggage; they keep getting their cars scratched in IKEA parking lots. However, you should rethink that.

If you have a habit of wandering around dark parking lots in bad neighborhoods with a Rolex on your wrist, looking for your brand-new sports car, you don't get to complain if you suffer what might seem like bad luck. When you inevitably end up getting mugged, it won't be a total surprise. You were being both naive and oblivious. Some people might call you an idiot who was responsible for the whole situation.

It's the same in a work setting: If you make a big announcement to management that you're going to handle some project, without knowing what's actually involved, you could end up wrecking your career, and it won't have a thing to do with bad luck. It will come down to lacking experience and judgment.

This could very well be what's going on with our friend the walking disaster.

Energy Vampires Who Drain Themselves

These energy vampires live among us and appear to be just like everybody else. They have spouses, parents, children, and friends, just like the rest of us. And their loved ones end up having to watch what happens, year after year. This can be extremely draining, to put it mildly. And that's the problem.

What do you do about somebody who manages to single-handedly cause themselves an endless succession of problems but never sees their own part in any of this? What do you do when your good friend, partner, or daughter-in-law keeps pouring their energy into a massive personal black hole? And, most important, what do you do when they keep having to turn to *you* when they need to replenish their energy?

The immediate response is concern. Not knowing what's going to happen.

What's next? What kind of problem are they going to get themself into this week? Going around feeling constantly worried about somebody you care about can be a huge drain.

One man I spoke to said that he was fully prepared to protect his partner from external dangers. But how was he supposed to protect her from herself? Her naivety got her in trouble every day of the week.

How long can this go on before you say you've had enough? How much of themselves are people supposed to sacrifice needlessly before their loved ones draw the line? Should you respond if somebody is heading for destruction without even knowing it?

These questions are highly relevant, since somebody who's always giving away pieces of themselves will eventually run out of self to offer their loved ones.

It's a beautiful thought, of course. This entirely unselfish individual, who never reflects on their own needs before committing to helping others. Isn't that the kind of person the world could use more of?

Like the familiar safety precaution says, *Put on your own oxygen mask before you help anybody else*. That is basically a warning that if you sacrifice everything for others you will lose yourself. And was that really the goal?

If you get used by others regularly—the usual suspects will be the narcissists and bullies out there—the reason could be poor self-esteem. This can be helped, of course, but that's probably best left to professionals. It'll take time, and I would recommend anybody who lacks the proper training to help find their friends a reputable therapist for treatment.

Compare it to stopping when you spot a car with its hood open on the highway. If you're a mechanic, who's trained to work on that specific make of car, you could actually do some real good. If not, you'd be better off towing the unfortunate driver's vehicle to the nearest garage. That's another way of doing good.

THE KNOW-IT-ALL

Somebody who gives advice all the time and interferes with what others are doing. They insert themselves into things uninvited. They always know better than everyone else, and they think they have the answer to everything. They happen to be experts at every subject.

Admit it. You've done it yourself. You've given unsolicited advice to people. In your case—and in mine, of course—it was a genuinely good-natured act. We really wanted to help and explain something to whomever.

But when other people do this . . . how annoying is it to have to listen to good advice *you never asked for*?

Know-it-alls generously share their opinions with others and will give lengthy accounts of their vast knowledge of everything on earth. They know the best way to cut the lawn, they know all about Argentinian wines, and they happen to be experts on Chinese history, Italian politics, segregation in North Korea, and the Australian automotive industry. All of that knowledge in one person! It hardly seems believable.

But there's more: Since they feel that they know best, they will occasionally also want to tell you, me, and everybody else what we ought to do in situation X, Y, or Z.

They'll get involved when we're building a patio behind the house, explaining how the dimensions look wrong to them, and they won't hesitate to walk up to the woman at the gym who's obviously spent years building muscle to point out the flaws in her squatting technique—even if they haven't ever touched a dumbbell.

When you're working, there's always another, better way you should be doing it. When you're raising children, know-it-alls will be happy to tell you about how you should be doing it according to A, B, or C.

It simply never ends.

How to Circumvent a Know-It-All

Some of these people are definitely the type I described in the chapter on habitual perfectionists. They can't help pointing it out when they perceive something to be incorrect. Others are simply Yellow individuals who can't help thinking out loud. They don't mean any harm, and they tend to forget all about it. Others are genuinely trying to be helpful and actually want to do some good. Perhaps they're exhibiting what's known as social drive.

The reason behind their annoying behavior is important, particularly when you're deciding exactly how enraged to get. If this person is genuinely trying to help you in the way that seems best to them, that's one thing, as opposed to when people just want to interfere and dominate others.

However, the problem these self-appointed advisors pose is really quite simple to solve. Except for your boss, whose advice you presumably have to follow, you'll find the only genuine obstacle in the mirror.

Think about it. If somebody tries to change what you're doing or not doing, why do you care at all about what they have to say?

If you'd never seek advice from this person, why would you listen to them when they try to involve themselves in your affairs uninvited?

Ignore what I told you earlier: Most of us simply dislike being told what to do. This is particularly true in situations where we already feel that we're in control.

I think many people will accept advice, and listen and nod out of pure courtesy. That's how I personally respond to tips I get from amateurs whose opinions don't really matter to me. When somebody who's never been onstage tries to tell me how I ought to give my lectures—while I've spoken to hundreds of thousands of people over the last two decades—I nod and then I switch off. But I wouldn't if the person in question happens to have more experience than I do. That would be completely different.

Or when dreamers who would like to write a book try to convince me that it helps your writing to have a few drinks first, because they read this somewhere—I was actually given this advice by a group of people years ago, half of whom admitted that they didn't even *read* books—I don't engage. There's really no need to respond to half-baked ideas like that.

Others might feel less sure about this and believe all advice to be well-meaning. Let's dispel that illusion right now. If you're not feeling confident about something, you might want to have your approach confirmed. But that doesn't mean you should be entertaining ideas from people who actually have nothing to do with it.

No, you'll have to decide what to do about that persistent know-it-all.

There are a few different options here:

Ignore them.

Thank them, but ignore their advice.

Confront them about not minding their own business.

The most entertaining option, of course, is confrontation. It can be both invigorating and educational. It's also rife with opportunities for potentially growth-inducing conflict. Further, it offers a chance to interrupt an unfortunate pattern in which your neighbor keeps lobbing pointless advice over the fence.

Here's what you might say: *Why exactly are you giving me that advice? Do you not trust me to know how to handle my own business?*

Here's a line I've used for years, with great success: *What would you like me to do with this information?*

You could also tell them that you'll get in touch if your current approach doesn't work.

Alternatively, you could demand that they show you their credentials in the field in question, and make it clear that if they don't, you won't pay any attention to their suggestion. (I like the sound of that one—I'll have to try it myself!)

If you have the time to spare, you could also mirror their behavior. Head over to your neighbor's place and show him how to do stuff. Snatch the lawn trimmer from his hands and give him a lesson on how to reach the awkward spots underneath the shrubs. If you're lucky, he might realize his mistake and the two of you will bond over a couple of beers instead. If he's annoyed that you're interfering, you could always tell him you're glad he knows how it feels. Then ask him to keep quiet from then on.

It might sound blunt, but it's actually surprisingly effective. Sometimes you simply need to call this behavior out—most normal people will see what they did. If you're lucky, they might even laugh at themselves for it.

Remember: Most know-it-alls aren't really trying to stir anything up; they simply have an unappealing urge to intervene.

Set boundaries for what you're willing to accept. And stick to them.

THE MOST COMPLICATED
ENERGY VAMPIRE OF ALL

I'm about to take a pretty serious risk here, and it's entirely possible this book will soon be crashing through your nearest window. We'll see how it goes, I guess. But let's be honest here, just you and me. Sometimes you'll lose energy, focus, and motivation for a very simple reason: You don't really know what you're doing. You don't see your own flaws and shortcomings, and you're unaware of the ways your behavior impacts your own energy levels.

Don't feel bad. We all have our less flattering qualities. That's true of me, you, and everybody you ever met or will ever meet. We're in good company. And life involves so much more than trying to monitor your own thoughts and actions. Who has time for that kind of thing? Stick with me, though, and you'll find out that there are enormous benefits to paying a little more attention.

Many of the things we do are done purely out of habit.

This goes for good things, less good things, and genuinely harmful things. They just happen.

Sometimes you'll be in a hurry to leave your house. You're late for a train, or your whole family is already waiting in the car. Whatever the reason, the last thing you want to be doing at that moment is looking for your keys.

That was me, for so many years. I'm usually a pretty organized person, but for some reason, my keys kept disappearing whenever I was in a hurry.

You know what it can be like. You run around your home like a lunatic, pulling out drawers, rummaging through all your pockets—some of which require at least five searches before you can be fully confident that your keys aren't in there somewhere. Sometimes you'll look in the pockets of a jacket you haven't even worn in three years. Perhaps, somehow, your keys have magically teleported themselves to your old winter coat from 2010.

The problem isn't so much the keys as the effect frantically looking for them like this has on you and your mood. When those blasted keys finally materialize, usually on some table you've already searched fifteen times while muttering the most appalling curses under your breath, your positive energy will be completely gone. If you're not incredibly stressed, you're probably actively enraged.

When you finally sit down behind the wheel, your whole family can tell that a live grenade just hopped in the car.

That used to happen to me a lot. It wasn't fun at all. Until the day I did something very simple: I nailed up a key hook in the hall. Next, I made a habit of always hanging my keys up in that specific place every time I *walked through the door*. That way I would always know where my keys were the next time I was about to *walk back out through the same door*.

My point is that we all have unexamined habits that disrupt our energy in everyday life, rob us of our focus, and bring our moods down to dangerous levels. And in the end, who suffers? Exactly. Our loved ones. They are the ones who have to witness outburst after outburst when we've lost it over something we did to ourselves. It's not a good look, my friend.

So spend some time considering these moments and see if there's something you could do to avoid losing energy and motivation at the wrong times. Some of these will be simple, while others are more complex. I'm not suggesting that this list is comprehensive. But we've got to start somewhere.

If you haven't already been taking notes while reading, this is the time to start!

The Most Effective Tool

A highly effective way to lose energy in the moment is to get into an argument with somebody. You know, all those times when you realize that you've completely misjudged a situation or just made a fool out of yourself by being . . . you. People you actually like a great deal turn their backs on you—and all you did was be yourself! (If you honestly can't recall any situations like that, you'll need to start paying closer attention, right now.)

I'm sure you've heard the expression *No pain, no gain*. It's often used in contexts related to physical training, but there are other situations that might also be quite painful, yet worth the effort.

One of the most important characteristics for success in life is self-awareness. In fact, with strong, solid self-awareness there's very little you can't achieve. Self-awareness is everything.

Why is this, though? Why is self-awareness one of the most powerful tools you have for achieving your dreams and goals? Also, what happens to people who don't cultivate self-awareness?

What problems can that cause?

We've all been in a meeting where we find ourselves gradually coming to the realization that nobody actually understands what's going on. Everybody else is talking, and nobody is listening.

The only exception is the folks who are staying completely silent instead. When you leave the meeting, all you can think is, *What's wrong with all these people?*

Other examples would be when your partner is simply refusing to listen to you or when you realize that some people just can't seem to understand what you're saying, no matter how clearly you speak to them.

If only they could all be more like . . . *you*.

Sometimes you'll feel like you're surrounded by idiots. Interestingly enough, it seems to me that some of us are surrounded by more idiots than others.

On the other hand, when you think of how difficult it can be to change yourself, it might seem futile to even try to change everybody else.

Is that really what social skills are all about?

Of course it isn't. Trying to change everybody else is pointless. Between you and me, it's also pretty naive.

What constitutes social excellence, then?

The ability to understand and predict the reactions others will have to your own behavior.

We all influence one another, all the time. Your actions influence the actions of others. All the time.

And this is the key to success: If you can figure out ahead of time what the person you're communicating with will do if you do X, Y, or Z, you will have good social skills.

The more often you get this right, the more probable it is that you're socially adept. Naturally, it would be even better if you weren't guessing at all but actually knew what you were doing.

Getting along well with others, regardless of who they are or how they behave.

Understanding and predicting the reactions your own behavior will elicit from others. That's the solution.

The Importance of Self-Awareness

If you take a closer look, you'll soon realize that the concept of social skills actually hinges on just one trait: self-awareness.

In order to know how people will react to the things you say and do, you'll need to know how they will be perceived. By others. You need to understand yourself. That's the key.

Self-awareness provides social skills, which, in turn, make you a good communicator.

What is self-awareness, then? If we understood this concept better, we might find it easier to acquire the magical knowledge.

Self-awareness is actually composed of several things:

1. the ability to see yourself clearly
2. an understanding of who you really are
3. an understanding of how you're perceived by others

When you look in the mirror, do you see what the rest of us see? Are you sure about that? What difference does what you think actually make? *I am what I am, and that's okay?* Well, certainly. You can always wander around being just the way you are. It's an option. You're perfectly entitled to be precisely the way you are and act the way you see fit.

But you should know that there will be consequences. And you might not like them.

Self-awareness provides social skills, which make you a good communicator.

Now we've finally arrived at the most valuable secret of all: the value of effective communication.

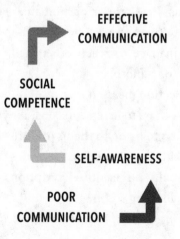

Communication as a Recipe for Success

A chain, as you know, is no stronger than its weakest link, and we're all links in a mind-bogglingly long chain. When the chain breaks, it will be because of either bad habits or bad communication. I'd be prepared to say that bad communication is the culprit about 90 percent of the time.

What happens when the chain breaks? It's actually rather simple. There isn't much we can achieve by ourselves in life. Most of the things we want to do will depend on or happen in collaboration with others, in one way or another.

Communication can be defined as the exchange of information, ideas, and knowledge between a transmitter and a receiver and involves the use of an agreed-upon symbolic code.

Ah, yeah, you might be thinking. *But don't we all actually communicate more than ever these days, thanks to all the countless platforms we use?*

We do communicate, that's true. But do we break through? Are we truly making a connection?

The word "communicate" comes from the Latin *communicare,* which means "to share or participate." Being able to share and convince others to participate is the whole objective. Whether we manage to reach others will decide how useful we can be to one another.

What does connection mean in this case?

It means getting others to listen and consider your message but also being willing to listen to them. And this is where the concept of social skills is so important.

How do they usually phrase job descriptions—regardless of what job they're looking to fill?

The person we want for this position is motivated and results-

oriented, i.e., Red behavior; *positive and inspiring,* i.e., Yellow behavior; *a strong team player and an excellent listener,* i.e., Green behavior; *and organized and highly disciplined,* i.e., Blue behavior.

All I can think when I see an ad like that is, *Good luck!* If you manage to find somebody with all those qualities, I'd be happy to hire them immediately. For what position? Any position. Every position.

At the end of the ad, they always cram in twenty more points, and one of those is social skills.

The trouble with social skills is that they're a bit like the famous sense of humor in that nobody believes their own to be lacking.

Psychological studies are unambiguous on this point: People who possess a high degree of self-awareness are generally happier with their lives. They have stronger relationships. They're a lot more creative. They're more confident, and they have better self-esteem.

But that's not all. They also perform better in the workplace. They're better communicators, they're more supportive of others, and when they become managers they make more effective leaders.

Why is this? Because leadership is a matter of communication. The best leaders are excellent communicators. They have great social skills. Because they possess . . . self-awareness.

We even know that people with good self-awareness tend to make more money than the average. If you need more reasons, you haven't been listening . . . [winky face].

On top of the things I've mentioned, self-awareness is the key to becoming a brilliant communicator and getting the best out of the people you meet.

No Pain, No Gain

Self-awareness can be quite painful to achieve, but it's worth it, nonetheless. Discovering how you actually function, whether through therapy, personality analysis, or asking others for feedback, can smart a bit. Trust me. If you ask me, though, that's no reason not to go through with it. The advantages are too great for you to refrain from getting as much self-awareness as you can, however humbling it might be.

Now, if the benefits of self-awareness are so great and if there are seemingly no drawbacks, why doesn't everyone work on developing it?

The answer is very simple: Most people think they already have it.

Behavioral science studies in which people have been asked about their self-awareness have revealed an interesting pattern. I don't usually refer to specific studies, but I think this one by the American psychologist Tasha Eurich is too much fun to keep to myself. Ninety-five percent of the respondents in the study turned out to rate their self-awareness as *above average*.

I'll repeat that: Ninety-five percent rated their self-awareness as *above average*.

Eurich included what's known as a 360-degree analysis. People who knew the respondents were asked, *Is this accurate? Is the description they've given correct?* The result? About 10 to 15 percent were said to have described themselves accurately.

There's an alarming truth hidden here. About 80 percent of us are lying about ourselves . . .

What's the right conclusion to draw from this? That self-awareness might be a more complex issue than you may believe. But it still doesn't matter.

Self-awareness provides social skills, which make you a good communicator. The foundation of success.

That's the answer to the question of why you ought to work to improve your self-awareness. Also, the less often you end up at odds with somebody because of bad communication, the fewer the occasions where you're left with a head full of questions about what just happened, the fewer the jobs you find yourself wondering why you didn't get, the less often you upset your granddad or never get a second date with somebody, and the fewer the times when you feel like you're surrounded by idiots, the more energy you'll have left!

Believe me. I've made some truly ghastly mistakes when it comes to other people, in both professional and private settings. It happened with colleagues, clients, and some of my best friends when I was younger. Some of these experiences happened when I was a teenager, and it still hurts to think back on them.

An Embarrassing Slice of Self-Awareness

I think I was about sixteen and I had a great friend—let's call him John. He was a mellow, good-natured guy, and we only really had one thing in common: music.

We were into heavy metal. The heavier the better. Iron Maiden, Black Sabbath, and the like were some of our favorites. We sometimes listened to Rainbow, too. In those days, bands used to release an album every twelve months or so. Whenever one of our favorite bands had a new release, it was a huge deal for us. We would sit at my place or John's place, stare at the album cover, and turn the music up loud. If the inside sleeve had lyrics, we would always read along as we listened.

We could spend hours just listening to the music. Our parents, as you might expect, were less enthusiastic: *That's hardly even music, and why do you have to play it so loud?* You get the picture.

But then Rainbow released an album that was a little softer. It didn't sound like metal at all. It was more like regular rock. Not cool. Wimpy. But still good.

And then John told me that one day he'd been playing this slightly softer Rainbow album and when he turned around he saw his mom in the doorway, kind of swaying along to the music. He stared at her in surprise, and then she said, *This is actually pretty good.*

Here comes the point of this story; it's something I've returned to in my mind over and over for almost forty years, ever since it happened. I remember the moment that followed with the same clarity I can see the room I'm sitting in now.

Maybe I was jealous that John's mom had finally, sort of, approved of our choice of music. Perhaps I wanted to be the center of attention. Perhaps I wanted to feel more important than I was. Perhaps I wished my mom could have shown a little interest, too. Maybe I was having a bad day. Most of all, though, I think I just felt it was a good story. Whatever my reasoning, what I ended up doing was quite unforgivable.

You see, when John and I and a third friend, whose name was Urban, were at my place a few weeks later, listening to that same Rainbow album, *I simply stole John's whole story*.

I told the same story to Urban, only set it in my own room

instead of John's. I made his listening session my own. Worse still: *His* mom became . . . *my* mom.

I ended the story by having my own mom tell me, *This is actually pretty good.*

Urban nodded and grinned. He didn't say anything. Maybe he thought something like, *Wow, what a cool mom this guy has!*

Then I turned to John, who was staring at me as though I had completely lost my mind. It wasn't until that moment that I realized that I had stolen the entire story from *him.* I remember it so vividly. How I just stared back, not knowing what to say to him.

The worst thing of all was that he didn't say anything. He just looked at me.

If only he had said something!

What's the moral of this tale of woe, then? Well, it goes something like this: To this day, forty years later, this experience has stayed in my mind. I've never figured out why it appears, but sometimes it's just there.

It has the same effect every time: I go silent. I feel my ears go red. And I feel ashamed. Forty years down the line. How about that?

I ran my mouth constantly when I was younger, and sometimes I said things I shouldn't have. That's an important aspect of my self-awareness. I need to think before I speak. I still live by that.

I'm so sorry, John!

Take a Test

How does one go about gaining self-awareness? If you'll excuse my self-promotion, I think the cheapest and simplest way is to take the test on my website surroundedbyidiots.com. That test will show you your colors and let you know how you can better communicate with others. That'll give you a good start in your new life.

1. Take a personality or behavioral test.
2. Ask others for feedback on how they experience and perceive you.
3. Be observant of your own behavior and try to understand why you do the things you do.
4. Read about personalities and behavior online.
5. Go to a lecture on the subject.
6. Read a book.
7. Read another book.

The point is that the more attention you give this subject, the more you will learn. I can guarantee that your journey towards increased self-awareness will be both entertaining and educational.

You'll learn about your flaws and imperfections, but the insights you gain will keep you from making the biggest mistakes. By learning to predict your instinctive behavior in any given situation, you can avoid a lot of missteps in life. Also, you'll be able to keep your energy rather than waste it.

You may even be able to avoid the energy traps I'll be discussing in the coming sections.

FAILING TO REACH YOUR GOALS

Let's set aside external things like unpredictable events and negative people for the moment. We can all agree that there's hardly anything more frustrating than not getting what you wanted. Not quite achieving the thing you deeply hoped for. That can really kill your hopes for the future. Setting increasingly challenging goals, time and time again, only to realize, over and over: *I'll never reach the finish line. I seem unable to overcome the smallest of challenges.* Is there anything else that drains your energy more than that?

We've all learned that we need to set goals in order to achieve anything worthwhile. We need to be done by five o'clock, or we'll miss the train. We need to go to the gym at least three times a week (and, importantly, work out while we're there) in order to reach our health-related goals. We need to study at least two hours a day for four weeks to pass the next exam. We need to call at least ten prospects every day to hit our sales targets.

Sometimes we reach our goals, sure. But alarmingly often, we don't. I've coached people who've stopped setting goals completely, because they don't know what to do in order to reach them. Or perhaps they do know but fail anyway. Some even claim that their goals weren't that important. However, all that is just self-deception. Each failure causes so much disappointment that they end up feeling better about not having any goals at all.

That's a rather depressing solution to a complicated problem.

Setting Dumb Goals

You may have heard of SMART goals. The idea is that setting up a clear structure for things will help you achieve success at whatever you're focusing on:

Specific: The goal should be a precise statement of the desired improvement.

Measurable: The goal must be quantifiable.

Attainable: It must be possible for you to achieve.

Relevant: The goal must relate to the big picture of what you're trying to accomplish.

Time-bound: Naturally, you have to be able to say when it should be done by.

The SMART acronym is usually attributed to George T. Doran. His idea won an audience, to put it mildly.

The problem with SMART goals is that although ticking things off of a list is enjoyable, this attitude is nowhere near inspiring enough. It only stimulates one hemisphere of the brain: the left one, which processes logical and rational thought.

Many people seem to believe that goals have to contain all five components of the SMART formula in order to be effective. They do this because it only addresses the left brain.

Why is this a problem, though? Look at the title of this book! It's about energy! SMART goals are practical and clear, but where is the energy, the inspiration, or the motivation? Where are the dreams?

Instead, I'd like to suggest an entirely different goal-setting method: DUMB goals.

Personally, I find American motivational speaker Brendon Burchard's DUMB method much more inspirational. "DUMB" in "DUMB goals" stands for the following:

Dream-driven: This might not need explaining, but dreaming is liberating and inspiring. There needs to be some grand dream behind it all if you're going to be able to achieve it.

Uplifting: It has to feel positive and invigorating. When your goal becomes a burden, it's no longer doing anything for you.

Method-friendly: There needs to be a functional method helping you achieve the goal, a system to follow that makes it easy for you to establish good habits.

Behavior-driven: It needs to be designed in a way that stimulates the correct behavior. Since any results will depend on what you *do* rather than on what you *know* or *can* do, this is absolutely vital.

Here's how Burchard explains each point. Let's begin with the most fun one: *dream-driven*. It might sound a bit ethereal, but the fact is, if you don't have a dream to guide you, there's not really any point in getting up in the morning.

John F. Kennedy's moonshot speech has become a thing of legend. It will take you a minute or so to read, but please read it slowly and think about what he's actually saying:

> But if I were to say, my fellow citizens, that we shall send to the moon, two hundred and forty thousand miles away from the control station in Houston, a giant rocket more than three hundred feet tall, the length of this football field, made of new metal alloys, some of which have not yet been invented, capable of standing heat and stresses several times more than have ever been experienced, fitted together with a precision better than the finest watch, carrying all the equipment needed for propulsion, guidance, control, communications, food, and survival, on an untried mission, to an unknown celestial body, and then return it safely to Earth, reentering the atmosphere at speeds of more than twenty-five thousand miles per hour, causing heat about half that of the temperature of the sun—almost as hot as

it is here today—and do all this, and do it right, and do it
first before this decade is out, then we must be bold.

What do you think? This isn't some vague inclination, like
Wouldn't it be neat if we could send a rocket into space with
some guys onboard? Let's see how far we can send them!

No, no. These guys *will* be going to the moon! Can you
think of a bigger dream, or a more inspired goal than that?

If Kennedy had set a SMART goal instead, I don't believe
any humans would have gone to the moon anytime soon.
Sometimes you need to be brave enough to have an impossible, huge dream if you're going to achieve anything that's
truly worth achieving. With plans that big, it'll be a lot easier
to keep your energy levels high.

Eliminating poverty worldwide—there's a grand dream
that's worth pursuing! Eradicating malaria once and for all
would be worth anybody's time, seeing as it's one of the
deadliest diseases in human history.

There's nothing wrong with reasonable and realistic goals,
of course, but they're not enormously inspiring, are they?
Achieving a genuine dream is better every day of the week.

The next point states that your goal should be *uplifting*.
The goal itself needs to feel amazing and inspiring.

Take health, for example. How many of us have set the
goal of losing some weight? Now, losing weight is good and
all, but how uplifting is the thought of losing six pounds?
Not enormously, in all honesty.

How about, instead of losing weight, you set the goal of
looking so good that when you walk by everyone will turn
their heads?

It's superficial, you're right, but guess what? We *are* superficial beings. Unfortunately, this example is something most of us can relate to, even if we might refuse to admit it in public. Losing something—six pounds—will never be as inspiring to us as becoming more attractive and sexier than we used to be. There's a goal that will feed you some positive energy!

Or what about leading a healthy lifestyle not merely to look great, but so that you'll get to spend more time with your beloved? Or hang around long enough to get to see your grandchildren grow up? That'll motivate you!

You need a *method* for reaching your goal or dream. Like, for instance, a specific diet that you can follow. Every day at X o'clock, you work out and do meal prep. You don't need to think too much—you just do it. Using a certain method will eventually become your routine or habit. Perhaps the specifics of your method don't matter too much, but even when you're setting your goal you'll know that there are ways you can do things to reach it.

Say you want to earn your degree and be in the top of your class. You plan specific study sessions, and after each one you get a special reward. Maybe you get to drink a beer, or play online games for half an hour. The point is that the system is set ahead of time. All you need to do now is follow it.

And the last point, B, stands for the idea that the whole package needs to be *behavior-driven*. What does that mean? Well, it means you should be able to reach the goal by means of your behavior. Your own actions should propel you towards it. What you *do* should matter. If you set the goal of being the tallest person in the world, you'll inevitably fail. There's nothing you can do to influence your height. There's no diet you can follow or exercises you can do that will make you taller.

However, if your goal is to achieve financial security, you

can influence the outcome by actively saving money each month, for example. What you do matters, but so does what you don't do. Like not spending all your student loans on partying, for instance.

That's a summary of DUMB goals. I think this is a very refreshing approach, and it has helped me get a lot further than I would have believed possible. That doesn't in any way mean that I have nothing left to achieve, just that I'm finding myself able to tick more and more of the boxes I want to accomplish.

And that's not too bad.

Realizing your dreams *feeds* you energy. Failing to do so *drains* you of energy. Not daring to dream up a more ambitious goal than dragging your carcass to work every morning does neither. At best, it's depressing. You deserve better.

Here's my advice: Dare to dream, and dream big! And make sure to reach your goals! One way of doing that is to take a look at your habits.

The Power of Habit

Admit it! You're a creature of habit. You might be wondering how I can be so sure about that. It's simple. We're *all* creatures of habit. Unfortunately, many of us are stuck in bad habits. We repeatedly react to our partners, our children, our bosses, and our employees in ways we wouldn't have chosen deliberately. Often, this leads to nothing but headaches.

Doing the wrong things can really steal your energy. What's strange is that we so easily do the wrong things and end up regretting it. When that happens, we ruminate, curse ourselves, and complain: *Why did I do so and so?* The funny part is, it just happened. Because it was a habit.

It could be leaving your keys in the wrong place. It could be spending too long on your phone at breakfast, which you do every day, which is why you have to drive like a maniac trying to get to work on time and then blame it all on traffic when you're late again. It could be habitually having an extra glass of wine every Friday evening, even though you really shouldn't, and then ending up eating too many snacks with your Friday night movie. On Saturday morning, you wake up feeling disappointed in yourself, again: *Why did I do that? Why do I never learn?* You recognize it, and you recognize the feeling. Sometimes you didn't even expect better.

Naturally, this could also apply to things you do at work. Your everyday routine begins with opening your inbox, because you always start your day doing precisely that. You want to tackle anything that diverts your valuable attention safely out of the way before you get your day underway. However, this inevitably leaves you bogged down in a bunch of issues that need resolving. You find yourself doing everything but what you intended to do until 2 p.m. That means that you're spending far too little time on your important project every day, the project you agreed to take on and that has a looming deadline. The stress will become painfully real eventually, and you'll end up having to go into the office on a Sunday to really take charge of the situation. Out of habit, of course, you open your email inbox, and . . . you get the picture.

Choosing a Habit

The solution is both simple and difficult. All you need to do is identify which of your habits lead to favorable consequences, like drinking an extra glass of water before lunch, and which ones lead to unfavorable consequences: browsing your phone at the dinner table so you're not paying attention to what your partner says to you.

Health is a good example here, because poor health won't just cause a loss of mental energy—it'll tax your physical energy, too. If eating too much and failing to get enough exercise causes you to lose energy, feel out of shape, and feel generally uncomfortable—apart from the consequences it can have in terms of your life expectancy—you'll need to *do* something. You'll need to *change* something.

Here's an important insight: Habits are a matter of *choices*. The choices you make. The things you choose to do or choose not to do. If your choice every morning is to press the snooze button three times between 6:30 and 7:00 a.m. and then practically drop to the floor, stagger to your car, and buy a donut and a large latte with all the extras on your way to work, you'll be very aware of how challenging it is to become somebody who will bounce out of bed at 5:00 a.m. to run for thirty minutes before breakfast. That's an active choice, too.

The problem is that it takes time. You won't lose a bad habit that has been developing for years in just a few weeks.

Good habits can be difficult to build, but they're easy to live with. Bad habits are easily acquired but difficult to live with.

What, then, is a bad habit? That part is pretty simple. A bad habit is anything you do that is directly opposed to your primary goals in life. In essence, then, this means that the same habits might mean different things for different individuals.

If your ambition is to stay in your current job, playing Minecraft until midnight every evening won't do you any harm. If, however, your goal is to get a degree in international finance, your online gaming won't get you very far.

If you're trying to save up for the down payment on a new home, it would be a bad idea to waste your money on unnecessary luxury items that you don't even need. If you already have that down payment put away, getting a new iPhone every six months might not be a terrible idea.

Essentially, you need to focus entirely on your goal. You know, that DUMB goal I was discussing a few pages ago. It will tell you which habits you should be avoiding and which ones you should acquire. Any habit that prevents you from reaching your goal is a bad habit.

Here's an example: Your goal is to fit in your wedding dress. You really ought to head down to your den and get on your treadmill for an hour every morning, before you have breakfast. That would make watching four episodes of *The Crown* until midnight the night before a bad habit.

Now, you may be thinking there's something fishy here. Watching television isn't going to make you put on weight. And that's true—but it will make it that much harder for you to get out of bed the next morning.

You want to have a successful career. Earn more money. You should be investing your time in leadership training. You're also planning to read at least ten books about leadership this year. What does this mean? Every time you're focused on unimportant things during work hours or listening to a podcast about something else, that's a bad habit!

This isn't easy, but just as before, the little things matter. Our new lives have to begin at some point.

The solution to bad habits is actually fairly simple to implement, but that doesn't make it easy. The first thing you need to do to break a bad habit is realize and accept that it *is* a bad habit:

1. The first component is a trigger of some sort. Something that creates the impulse to behave in a specific way.
2. After this comes routine behavior. Something you do the same way every time. A habit is really nothing but a repeated action.
3. Last of all comes the whole reward thing. This is something that gives you short-term encouragement to repeat the things you did in step 2.
4. Now, this is where the danger lies: When a specific behavior has been repeated a number of times, your habit will be established. At this point, things change. You'll crave the reward, and go straight to step 2 without any trigger at all. That's how a bad habit is made.

Okay, we've gotten the theory out of the way. How does all this work in practice? Imagine that you have a habit of stopping at 7-Eleven on your way to work to buy a triple latte with extra syrup for five dollars, but that you'd like to break that habit: First, you have to admit that it's a bad habit.

This is what happens: You see the 7-Eleven (that's your trigger) and your autopilot kicks in and you go inside and buy your coffee (that's the routine behavior). The reward, step 3, is drinking the coffee. You find it very tasty. It gives

you a dopamine high, and you experience short-term satisfaction.

After a while, however, you'll find yourself thinking of
that tasty coffee with the extra vanilla syrup. At this point,
you'll be craving that specific coffee. That's when you find
yourself leaving your desk to go downstairs to the shop deliberately. Note that you'll still enjoy the coffee. However, it
might not be what you ought to be drinking if your goal is to
limit your calorie or caffeine intake—or save money, for that
matter. A $5 coffee every day is over $1,800 in a year.

How Do You Break a Bad Habit?

If you take a look at your action plan for, say, saving money
and you don't find any triple lattes on your list, that's your
answer right there: It's not helping you reach your goal, so
it's a bad habit.

You can also use this approach to address bad habits that
are already established. Stop walking past that 7-Eleven.
Hold on now, though: There are other coffee shops along the
way, aren't there? Yes, but you're more alert to this now. You
won't get lured into that habit again.

Here's what you can do:

Remind yourself of whatever your goal is. Health, finances,
career, relationships—anything at all. After this, just be honest with yourself. In order to break a bad habit, as I said, you
have to acknowledge it first. After this, you'll need to write it
down and, finally, get clear on what would make for a better
habit in the same exact situation.

It's simple. But it's not easy.

My bad habit is . . .	An alternative course of action might be to . . .
Write down the thing you do that isn't helping you reach the goal you stated above, for example: I go on spontaneous shopping trips when I don't need to, without any idea of what I really need.	*Write down what you could do instead, for example:* I'm going to keep a list in the kitchen where I will regularly write down the things I actually need. Also, I'll never put anything in my shopping cart that's not on my list. No matter what the kids nag me for in the supermarket.
I get home and start planning to go to the gym. But I never find all the things I need, and I usually give up.	I'm going to pack my gym bag the night before and use the following checklist to make sure to pack everything I'm going to need: Shoes Towel Water bottle Phone Knee brace Headphones XYZ
I start every workday checking my email, which causes me to end up reacting to other people's demands all morning.	From now on, I'm going to observe specific email times: 10:00 a.m., 1:00 p.m., and 4:30 p.m.

Usually, no one solution will work for everybody. That's why you need to take a good look at yourself and make up your mind; what's the reality in your specific situation?

Breaking a bad habit requires an active decision. And establishing a new habit takes time. Those bits are nonnegotiable.

Learn to observe your own behavior. Spend a few minutes

each day examining all the things you've done. How much of it is routine, i.e., habits, and how many active decisions are you actually making?

The fascinating part of all this is this: When you feel like you're the one deciding what you do, rather than your subconscious habits, it will give you a wonderful sense of control.

That, my friend, will give you a boost of the best kind of energy!

The Fine Art of Procrastination

This section is a real drag, and it took me several weeks to even get started on it. You see, I didn't quite know how I ought to approach the subject, so I kept myself busy with other stuff for as long as I could. It was only when I realized what I was doing that I managed to get started on doing the actual work. That's irony for you.

However, I'm in excellent company. People have been procrastinating on things for centuries. The phenomenon is actually so ageless that philosophers like Socrates and Aristotle devised a word for this behavior: *akrasia*.

Akrasia is acting against better judgment. It's when you do one thing despite knowing you really ought to do something else. Loosely translated, *akrasia* means delay, or a lack of self-control.

How many books have been written on the topic of personal productivity? I don't know, but I've probably read north of fifty myself. Some of them were good, while others just gave me a headache.

Personally, I don't believe in trying to change your nature, but I do believe in getting things done so you don't have to think about them at the wrong times. That can cause massive energy drain, you see. Procrastinating on things is definitely not a good way to manage your life if you want to feel strong and full of positive energy.

You know how it goes. You work like a maniac all week long, getting a bunch of little things that have been bothering you out of the way. The only thing you don't do is that complicated, slightly worrisome, but frightfully important work task, the one thing that would fix so many other issues. Maybe you're not feeling motivated; maybe your confidence isn't where it needs to be for you to tackle it. Maybe you simply don't know how to do it. Or maybe you do know how to do it, but it's just so awfully . . . hard to get started.

Friday afternoon. It's far too late in the day to get started on that nasty thing that's weighing on you, so it'll have to wait, unfortunately. And even though you worked like a maniac all week and got lots of stuff done—perhaps you crossed ninety-nine things off your list—the thing that'll be worrying you all weekend will be that hundredth task. The one you *didn't* complete.

Ring a bell? This means you'll spend huge amounts of mental energy, all weekend, on *not doing the task*. That's the *consequence* of your procrastination.

Procrastination is when you unnecessarily and voluntarily postpone something despite knowing that it will cause negative consequences. The word originated in the Latin word *procrastinatus,* which itself evolved from the prefix *pro-,* which means "forward," and *crastinus,* which means something like "to tomorrow." In other words, when somebody says, *I'll do it tomorrow,* they can be accused of procrastinating.

This involves delaying everyday chores or postponing important things like attending a meeting, handing in reports or schoolwork, or bringing up a difficult issue with your partner. Although procrastination is commonly perceived as a negative because of the impact it can have on your productivity, it is different from other situations, like when you're waiting for new information in order to make an informed choice.

Pastry Today or a Six-Pack Tomorrow

What happens in our brains that makes us avoid the things we know we ought to be doing?

Behavioral scientists have discovered a phenomenon called time inconsistency, which helps us understand why we can procrastinate even when we have the best of intentions. "Time inconsistency" refers to the brain's tendency to value immediate rewards higher than future ones.

Imagine that you had two selves: your present self and your future self. When you set goals for yourself—like building muscle or writing a book or learning a language or asking that guy you fancy out for a date—you're actually setting plans for your future self. You imagine how you'd like your life to look at some point in the future. Maybe you took my message from earlier to heart and have set a really juicy DUMB goal.

Researchers have found that when you consider your future self, your brain has a fairly easy time seeing the point in doing things that grant long-term advantages. Your future self values long-term rewards, because it is the version of you that will reap the benefits of your current efforts.

While your *future* self can set goals, only your *present* self can actually take action. This is where things get messy.

When the time comes to decide in the moment, you're no

longer making a choice for your future self. Now, in the present, you're in charge, and your brain will focus mainly on the needs of your present self.

Research studies have also established that the present self—surprise, surprise!—very much prefers instant gratification. It's not big on long-term profit. As a result, we postpone what we ought to do in favor of doing what we want to do.

This means that our present selves and our future selves are often at odds with one another. Your future self might want to be svelte and fit, but your present self, right now, is more interested in eating pastries.

Similarly, many young people know that the retirement savings they make in their twenties and thirties are vital but also that the benefits involved won't come for many decades. It's a lot easier for the present self to see the value in buying a pair of new shoes than putting away one hundred dollars a month to enjoy in seventy years.

This is one of the reasons why you might go to bed full of motivation to make a change in your life but wake up surprised at how much less important it seems now. Rather than doing what you intended, you fall victim to the temptation of doing something much easier, whatever that might look like for you.

How the Four Colors Procrastinate

Now, nothing is ever quite that simple, of course. Naturally, different people procrastinate in different ways, for different reasons.

Figuring out which category you belong to can help you

overcome your procrastination habits—and maybe even get some work done ahead of schedule occasionally. Just a thought.

Now, let's get serious: We're all prone to falling into this trap. In fact, even hugely successful people can be pathological procrastinators. This doesn't mean, however, that everyone does it for the same reason or overcomes the challenges involved the same way. The key to conquering your own procrastinating nature is to figure out which group you belong to, so that you can break with your own patterns and get the project done early for once.

In the following sections, I'll give accounts of how each of the four colors relates to procrastination.

Red

Reds often say things like, *I do my best work under pressure.*

There's actually a grain of truth to this—although it's a pretty small grain.

These types tend to coerce themselves into focusing by limiting the time they have to do a certain task. They'll often start on things they don't feel like doing late, because they talk themselves into believing other things are more important.

For many of them, the true reason for this is a fear of perfectionism. If they limit the time available, there's no way the task can be done to any unreasonable standards anyway, right? Quick and sloppy is the solution, but at least it gets done in the end. Regardless of the reason, it's probably not a sustainable approach to keep pressuring yourself like this.

Their greatest challenge: getting started early enough

so that they don't have to rely solely on their ability to rush through a project.

A possible solution: If you're a Red, try turning your whole structure around and setting a start date. When you focus on when you're going to *start* on a task, rather than when you hope to *complete* it, you'll be removing a huge weight from your shoulders. It'll free up more energy for the right things.

A caveat is in order here: Many Reds have a very basic mindset when it comes to priorities. I call it toughing it out or running away. They either work like crazy at something or ignore it completely. On or off. Those are the only options.

Yellow

These procrastinators are huge victims of "shiny object syndrome." They constantly keep coming up with new projects they want to pursue—only to abandon them a week later.

It could even be just a couple of days. Or hours. If they don't get started, something else might very well outcompete that initial idea in the struggle for their attention. They're fascinated with the latest trends and are quick to implement but seldom get around to following up.

These individuals are actually good at making decisions and taking action. However, they end up wasting a lot of time unintentionally, and their efforts tend to fade as they don't align with work consistently for long enough to ever really see any results.

If you're a Yellow, your biggest challenge is this: completing things.

Here's how you solve it: Make things stick. I mean that literally. Write down new ideas for projects on a sheet of paper—but *don't start on them* until you've finished whatever it is you were doing when you thought of them.

Green

These people always claim to have too much on their plates. They're pros when it comes to filling their calendars, and they often feel exhausted just from thinking of everything they have to do. The most common excuse the rest of us hear from them is probably *I'm just so busy*. Whenever the word "busy" is used as an excuse not to do something, it's probably an indication that something else is going on. This is most often caused by the Green's tendency to avoid anything they don't feel like dealing with.

Rather than taking on a challenge head-on or admitting to themselves that they don't want to do something, they find it easier to blame their other priorities. With a bit of luck, they can even get away with it.

If you're a Green, your major challenge is this: stop causing chaos that allows you to avoid dealing with the things you know you ought to be handling right now. Oftentimes, the thing they're procrastinating on isn't a task but instead involves resolving a conflict or something along those lines.

Your solution: set aside some time for introspection. Ask yourself: *What am I—really—avoiding? And why?*

Blue

This procrastinator strives for excellence, and when they don't do the things they should be doing they tend to be particularly hard on themselves. They often blame their passivity on laziness or stubbornness rather than simply admitting that they're tired. What they really need to do is be more compassionate towards themselves.

If you're a Blue, your main challenge is this: taking a break. (I already know you're going to say that you don't have the time for that.)

Your solution: recharging. Try to take a walk, to give yourself the space you need to start replenishing your energy levels. Read a book. Rejuvenate yourself.

Making Your Unreliable Self More Reliable

Unfortunately, you can't rely on long-term rewards to motivate your present self. If you get yourself believing that you can somehow manage X situation through sheer discipline, you'll only be fooling yourself. Instead, you need to find ways to move future rewards and punishments into the present. You need to turn future consequences into present consequences.

This is exactly what happens in the moment when somebody manages to finally stop procrastinating and move to action.

Let's say you have a report to write. You've known it was coming up for weeks, but you've kept pushing the start back, day after day. You can feel that constant anxiety and concern whenever you think about that damned report, but the pain is still not sufficient to make you do anything about it. Then suddenly, one day before your deadline, you realize with horror that what had been a future consequence—your boss's outrage at your having dragged your feet too long—is transitioning into the present. Within twenty-four hours, your ruse will be up, and your promotion could be on the line. You realize that you have no choice; you work like a lunatic for nine hours straight and manage to compile that blasted report just hours before it's due. It even turns out pretty good.

The pain of postponing the work finally intensified, and you began to act. Well done! But just imagine the anxiety and wasted positive energy you went through before you got there.

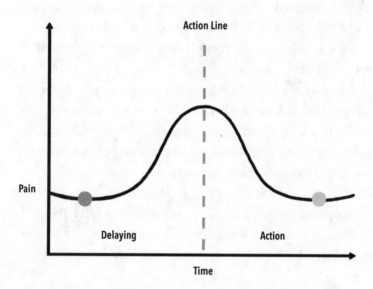

The model above was designed by James Clear, the author of the international bestseller *Atomic Habits*. He describes this mechanism incredibly well.

As soon as you act, the pain begins to recede. In fact, it's often more painful to be in the procrastination stage than it is to be in the work stage! The anxiety can feel like it's about to eat you whole. Point A in the diagram above is often more painful than point B. The anxiety you go through as a result of your sad attempts to postpone the inevitable tends to be worse than the effort and energy that go into performing the task itself. You know what you need to do; you just . . . don't do it.

If you want to stop procrastinating, you need to arrange things to make it as easy as possible for your present self to get started, and trust that your motivation and pace will pick up once you're actually doing the work.

If you can find a way to make the advantages of long-term choices more immediate, you'll have an easier time keeping yourself from procrastinating. One of the best ways to move future rewards into the present is a strategy called temptation bundling.

Temptation bundling is a concept that was developed by behavioral economist Katherine Milkman at the University of Pennsylvania. Put simply, this strategy hinges on combining a behavior that benefits you in the long term with a behavior that feels rewarding in the short term.

The basic idea is this: Only do something you *love* at the same time as you do something you want to *procrastinate*.

What follows are some common examples of temptation bundling. The principle is simple: Kill two birds with one stone.

- Only listen to audiobooks or podcasts that you enjoy when you're on your exercise bike.
- Only watch your favorite TV show while you iron or mend socks (is that still something people do?).
- Only visit your favorite restaurant when you're in the company of somebody you can talk shop with.
- Only go to the nail salon if you can work on work emails while you're there.

I know, the examples are a bit convoluted—but you'll just have to use your imagination.

There are plenty of ideas for making procrastination more uncomfortable as well. If, for example, you work out alone, it won't have much of an impact on your life if you skip a workout. Your health isn't going to crumble just because you missed one single training session. The price for postponing your training won't get to be enough for you to notice until you've missed weeks or even months of workouts at the gym. However, if you commit to working out with a friend at 7:00 a.m. every Monday, you'll immediately feel the cost of skipping a workout more acutely. If you have a good training buddy, they'll get annoyed with you for missing it. Missing a single training session will leave you looking like a fool. Besides actively helping each other, you can always get your friend back when they try to skip a session for some reason.

Another approach is to make a public pledge: If you break your pledge to go to the gym, or take your wife out to dinner, or help your twelve-year-old with their homework, or not to eat chips more than once a month, you'll commit to paying a certain amount of money to some charity organization you have a serious distrust of. Basically, negative consequences are attached to any failure to do the right thing.

Another way to stop procrastinating involves influencing your future actions in advance. You can regulate how much food you eat by buying smaller packages. It might mean you're paying more for the quantity you get, but at least you'll know you won't overeat. Remember that your unique goals have a huge impact on which activities are helpful and which ones are detrimental.

You can stop wasting valuable time by removing games and social media apps from your phone.

Similarly, you can prevent mindless channel surfing by hiding your television in a cabinet and only taking it out on certain days. You could even give your remote control to your grouchy neighbor and have him hide it from you. He'll almost certainly be happy to help.

You can ask to be added to the blacklist of casinos and online gambling websites to prevent future gambling excess.

You can build up a financial buffer by arranging for an automatic transfer of funds to your savings account.

These are all examples of planning that can help minimize the danger that you'll end up procrastinating.

Another good approach is to break tasks into smaller, more doable chunks. British author Anthony Trollope was legendary for being enormously productive. Any writer will no doubt have heard of him and his incredible writing speed. He published sixty-five books in all, along with a bunch of short stories and several plays.

How did he get all that done? Rather than count finished chapters or even whole books, he measured his progress in fifteen-minute intervals. He set a goal of writing 250 words in each fifteen-minute work session and spent three hours each day working under that regimen.

This approach provided him with the instant feedback of success every fifteen minutes—four times an hour!—while he was actually working towards the larger goal of writing a whole book. If his writing session ended in mid-sentence, he stopped right where he was and finished the sentence the next day.

In case you're a writer and you're reading this without feeling the slightest bit impressed: While he wrote all those books, Anthony Trollope also held down a fairly demanding full-time position for the Royal Mail in the UK. I've seen some of the novels he wrote, and they're huge books. He wrote sixty-five of them. No mean feat.

Small steps of progress along the way will help you maintain your pace in the long term, which will make you more likely to finish big projects. Good, right?

The quicker you can finish a productive task, the sooner you'll have established a pattern of productivity and efficiency.

Being unhappy with yourself is a waste of energy. So where does all this leave us? You'll be happy with your achievements, and being happy feeds you—yes, you know it—energy.

WASTING TIME IS WASTING ENERGY

Is there anything worse than finding yourself constantly short on time? It can be so stressful that it makes you sick just thinking of it.

We've all been there. So much to do, and so little time to do it. It's a draining equation. It robs you of your energy quite efficiently. Is there some way you could make better use of your time? As a matter of fact, there is. More than anything, this is a matter of how you relate to the very concept of time.

Would you like to know who your greatest enemy is in this battle for your time? Hold on, and I'll get you a mirror.

The most common excuse I hear from the people I meet is that they're definitely going to do all that important stuff—

when they can find the time. It's all going to happen soon. Down the road. When there's more time.

Willpower isn't enough—I discussed that earlier. Even if you're a pretty productive person, I'm sure you'd like to increase your productivity even more. The problem with all the time management systems is that they're all based on logical thinking. Prioritize this, delegate that.

I'm sure that's all very well. It's just that we're not logical and rational. We're emotional. If you've set aside a Tuesday evening at home to catch up on work, but your partner comes in for a quick chat, your whole system will go out the window. Because you're an emotional being, you'll invest your attention in your partner, rather than your work. I have nothing to say about your spending time with your family, except this obvious fact: The work won't be getting done.

The most common approaches to time management involve some variation on prioritizing. Ranking various tasks by how urgent and important they are. While there's essentially nothing wrong with prioritizing, there's an obvious flaw to this approach: It can't actually give you more time.

All it can really do is move the tasks in your to-do list around, so that what used to be number three becomes number nine. You're simply borrowing time from Peter to pay Paul. The problem here is that you actually end up wasting even more time by setting priorities. You still have just as much to do; you just have even less time to do it than before.

The right question to ask yourself to avoid this kind of high-level energy drainage is this:

What's the best thing I can do today to make things better tomorrow?

I'm going to give you a method now that *isn't* based on

RIGHT THINGS DONE RIGHT MATRIX

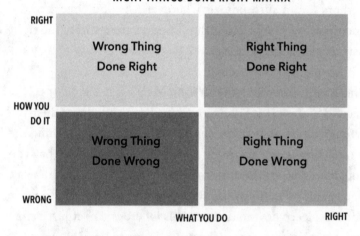

prioritizing things but rather on removing things from your to-do list that should never have been there in the first place. I've used this method myself with great success for more than two decades.

On the left side are the things you should never do. Ever. Note: You're taking them *off the list forever*. That's why I'm calling them the *wrong* things. If, for some inexplicable reason, you insist on doing the wrong things, you can, as you see, at least decide whether to do them the wrong way or the right way.

On the right side are the right things. These are the things you should be doing. You can do them either the right way or the wrong way. It's pretty simple, isn't it? There's no need for it to be any more complicated than this.

The Right Things in the Right Way

If you do the right things the right way, it will make you one of the top managers, assistant nurses, plumbers, influencers,

IT engineers, business owners, driving school instructors, authors, brain surgeons, or whatever it is you choose to do. You do exactly what you're supposed to, in precisely the right way. It works like a charm.

The Right Things in the Wrong Way

Second best is getting the right things done but doing them the wrong way. Why is this second best? Well, the right thing the wrong way is still the right *thing*. Since it's unlikely that you could become the world champion at everything right away, you might as well start doing X as often as possible, to make sure you learn how to do it. This is where you're at just before you enter the last stage—the right things in the right way.

The Wrong Things in the Wrong Way

Spending time on things that won't get you where you want to go and doing them poorly on top of that—no thank you! Setting yourself up for a load of work you don't know the first thing about and doing an awful job of it? There's no denying the countless millions of hours that end up in this box every year, all over the world. Your friend asks you to help her wallpaper her new apartment. You're happy to help, but you don't have the faintest idea what you're doing. Before you know it, you'll be covered in glue, with wallpaper plastered at all kinds of angles. You've never done any wallpapering before, after all. (The only good news is that she's unlikely to ask you again.)

The Wrong Things in the Right Way

This box is a dangerous trap. It might actually be the best way to waste time ever invented. Doing the wrong thing well. You might be thinking it's at least halfway right, which doesn't sound so bad? However, doing the wrong things the right way is the worst way to spend your time, due to the simple fact that it gives you the deceptive idea that things are going well. It's very easy to be tempted to do something that you feel you are good at.

But think about it. Getting good at something that won't actually help you? You work in an office, and you're an expert at fixing the printers when they get jammed. You've figured out how to get them up and running again. Could you possibly imagine any bigger waste of time and resources than becoming the department's auxiliary IT guy when you actually have a job of your own you should be doing? Getting really good at something unrelated to the task at hand is madness.

What you choose to do in your spare time is your business, of course. Then you're free to indulge in whatever you enjoy and don't need to consider whether it's getting you to where you need to go or not. However, if you've promised your partner you'll mow the lawn by the weekend and you start sorting screws in the garage instead of getting the lawn mower out, you're just wasting time.

What could be more inefficient than perfectly doing a job that didn't even need to be done in the first place?

This brings us to the actual point of this section. You want new, positive energy, right? You don't want to be spending your life doing things that drain you of the hard-won energy you actually have. This means you'll need to keep a lookout for time sinks.

Time Sinks

The two boxes on the left of the chart below are time sinks.

Sometimes there's simply no avoiding time sinks. If you

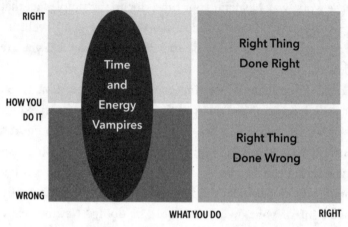

work in an office and the printer gets jammed when you need to use it, you'll have no choice but to start pulling the trays out and looking for that annoying stuck sheet of paper. But does this mean you should be spending your spare moments learning about printer technology? Hardly.

Wouldn't it be great if there was some way you could determine what the wrong things to do are . . . ahead of time? As it happens, there is.

How to Know What the Right Thing to Do Is

Essentially, the right things to do are the activities that bring you closer to your goal.

Here's an example from work: Your task is to increase the company's sales by X percent. You should be spending your time prospecting for new clients, making phone calls, and visiting clients to perform extensive needs analyses. Since your intention is also to do it the right way and actually bring in some business, you'll also spend a great deal of time writing up estimates and performing follow-up activities. You'll be constantly refining your sales techniques. That's how sales growth happens. Spending time on customer-processing activities without making any sales would be doing the right things the wrong way.

An example from a nonprofessional setting: You're building a patio for the house. You measure and plot it out, maybe making a sketch of your desired outcome. Since you've done this before, you know what you need: concrete plinths, gravel, joists, and so on. You calculate what materials you'll need and try to estimate how long it's all going to take. After this, you put your plan into action. You also spend some time on rather dull, yet essential, preparations by digging up the old lawn. If you have the right tools and the right materials, the whole operation will proceed smoothly.

However, if you get lots of decking lumber and screws but keep forgetting to pick things up at the hardware store and have to go back and forth five times, it's questionable whether this will ever be an efficient project. Doesn't everyone forget stuff? Of course, but driving around all day isn't a useful step in project "build a patio." If you do a sloppy job on the foundation, the patio will start sagging after a year or two. This would be doing the right thing the wrong way. It would also be a huge waste of time.

Now, you might be thinking that all this isn't such a huge deal. It's only a little patio project. And you're right; it's not necessarily a big deal. At least, assuming you're one of the lucky people who happen to have *too much* time on their hands, as opposed to *not enough*. If that's you, you've just been wasting time on the wrong thing—reading about how to save time is obviously wasteful if you find yourself having trouble filling your days.

I'm joking, of course.

The Missing Piece for Truly Maximizing Your Time

In order to make absolutely sure you know what the right thing is, we'll need to factor in the complex variable known as time. Let's say you need the patio finished this week. That will suddenly change your options significantly. You might have to consider outsourcing the whole job to a professional. That will get it done quicker, and usually better, too.

Therefore, the correct definition of the right thing to do is this: the thing that brings you closer to your goal *at the intended time*.

This means that the correct diagram should actually look like this:

The right thing at the right time depends on your goal. That amazing, exciting goal that there's no way you'll forget.

RIGHT THINGS DONE RIGHT MATRIX

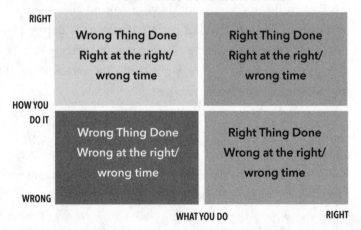

That determines what you should be doing on the days when you have a little time left over.

What's the right thing to do *right now*?

Something that's wrong in one moment might be right at another time. Something that's wrong for you might be right for somebody else. It's confusing, I know. That's precisely why timing is so important.

This isn't an exact science, either. You can do whatever you feel like at any given moment, too. You're under no obligation to do things the way I've suggested. However, if you want to get the things you've decided to do done *when* you decided to do them, it makes sense to ask yourself this:

What's *the right thing to do* right now?

Stick a yellow sticky note on your computer screen. On your bathroom mirror. On your kitchen fan. On your steering wheel. On the inside of your sunglasses.

Set an alarm on your smartphone, so it will go off once an hour during your work hours, to ask you, What's *the right thing to do* right now?

Stop wasting time as though it were an unlimited resource. You might say that life is long. And it is. However, it's also quite short. And I can't imagine how dreadful it would be to face the end of it thinking that *I used the only life I was given for the wrong things*.

It's time you took your time seriously.

Nothing is more valuable than the time you have. It's an asset you can never get more of, that can't be restored once it has gone by. You can't stockpile it, and you can't trade for or purchase more time.

Time is actually the single most important resource you

have. While you can feasibly get more of everything else, time is constant.

When you're young, it's easy to imagine that there's so much time that nothing you do really matters: *I'll just work twice as hard tomorrow instead!* But that's just self-deception. You could have done that anyway and had an even bigger edge on everybody else. The older you get, the more often the rather unpleasant thought that time is not unlimited will come over you.

Do you feel that you use your time for important things? Do you feel that you spend it on valuable activities? Are you doing something positive with the time you have? Does it energize you to be spending your waking hours on the things you're actually spending them on?

If your answer is yes, I can only congratulate you. If the answer is no . . . you need to rethink things.

Think again, and get it right. And stop wasting time and energy on the wrong things.

How to Follow the News Without Getting Depressed

There's no other way to put this: You shouldn't spend as much time on the news as you do. The reason is simple: Almost no news, in any media, is objective. However, if you don't follow the news at all, you'll end up being uninformed. There is an almost endless flow of news on offer, and it's a good idea to be selective.

The thing is, there aren't any truly objective people. Any individual you ever meet will be subjective or partial in some way. Human beings respond emotionally to basically everything we experience. It's simply a fact. When we do that, we *feel*, rather than *think*.

News is curated and reported on by human beings, and for this reason you shouldn't have absolute faith in anything you see or read. Just look at how a left-leaning newspaper describes something compared to how a right-leaning newspaper describes it. They'll report on the same story in two different ways. Some things will be omitted, others will be added, depending on who is writing each particular story. Who's right, and who's wrong? I don't know, and that's not even the point.

Besides, almost all news is negative, and you can't ignore the impact that will have on your energy levels as you head into important situations.

According to my own observations, up to 90 percent of all news stories in the media are negative. It can vary to some extent, but when I read a regular daily newspaper I always arrive at more or less the same result. The same goes for the news on television. A depressing majority of the things we watch have negative, or even catastrophic, implications.

The reason for this could very well have to do with evolution. Our ancestors' survival depended on their focusing on the negative events that unfolded around them. Whether it was a coming storm, an approaching predator, or some other threat, anything negative was potentially life ending.

Based on the fact that around 90 percent of our news feeds is negative content, we seem to still be prioritizing negative information in modern society. Most of it is absolutely beyond our control.

Sensationalism also happens to be a consistent element of all news reporting. It actually seems to be something most media require of their journalists. The media itself often actively exploits our innate bad news bias, a practice that might do more harm than good. However, in this information-dense age they need to exploit every possible angle to gain our attention.

Take plane crashes, for example. They always make the headlines, although car crashes seldom do. And still, far more people die in car crashes every year than in plane crashes. The reason for this bias in reporting is that a single plane crash kills more people than a single car crash. Plane crashes also make for more bombastic headlines, which will encourage more people to click the links to the article.

Many writers express great fears about the dangers of nuclear power. These dangers exist and mustn't be overlooked. However, nuclear power is the form of energy that has caused the fewest human deaths of all known energy sources. Apparently, this is a statistical fact. I had a hard time believing it, too.

We know that the conventional media (TV news and newspapers) are fighting hard to survive in the face of the threats posed to them by the Internet, which is becoming increasingly dominant in its role as the source of our information and news. I'm not here to argue whether this is a good thing or a bad thing; I'm just pointing out that it has certain consequences.

Many American journalists feel that the Nielsen ratings (a viewership measure used in the USA) are the single most important reason why news reporting is so often either sensationalistic or simply inaccurate. As the viewers aren't in a position to determine what's inaccurate or sensationalistic, their attention ends up being the determining factor in the ratings they give, and high ratings, in turn, increase the number of viewers, which, in turn again, attracts more advertising revenue and investment.

As a result of this, many media outlets prioritize emotionally impactful news reporting. Studies have even shown that headlines for bad news captures up to 30 percent more attention than headlines for good news. It's also been established that negative words tend to correlate with a higher frequency of clicks.

How does this work in your particular part of the world? Well, human reactions are universal, and we all function more or less the same way in this regard.

You would be unwise to dismiss the psychological impact that bad news can have. Many doctors even claim that constant news consumption can actually induce a state of physiological stress.

It's important to be able to keep two thoughts going at once here. We need to realize that individual journalists aren't really to blame for the way the system works. We can only speculate on how things ended up this way, but most journalists have no other choice. Their only option is to play the game like everyone else.

By the way, do you remember what I wrote in the beginning of this section? About how all human beings are subjective? Well, so am I. Therefore, it would probably make sense for you to take my words with a grain of salt, too. Like everyone else, I'm driven by my emotional reactions to things.

I wanted to try an experiment, to investigate whether all these reports were actually onto something. Can excessive news consumption negatively impact our well-being? Here's what I did: A few years ago, I took a break from the news. These days, I don't read anything from printed newspapers or popular newspaper websites and I don't watch any news on television. If I'm listening to the radio and the news comes on, I switch to another station. Or turn it off. Enjoy the silence. It's quite underappreciated, I feel.

I can tell you this: I've never felt better, or more focused, in my entire life. I'd like to suggest you try a thirty-day news detox. Afterwards, you'll be able to compare for yourself and see if you responded like I did or if negative news doesn't impact you.

I avoid a great deal of misdirected focus and anxiety by only consuming a minimum of news and instead diverting my attention to nonfiction books, new things I want to learn, and the pursuit of personal growth.

Whatever I'm doing, I find that for the last few years I have gained a new level of focus and dedication to the task at hand now that I'm not carrying around a vague sense that the world is about to end. It's also helped me come a lot closer to realizing my dreams.

This isn't about trying to deny that there is evil in the world. Rather, it's about not letting this fact consume you from the inside.

Try it for yourself. I think you'll discover that it will bring you an inner peace you might not have believed was possible.

Social Media

I feel I should begin this section with an admission: I, the author, use social media to stay updated about certain things, to inform people about the things I'm working on, and to spread knowledge to, and I hope entertain, my followers. I'm on LinkedIn, Facebook, and Instagram. I'm not in any way opposed to social media when it is used as a tool, but just like with good wine, I know how much of it I can handle and how much of it is too much for me.

Social media can obviously be lots of fun and highly energizing, but using it doesn't always end well. Gaining insight
into how social media actually works and the influence it has
on you is a good way to avoid unnecessary energy drainage.

Human beings are social creatures. We enjoy one another's
company, and being among people we like contributes significantly to our mental health and happiness. Participating in
social contexts can alleviate stress, improve self-esteem, and
prevent loneliness, and it probably does a whole load of other
good things, too. Basically, not feeling too isolated is good for us.

This might seem ironic, as the technology was invented
to bring people closer together, but spending too much time
on social media can actually make you feel lonelier and more
isolated.

When Just a Glass Is Plenty

Naturally, there are many positives involved, and it's worth
reminding ourselves of them. Social media helps us with the
following: communicating and staying updated with friends
and family all over the world; finding new friends; networking; communicating with strangers about important subjects;
finding outlets for our creativity; gaining inspiration; finding
entertainment; and, importantly, learning new things. About
anything at all.

So far, so good. However, you should beware of the rather
serious downside to being exposed to all this temptation.

When You've Had Too Much

Since this is, after all, fairly new technology, there's not an incredible wealth of research into the long-term consequences

of the possible overuse of social media. Studies have found a correlation between social media use and an increased risk of depression, anxiety, loneliness, and various self-harm practices.

Social media can amplify negative feelings about your appearance, your career, your friends and family, and even life in general. Even if you're very much aware that the pictures you see on Instagram present an embellished and inaccurate version of reality, it can still be difficult not to compare them to your own life.

You browse through somebody's neat, filter-processed pictures of their vacation on some tropical beach or read about somebody else's exciting new marketing position. You can literally feel yourself clouding over with envy: *Why am I stuck here, in this house?*

And although FOMO, or fear of missing out, has certainly been around longer than social media, platforms like Facebook and Instagram seem to strengthen this impression that everybody else is having more fun than you or leading better, more interesting lives than you. This will be particularly true if the people you've decided to follow happen to be dramatic or narcissistic individuals. Both of these types are experts when it comes to presenting themselves as successful on social media.

FOMO is the effect that causes you to keep picking up your phone to check for new updates or react to every notification. This behavior can occur even while you're driving, missing sleep at night, or having dinner with your family.

Strangely, it seems that spending a lot of time on Facebook, Snapchat, Instagram, and so on will actually strengthen rather than weaken your sense of loneliness. Cutting back on your social media use can make you feel less lonely and isolated and improve your general well-being.

Nothing will alleviate your stress and raise your mood more quickly and efficiently than face-to-face contact with somebody who cares about you. The more you prioritize your social media interactions over personal relationships, the more you will be at risk of developing (or aggravating existing cases of) mood disorders like anxiety and depression.

Again, this phenomenon is fairly new, so there's plenty we do not yet know about it. New studies are being published all the time, so who can predict what we will have learned a few decades from now?

How to Behave in the Virtual Universe

Social media also happens to be available every hour of the day and night, which gives it further opportunities to hijack your nervous system. Constant notifications and messages impact our concentration and focus, disrupt our sleep, and make us slaves to our phones, to some degree.

It takes up to twenty minutes to regain your focus if you're working on a complex task when an interruption occurs. That's why it's essential not to allow yourself to be distracted for no good reason.

Know this: Social media platforms are designed to capture your attention and retain it for as long as possible, just like newspapers are. And we have that cursed phone with us everywhere we go. We want to just take a quick look. Just a little peek, to see if something has happened.

Your expectation of getting a like, a share, or some positive reaction to a post will trigger a dopamine release in your brain. This is the same reward chemical that you get when you bite into a piece of chocolate or smoke a cigarette. It doesn't matter if what we're doing might be harmful in the long term; we still like the reward it will bring in the present.

If you spend more time on social media when you feel depressed, lonely, or bored, it might actually be a way for you to distract yourself from negative stress or simple boredom.

We're all different, and there's not a specific amount of time you can spend on social media that's somehow more or less healthy than any other amount. It's probably related to the effect it has on your mood and well-being. For one person, five hours might be beneficial, while five minutes might be all it takes to bring somebody else's mood to dangerously low levels.

My own sense is that if you're spending more time on social media than you spend with friends from the real world, this is a warning sign that you'd be wise to take seriously.

Social media use also seems to have become something of a substitute for regular social interactions. Even when you're out with friends, you'll still feel the urge to check social media all the time, and often your motivation will be a sense that others might be having more fun than you are.

You also know very well how it makes others feel when you spend your dinner browsing your Instagram feed for something more entertaining instead of talking to them.

It's r-u-d-e.

Silent Mode Might Be the Best Mode

Now calm down. There's no need to panic.

You don't need to massively cut down on your social media time. Personally, I think the important part is to pay attention to how you actually use social media when you use it.

There are apps that will track the amount of time you spend on certain social media platforms each day. Take note of how many hours you're actually spending there. Sit down, have a coffee, and get over your shock: It's likely more than you expected. Next, set a goal for how much you'd like to reduce that time.

Turn the phone off at certain times during the day. In many countries, laws have been passed against fiddling with your phone while you drive. But other good times include when you're in meetings, at the gym, having dinner, spending quality time with a friend, or playing with your kids. A (very) personal tip: *Don't* bring your phone into the bathroom. For two hundred thousand years, people were perfectly content to go there without one. Nobody ever bit the dust from a lack of social media while doing their business.

Don't bring your phone or tablet to bed. Leave it in another room overnight, to charge. (This is incredibly liberating—you have no idea!)

Turn off the notifications. It can be hard to resist all that beeping and buzzing. It's not your fault you respond to it; it was designed to *make* you respond. However, turning the notifications off can help you regain control of your focus. After all, it's not as though you don't have other things to do. Like work, for example.

Also: If you've developed the habit of checking your phone every few minutes, you should start weaning yourself off of that by limiting checks to one every fifteen minutes. Next, move on to thirty-minute intervals, and then hour-long ones. There are even some apps that can limit your access to your phone automatically.

Try removing social media apps from your phone so that

you can only check Facebook, Twitter, and so on from your tablet or computer. That will make it too complicated for you to abuse it.

Personally, I removed Twitter from my phone years ago, after realizing that I would miss everything each night because of how fast the conversations develop there. But goodness, I certainly got a lot more done at work when I stopped trying to keep up with all that.

If this sounds like too drastic a step to take, you can remove one app at a time and see how badly you end up missing each one. Who knows—perhaps you don't have a desperate need for cute pictures of kittens, after all?

What Are You Doing Here?

Many of us use social media purely out of habit or simply to kill moments of boredom. I do that, too, and it bothers me whenever I catch myself doing it.

If you use social media to find specific information, get in touch with a friend you haven't heard from in a long time, or post pictures of your kids, your experience will probably be quite different than if you open it up out of boredom, or to see how many likes your post got, or to see if you're missing out on something. Maybe you *are* missing out on something. And so what if you are? Most of the things that happen on those platforms are things you'll never need to know about, anyway.

The next time you open your favorite app, consider what you're really doing there.

If you're feeling lonely, ask a friend out for coffee instead. Or knock on your neighbor's door and ask if they need help with anything.

Are you feeling depressed? Take a walk, go to the gym, or do some gardening. Bored? Get a hobby. A good one.

Join a club or an association. Don't let social inhibition get in your way. There are proven techniques for overcoming insecurity.

If you feel like you have nobody to spend time with, try reaching out to some acquaintances. They might be just as uncomfortable about making new friends as you are—and if they are, you'll have something to talk about: how difficult it can be to find something to talk about. Invite a coworker over for lunch, or ask a neighbor or classmate to go out for a cup of coffee.

Compliment a total stranger on their smile. See what happens. Avoid doing it in a flirtatious way, though. I don't want to get you into trouble. Look up from your screen and try to connect with the people you cross paths with on the bus, in the coffee shop, or in the park. Make a joke. Just smiling or saying hello to somebody will make you feel better—and you never know where it might lead.

You can interpret that any way you like. But there's no need to participate in everything on social media if you feel that it's draining you of your energy. Remember that you always have a choice.

Good luck!

9

A Survey of the Four Colors

I f you're absolutely exhausted from reading about all the various energy vampires, this might be a good point to put the book away and take a break. Head out into the fresh air and try some of the ideas I've given you. However, I did promise you that I would introduce you to the four colors, since I've referred to them so many times in this book. Understanding the four colors is important because even fully normal behavior can be quite frustrating if you can't make sense of it. When you meet somebody who has a thing for details, but you've never really even understood what Excel was for, you're already headed for a loss of energy. If you prefer it when things are predictable, but have a friend who always stirs stuff up and acts on her impulses, you might feel your pizzazz escape when she walks into the room.

This will depend to some extent on who you are, and to some extent on how well you can adapt to different behavior patterns—without losing it completely, that is. I thought we should take a look at the four colors and see what potential energy vampirism they can cause.

To do so, we'll need to begin with a quick survey of the four personality colors. If you've read any of my other books, you'll be somewhat familiar with these ideas, but even if you feel like you know this stuff well, I'd like to encourage you to at least skim the next few pages. There's no harm in repetition, and there's material here that I've never mentioned before. Join me.

A SIMPLE WAY OF MAKING SENSE OF HUMAN BEHAVIOR

As I mentioned in the introduction to this book, this is a method in which human behavior is categorized according to four colors: Red for dominance, Yellow for influence, Green for stability, and Blue for compliance. These are the basics of the DISC assessment, which is used all over the world.

As you can see, each square encompasses two dimensions:

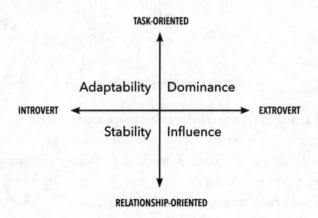

task orientation versus relationship orientation, and extroversion versus introversion. The colors are simply a helpful memory aid. It's easier to remember that a certain behavior profile is Red-Yellow, rather than calling it high D over I with low C.

Each color combines two dimensions, which means that a color covers two measures at once. It's simply a question of which axis you're on.

Task Orientation versus People or Relationship Orientation

This is the easy part to figure out. If you'll allow me to simplify things a little here, this axis can be connected to people's different interests or focal points. Some are more interested in things, while others are more interested in people.

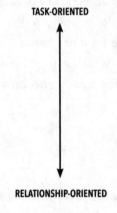

The effect of this is that a task-oriented individual will tend to enjoy working with objects, like tools, cars, or computers, while a relationship-oriented person is more likely to enjoy working in settings where they will interact with people, like health care, service roles, or sales.

There's no good or bad here. The situation you're in determines which orientation is advantageous. As usual, self-awareness is the most important thing.

Extroversion

There's a simple way to define the other axis, based on how extroverted or introverted individuals replenish their energy. Extroverts like being in the world, moving about, staying active, and getting up to stuff. They seldom have any challenges communicating with others, although extroversion shouldn't be conflated with being socially outgoing as such.

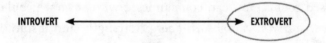

They often speak quickly, and the words just come to them. The floodgates open and practically anything could come out of their mouth. Many extroverts act spontaneously, and they may not always know what they're about to say. Thought and action—or speech—often occur concurrently. This can be both energizing and entertaining, and you can definitely say that extroverts gain energy from keeping busy and following their impulses.

They can be quite driven, and tend to express themselves somewhat dramatically. When an extrovert tells you about their travels, the story will be about either a visit to paradise or a journey through the shadow of death. They'll be unhappy from time to time, but it's not what they generally prefer. Average is pale and dull, and not something they would ever strive for.

Depending on where exactly they are on the extroversion scale and depending equally (at least) on where they are on the other axis, they might enjoy being in crowds. They have no qualms about being the center of attention. Closing an extrovert up in an office, shutting the door, and saying, *Good luck with the project, I'll see you next Easter!* would essentially be like slowly depriving them of oxygen. Although they need to focus and stop running around all the time in order to get the job done, this would still be a bad way of handling an extrovert.

No, they prefer open-plan offices. The more open the plan, the better.

Why is this? It's simple. It means they can be where the action is. The energy flows differently than it does in stuffy, closed rooms. You can communicate with several people at once, and you can absorb energy, strength, and inspiration from all directions at once.

Tear down all the walls! Let's all work together, like one big, happy family!

Of course, this is far from productive, but I'm not discussing productivity here. I'm talking about the kind of environment that appeals to extroverts.

Multitasking is a bad habit that's particularly typical of extroverts. I'm sure you've heard the expression *keeping all the plates spinning*. I'm prepared to wager a dollar that the person who came up with that expression was an extrovert. However, the problem will be obvious to anybody nearby: Lots of those plates get broken along the way. It's one thing to keep them spinning and another thing entirely to catch them and put them away in the right places. Quite often, some of those plates will shatter on the head of the extrovert's completely innocent coworker when the former is out on the town, experiencing the world.

Personally, I'd say I find extroverts quite easily distractible. The results end up however they end up.

One of the reasons why extroverts allow themselves to be distracted all the time is the fact that they're so partial to novelty and change. Extroverts gain energy from constantly trying out something new. Out with the old, in with the new. But what if there's nothing wrong with the old? What if it happens to work really well?

That's not going to convince them not to change things up all the same. What we're dealing with here is the kind of person who loves change and who actually feels drained when they have to maintain a routine and experience constant repetition. They want to try new ideas, and that's what they are going to do.

According to the DISC theory, Reds and Yellows belong in the extroverted area. Guess who they find the most draining?

That's right: introverts.

Introversion

While extroverts seek to replenish their energy from sources external to themselves, introverts find their energy sources within themselves. It's a common misconception that this somehow means that introverts don't like people or dislike social interaction. What it actually means is simply that interacting with others drains them of energy and thus they react very differently than extroverts.

Introverts can enjoy spending time with others, particularly people they know very well and would choose to spend time with—but they like being alone even better. They don't mind working in absolute silence in a closed room at all. In fact, they strongly prefer this over working in open-plan offices. The people you see working with headphones on in open office spaces are almost certainly introverts. The headphones aren't to tell everybody else to stay away; they're just a measure to maintain at least a degree of concentration in the chaos of the office.

An introverted individual will not be as easily distracted as an extrovert, but they still prefer to work in a more concentrated fashion, one thing at a time. They don't enjoy having people around them as much as extroverts do.

A few years ago, there was a study that came to the entertaining conclusion that, for introverts, working in open-plan offices was a little like spending the whole workday slightly intoxicated. Amusing as that may be, we should also accept that these kinds of environments cause them to lose some of their concentration.

Not every environment will suit every person. It's not surprising, really.

The same applies to multitasking. Introverts prefer to avoid it completely. This is mostly because they prefer to do one thing at a time, but it's also because they don't bore as easily as extroverts. Introverts don't mind working away in the same old way. Sometimes this can be an extreme strength, but sometimes it can cause problems.

Introverts, basically, are more controlled in their behavior than others. You can also tell it from the way they speak. They use fewer words and think for longer. As I mentioned, extroverts open their mouths and spew anything at all, but introverts prefer to wait to voice their opinions until they're done thinking. Or exploring their feelings. Generally speaking, they act with less spontaneity than extroverts do.

There's an interesting effect when introverts finally do open their mouths. They won't offer any direct statements or clear proclamations; rather, their speech will resemble a long, sometimes painful, circular train of thought.

If you ask an introverted project manager how their project is going, it can take some time to get an answer. However, when their response finally comes, it can sound something like this: *It's interesting you should ask! Considering the qualitative standards we're basing our work on—I mean the ones that were set during the last steering group meeting, which was actually interesting, considering the fact that there were only eleven out of twelve representatives present, which naturally has an effect on the legitimacy of the decision, since we did decide during the* previous *meeting that all representatives have to be present for the meeting to have the authority to make decisions like that—but on that basis, I feel that these KPIs are still something we ought to be able to manage in a satisfactory manner . . .*

Now, is this good or bad? I can't really say. I'm just explaining how these things work. The situation will always determine what makes the most sense in any given moment, so there's no clear-cut answer.

How would an extroverted project manager answer the same question? Let's try it out!

How's the project going?

To hell!

Who are the number one energy vampires for an introvert? You got it right again: extroverts. Introverts and extroverts are very different from each other, in many ways. Things can easily get very complicated between them unless they act with caution.

However, extroversion and introversion both exist on a continuum. It's uncommon for somebody to be at the extremes of this axis; most people are closer to the middle.

Being Somewhere in Between—Ambiversion

There are also people who are ambiverts, meaning that they display both introverted and extroverted tendencies. The direction an ambivert leans towards will also vary hugely depending on the situation they're in.

Being an ambivert also means having a certain advantage over those who are strictly introverted or extroverted. Since ambiverts have a personality that isn't too far in either direction, they actually have an easier time adapting to different situations. This also makes it easier for them to make connections—deeper ones at that—with larger numbers of people.

By gaining a better awareness of where you belong on the introversion/extroversion scale, you can develop a better sense of your own specific tendencies and apply your strengths more effectively.

If you think you might be an ambivert but can't tell for sure, you can take a look at the following statements. This isn't a precise tool; think of it as an aid for gaining deeper self-knowledge. If most of these statements apply to you, you're probably an ambivert.

1. I can work alone or in a group. I don't really mind either way.
2. Social settings don't exactly make me feel uncom-

fortable, but I do eventually grow tired when there are too many people around.

3. Being the center of attention can be a lot of fun, but I wouldn't want things to be like that all the time.

4. Some people think I'm a quiet type, but I think of myself as very sociable.

5. I don't need to be in motion all the time, but sitting still for too long gets boring.

6. I can lose myself in daydreams just as easily as I can lose myself in conversations with people.

7. Small talk doesn't make me uncomfortable, but eventually it gets boring.

8. Sometimes I trust people, but other times I don't. I don't really know why.

9. If I spend too much time alone, I get bored, but if I spend too much time around other people, I end up feeling drained.

10. I feel able to understand the details while I'm trying to progress through a process.

The challenge of being an ambivert is knowing when you should lean towards one end of the spectrum rather than the other. Ambiverts with poor self-awareness often struggle with this, and they can feel strangely torn, like the famous donkey that's exactly midway between two haystacks. For example, a self-aware ambivert visiting a networking event will lean towards the extroverted end of the scale, even after a long day when they have had enough of interacting with people. Failing to adapt to the situation can be frustrating, inefficient, and even demoralizing for an ambivert.

THE DISC THEORY: A STUDY IN ENERGY LOSS

What does all this actually have to do with energy vampires? Join me, and we'll find out. Based on all the things we've just been looking at, our interpretation of the DISC model becomes a lot clearer. Knowing what both those axes actually represent makes us able to see the different colors in the right light. It will also become clearer why members of one type will so regularly find themselves frustrated with members of another. We've all had experiences where we've met somebody who was perfectly normal but still found ourselves thinking that they were a complete pain to deal with. We can't always say exactly why this happens, but trying to figure it out and adapt to it can consume a great deal of energy. But these people are also a lot easier to deal with than dramatic individuals, for example. Or bullies, for that matter.

If you want a clear description of how the different colors relate to each other, there's a good diagram on page 19.

This is important for a number of reasons. One of these is that although a person may have a *behavioral profile* that's dominated by a single color, a number of interpretations must still be made. Another is that it can help address a common question: *Are there really only four kinds of people?*

The answer is very simple: of course not. As you can tell from the diagram I mentioned earlier, while a Red is always a Red, it can still mean different things. A person who is at the extreme of the top right corner is very Red—perhaps exclusively Red. That individual will behave a certain way. We'll understand what they mean almost immediately. But somebody who belongs in the extreme of the bottom left corner of the Red square will seem quite different in several ways. Where you fit in on *both axes* will have an impact on your *behavioral profile*. In other words, this model really only gives an outline of the different basic ingredients.

As you've probably noticed, I'm emphasizing the term "behavioral profile." This model isn't a personality test. It's a self-assessment tool that can be used to describe behavior—but that's all it is.

How much of human behavior can we really chart through psychological studies? There's no definitive answer to that question. Human beings aren't lab rats; they're highly complex creatures who are very difficult to describe.

I'm not trying to claim that the DISC theory offers the best method in existence; I'm focusing entirely on describing how the method works. When it's used correctly, I'm convinced that the model can be useful for understanding human behavior and thereby help people improve their self-awareness.

To save you having to flip back to the beginning of the book, I've included the list of traits that characterize the different colors again on the following page.

Looking at the various traits in the list will soon reveal that there is some overlap between some of the colors. Red and Yellow both include a lot more active characteristics, while Green and Blue include more passive ones. This doesn't mean that either is somehow better than the other—they're just different.

In the Red column, we can see a lot of attributes that might be problematic. The more of them you can tick, the more Red you have in your behavioral profile. The farther you go to the left in the Red box, the fewer Red properties will be found, and instead, a number of Blue properties will begin to appear *alongside* the Red ones that remain. If you go in the other

RED	YELLOW	GREEN	BLUE
Aggressive	Talkative	Patient	Conscientious
Ambitious	Enthusiastic	Relaxed	Systematic
Strong-willed	Persuasive	Self-controlled	Distant
Goal-oriented	Creative	Reliable	Correct
Pushing	Optimistic	Composed	Conventional
Problem-solver	Social	Loyal	Seems insecure
Pioneer	Spontaneous	Modest	Objective
Decisive	Expressive	Understanding	Structured
Innovator	Charming	Long-winded	Analytical
Impatient	Full of vitality	Stable	Perfectionist
Controlling	Self-centered	Prudent	Needs time
Convincing	Sensitive	Discreet	Reflecting
Performance-oriented	Adaptable	Supportive	Methodical
Powerful	Inspiring	Good listener	Seeks facts
Result-oriented	Needs attention	Helpful	Quality-oriented
Initiator	Encouraging	Producer	Scrutinizes
Speed	Communicative	Persistent	Follows rules
Timekeeper	Flexible	Reluctant	Logical
Intense	Open	Thoughtful	Questioning
Opinionated	Sociable	Conceals feelings	Meticulous
Straightforward	Imaginative	Considerate	Reflecting
Independent	Easygoing	Kind	Reserved

direction, i.e., down, towards the left end of the Green box, that makes you an introverted individual whose primary interest is relationships.

Statistically, only about 5 percent of the population would exhibit just one color after going through a DISC assessment. This is why relatively few individuals will identify as exclusively Yellow or exclusively Green.

This is how we have to approach the whole DISC theory—and, actually, every known theory that sets out to do the same thing—we need to understand more in order to apply the method appropriately.

The claim that people are too complicated to be defined by a sheet of paper is correct—but only correct to a certain degree. It's definitely the case that you can never understand any single individual 100 percent, but it's also true that we can document a great deal—and keep an open mind about the things we can't capture completely.

However, the more we understand about one another, the easier it will be for us to handle the people we perceive as energy vampires, who hinder our performance in everyday life. Let's look at the situations where it works the best and, naturally, the ones where it crashes and burns—which it definitely does from time to time.

Matching Colors

What you see below is a simple structure of energy vampirism. It relates to people who have different orientations along the task versus relationship axis. While this can no doubt be frustrating, it seldom causes any serious problems. Naturally, a Blue can find it frustrating that a Green doesn't exercise the same level of control over the minutiae. At the same time, a Green can get frustrated in the opposite direction, over the Blue's fixation with detail.

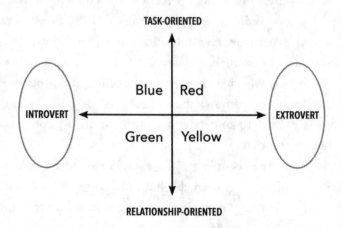

I'm not claiming that this mismatch is insignificant, but the situation is greatly improved by the fact that both of them are introverts. They recognize each other's energies, they see themselves reflected in each other, and they can tell that they are more alike than different. Combined with the fact that they're both fairly mild mannered, this will help them avoid any serious conflicts. Blue and Green is actually a pretty good match.

The picture on the other side is a similar one. People with the extroverted profiles, Reds and Yellows, recognize and vibe with each other's extroversion. They both like action, and they hate sitting still. They prefer immediate feedback and spontaneity.

Sure, the Reds will often decide that the Yellows are chatterboxes, and the Yellows might well find the Reds to be a bit too harsh and cold, but as I said, they both have the most important characteristic—extroversion—in common. This is actually the best match of all. It's better than Yellow-Yellow, and it's *much* better than Red-Red. You'd be alarmed to see what can happen if you crowd too many Reds together in the same room. It could register on the Richter scale.

However, what's the situation if we look for similar combinations along the other axis?

Working on Different Clocks

When we look at how task orientation and relationship orientation influence interactions, we'll discover an interesting situation. Having the same orientation here is nowhere near as useful for collaboration as it is along the other axis. When we remove the connection in terms of extroversion or introversion, problems can occur.

The most obvious example of this is the fact that Red and Blue might look like a pretty good match on paper. If we imagine them in a work setting, this makes sense: They both prefer to talk about work, anyway. Both of them focus on the tasks at hand, rather than getting into messy relationship issues. It ought to be smooth sailing, no? They're focused on the things, that's true.

But there's one rather significant detail that gets in the way here.

Their perspectives on time.

Reds, as we've seen, are always in a hurry. They hate waiting, and they prefer getting everything done yesterday. Quality is less important to them, as long as the result is passable. Whatever that means. How something gets done

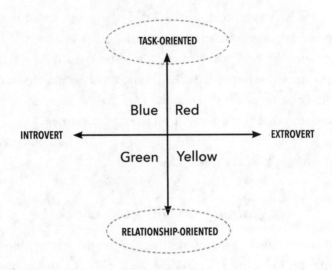

isn't their priority. What matters is making progress, of any kind. The goal is everything.

Blues, for their part, disregard the time factor entirely. To them, a deadline is simply a way to keep them from achieving the highest possible quality. In most cases, Blues will frustrate Reds endlessly. But they can work together, on some level, and that's because they're not relationship-oriented. There will be some friction, but it won't dominate their interactions completely.

Now, when Greens have to interact with Yellows, it's a whole different story. Both of them are relationship-oriented, and this will make them approach each other with greater caution. Yellows are brilliant speakers, who love the limelight, and Greens are brilliant listeners, who hate it. Yellows, of course, will stick their feet in their mouths repeatedly. When they do so, they'll rely on charm and general congeniality to smooth things over.

Greens, for their part, will seek to avoid conflict at all costs and be generally agreeable individuals. Many people find that Greens are incredibly nice to be around. There's really only one other color that has trouble with them, and we'll be looking into that in a moment.

However, all in all, while both these combinations have their challenges, they're in no way hopeless. As I've already mentioned, this is based on pure Red, pure Yellow, pure Green, and pure Blue. It's likely that most of them will be some distance from the extremes of each axis, and generally speaking, this means there's no real cause for concern. Any color can be an energy vampire, depending on whom they're interacting with in the moment.

However, although these interactions can cause some energy loss, there's a good deal of hope for most of them. They will have things in common, and with some self-awareness and a bit of goodwill from each side they should be able to interact nicely.

However, what happens when we pick opposite points across both axes?

Fight of the Century

Let's turn up the heat and match people across both axes— this will give us some real friction to look forward to. The following diagram explains everything you need to know.

When two people are at different sides of extroversion versus introversion *and* task versus people orientation, you might well end up with a major problem on your hands. We have two very simple mismatches here. The simplest kind of mismatch is when you match somebody who's strictly Green with an individual who exhibits only Red behavioral traits.

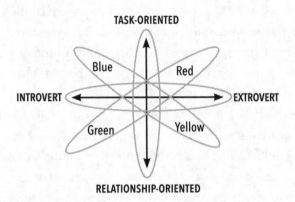

This is somewhat unfortunate, particularly for the friendly and conflict-averse Greens.

Remember the Green profile? Friendly, security-oriented, change-averse, calm, modest, cautious.

Their Red counterparts? Pushy, willful, innovative, impatient, intense, opinionated. The scene is set for the fight of the century. Or is it? And who is set to lose the most energy from this encounter?

WHAT COLOR IS YOUR ENERGY VAMPIRE?

Red Flags

Okay, let's begin with dominant Reds. These people are often challenging for everybody to deal with. In fact, even other Reds feel that they can be quite difficult, as they always seem to need to win and are never prepared to back down. Sometimes they argue just to argue, and they can be quite annoying to everybody around them. Reds always end up in conflicts of some kind, eventually. It's just in their nature. However, they aren't always

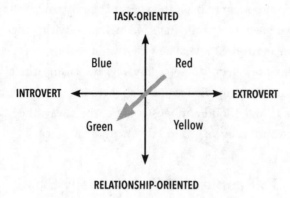

aware of this. An old boss of mine used to do exit interviews with people leaving the organization. He was often told that his employees had found it difficult to work with him because he had been angry so much of the time. He couldn't understand it—in his mind he hadn't been angry in a decade.

The unofficial motto of Reds is *fast and flawed,* and their unwillingness to address small things will often come back to bite them quite severely.

Who has the hardest time around Reds? By staying on the move and demanding the impossible, they can be incredibly difficult to deal with, particularly for Greens.

Greens want things to be calm, and safe, and—above all—predictable.

Reds are anything but that.

Reds have no real concept of stability or security. They want results, and they don't care how they get them. As long as they do. Preferably yesterday. Having to follow the rules makes them see red. They are notorious rule breakers, but they often have an explanation, or excuse, ready in case any problems arise after the fact.

They also seem to have an excess of energy, and if they lack self-awareness they will have no patience with others who need the occasional rest. They might not set out to cause conflict, but they keep doing it anyway, by raising their voices and demanding obedience at the slightest sign of resistance. If they have to get loud and messy to get their way, they'll keep doing it until they've ground down any resistance.

Do People Like This Actually Exist?

Let's say, for the sake of argument, that you're mostly a Green. How will you respond to the threat posed by a Red?

If you've never met a Red person before (this is entirely possible, as this is the least common color), your initial reaction will be shock (*What on earth is going on?*), your second reaction will be disbelief (*Do people like this actually exist?*), and your final reaction will be panic (*How do I get out of this?*).

THE RED ENERGY VAMPIRE (FOR THE GREEN)

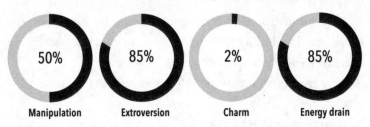

Manipulation	Extroversion	Charm	Energy drain
50%	85%	2%	85%

You'll risk suffering a kind of temporary thought paralysis. Since your natural instinct is to rely on your feelings, you'll be overwhelmed by the strongest emotion you're experiencing.

It's quite likely that it will be negative.

Frustration, unhappiness, worry, and even anxiety can occur.

I've met many groups that primarily consisted of Green individuals. (Green is the most common color in society.) When I've explained to them about Reds, the Greens sometimes looked at me like I'd lost my mind. On one occasion, they determined that their boss was a Red. They soon nicknamed him the Red Devil. No, this isn't a joke. They actually felt that Red behavior was genuinely diabolical.

I hardly need to point out that this can lead to huge energy loss.

How to Survive

As a Green, in order to cope with a Red whom you neither can nor want to remove from you, you need to manage your negative emotions. This is easier said than done, of course, but remind yourself that the Red doesn't necessarily have anything against you personally. They just have this slightly dominant, brash way about them.

Let's suppose it's a work relationship you're dealing with. You need to sit down and have a serious talk.

Telling them that you're hurt and need to discuss your feelings won't be a helpful way forward. No, that would just be an effective way of getting the Red to refuse to come to the meeting: *Mushy stuff. Yuck.*

What you need to do is try to understand how Reds think. They like to keep a quick pace, they prefer not to follow orders, and they don't think it matters whether people raise their voices or not.

Tell them that you want to talk about how you can get *better results* in *less time*.

That's all. After that, you're in.

Once you're both sitting down, you can hold the Red's attention by expressing, *in as few words as possible,* how you're not making the most of your work hours. Explain that the two of you should be able to work more efficiently together than you do.

Also—*this is vital*—you have a suggestion for a solution.

The following is important: Reds hate it when people whine. Complaining and expressing emotions is a sign of weakness to them, and they won't look kindly on it. However, if you offer a solution to the problem, you'll already have won half the battle. Remember, this is a highly impatient person. The conversation won't need to be much longer than seven minutes, perhaps even less than that.

You'll have to explain that you feel that your relationship is cold and unwelcoming. But you shouldn't use those words. Instead, tell them that the best way for them to reach you and help you deliver the best possible performance is to give you more time to adapt when things change and to ask you how you're doing on a personal level from time to time.

What you're trying to do is to point out a problem, while also offering them a quick and easy solution to it. Note: There's no point explaining that the Red's dominant manner stresses you out or causes you anxiety. How you feel will be of limited interest to the Red. But if you can point out how they aren't achieving what they want by behaving in a particular way, they'll suddenly have an incentive to think things over. If they can bring about better results or greater efficiency or achieve more of whatever they're looking for, they'll be prepared to listen.

Your solution is actually very simple.

Give me a heads-up when you come up with a new idea.

Don't demand an immediate response.

Put your hands in your pockets when you speak to me (so they can't gesture at you aggressively—nobody likes that!).

Ask me how I'm doing once a week. And listen to what I say. That's all.

When you've done this, you can wait and see if their new behavior actually manifests. If it does, the time might be right for you to take the next step and ask for other things. Repeat the same approach, but change the contents.

What you *must* bear in mind is that the Red won't hate you, attack you, or try to eat you alive. They just happen to be incredibly intense, and their personality is just very different from yours.

Okay?

If you can establish this kind of relationship instead, you'll rediscover a lot of the energy you might have thought was gone forever.

The Green Masses

Since a majority of people exhibit predominantly Green behavior (about 45 percent of all assessments end with the Green bar

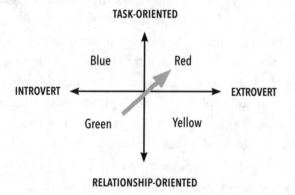

being the highest), it's less common for people to react strongly to Green behavior than to Red behavior. However, the people who do react to it will tend to react even more forcefully.

While Greens seek stability, they can often cause anxiety in some people. They avoid all kinds of confrontation, but by doing that, they'll also manage to spark conflict that can seem absolutely unresolvable.

They go to great lengths to never upset anybody, and they try to agree with everybody they meet on everything. As a result, nobody really knows where they stand on anything.

They seldom want to do anything, but they're unable to say no to things.

They are very good listeners, who truly hear what people have to say to them, but they tend to only remember the negative things.

They hate change, even when it's absolutely necessary. It's very rare for them to be able to truly explain why. They seldom offer any concrete arguments, but their general outlook is nonetheless that they don't want anything to change.

It's not uncommon for others to perceive them as a homogenous Green mass, because they're all so afraid to stand out. They turn noncommitment into an art form. They're basically the essential conformists.

Another big problem is that they're not always fully honest. This may seem strange in light of how they aim to please everybody, but Greens actually tend to both sugarcoat bad news and lie to people's faces about things. Since they don't say what they think, they can agree with the strangest of statements or make all kinds of promises they have no intention of keeping. All because they can't face the conflict that would arise if they told the truth.

People in a certain color profile feel incredibly drained by this inexplicable behavior. I'm talking about Reds.

Greens Make Reds Blow a Fuse

Just like I said before: The more Red there is in your profile, the greater the headache you'll suffer from Green behavior. However, being a predominantly Red individual, you'll be prone to suffering very strong irritation in response to basically anything.

What am I saying? *Irritation?* You'll be literally enraged at the Green partner/colleague/relative, on a daily basis. Since you're moodier than anybody else and since you're not afraid

THE GREEN ENERGY VAMPIRE (FOR THE RED)

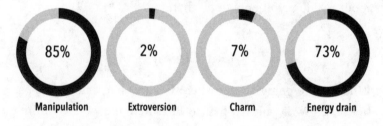

85%	2%	7%	73%
Manipulation	Extroversion	Charm	Energy drain

to show it, you'll end up at odds with this person constantly. This will wear on your focus, your energy, and your desire to have anything to do with them at all.

Reds only really have two modes: on and off.

Reds can work hard and go to extreme lengths, as long as they believe in what they're doing. If they lose faith, they just let go completely. When that happens, the chips fall as they may. They tough it out or run away.

A Red will yell at the Green. They'll raise all kinds of hell and make all kinds of threats, just to get their way. I know some Reds who explode completely just from having to confront somebody's evasive and defeated body language. It can happen without anybody even firing so much as a verbal shot.

The problem with these constant outbursts is that even if the Red is fairly immune to negative experiences, it still takes a toll on them. Also, getting angry with a Green coworker or daughter doesn't really achieve anything. It's like yelling at a pebble. The pebble might hear you, but it's still going to obey its nature and just remain stationary wherever you found it.

If you're a Red, your energy levels will rise, but it won't be in the way you want them to. What you want to do is release negative energy and replace it with positive energy. I'm about to show you how to do that.

Get Clever

What you're going to need here is a massive amount of patience. Now, if you happen to be a Red and you're finding yourself wishing you could call me and demand I give you the solution to this dilemma immediately, since it would save you half a minute of reading, and you're also feeling an uncontrollable urge to shout that you're *certainly* patient, I'd just like to set this straight, once and for all: No, you're not. You're not fooling anybody.

Take a few deep breaths, go back to your corner, and think it over.

You want something. What is it?

Maybe you want the Green to communicate with you. It could be your husband or wife. It just seems virtually impossible to get anything at all out of them. Your communication has broken down, and you know you've been a little too aggressive in your attempts to coax whatever it is out of them. You'll have to think things through.

What is it Greens seek more than anything? Predictability. Okay. That means, then, that wild surprises will be perceived as a negative. Actually, you shouldn't even trust your own estimation of what a dramatic surprise would be. Let's play it safe and assume *any* surprise is a negative. That's the baseline.

Instead, you should soften them up with a gradual approach, which allows them to get used to the idea first. Don't try to make them respond immediately just because you're too impatient to wait. Practice waiting.

Suppose you want to suggest a vacation destination and you genuinely want your wife to agree to it.

What do you do? Well, you obviously didn't get your hands on this book in time. You've already booked the trip, and you're leaving in ten days. It was supposed to be a fun surprise! But now, you've realized she might not feel like going along with it. So what do you do?

This is where you need to get clever. Rather than rushing up to her with the tickets and making her anxious, which will only end up annoying you again, you approach the whole thing differently.

The same evening, you tell her you've been feeling a bit run-down lately, what with how hectic work has been this quarter, and that you'd love to have a break.

That's all for now.

Let me be clear about this: You don't say anything else *that evening*.

I know. Your instincts are telling you that's not enough. However, rushing things along would be a big mistake.

The next evening, you ask your wife if she's also a little exhausted from work herself. She's been working hard, too, especially considering how much extra time you've been putting in at the office. Whatever her response is, *you stop there. Do NOT proceed.*

The evening after that, you come out and tell her that you'd really like to go on vacation with her. Get away somewhere, maybe get some sun? Imagine chilling on the beach with a drink and just relaxing. (You don't make any mention of wanting to spoil her and how you've already booked a spa session, a guided tour, and an exciting walk in the mountains.) That's all.

If she hasn't rejected the idea outright and called it ridiculous, you can show her some options the next day. If she seems open to taking a trip and you feel confident that she's being sincere, you can go on and suggest something. After this, you both sleep on it.

On day four, perhaps you'll suddenly discover a great deal on the trip you've already booked.

Now your trip will be good to go.

Now, hold on a minute, some of you might be thinking. *That's just manipulative!*

Well. I'd call it adapting your message or, possibly, selling it. Your intentions are good, after all. This is the way you can get a Green individual to agree to your plans. You shouldn't confront them with a fait accompli—that will only reveal your thoughtlessness. They would perceive it as an ambush.

Unfortunately, no systems are absolutely foolproof. This is

advice I've been giving to Red individuals for more than two decades, and although they often accept it in theory, plenty of them won't even make the effort to try it out. Why? Because it requires too much time and energy on their part. And, after all, this is a book about energy vampires.

That's one of the major challenges the DISC theory identifies: Red and Green. You can get them to complement each other, kind of like yin and yang. However, they sometimes end up like cats and dogs. But that's still some kind of energy, I guess.

Next, I'd like us to move on to the biggest challenge of all: Yellow versus Blue.

This is the combination that produces the most serious loss of energy.

Blue Chills

There's no way to sugarcoat this. A truly Blue individual will seem like a total robot to some people.

Sure, Blues are interested in facts, but sometimes they dig in way too deep. When everybody's long since left for home, they'll still be working on the last three-tenths of a percentile, striving for some kind of divine perfection, and then still end up vaguely unhappy with what the team achieved.

Yes, it's true that they're very rarely wrong when they actually do open their mouths to speak. Being motivated by quality and excellence and being incredibly perceptive, they can have a hard time keeping from pointing out everybody's flaws. People don't appreciate that at all. In fact, they hate it.

However, in other situations, Blues simply watch as people

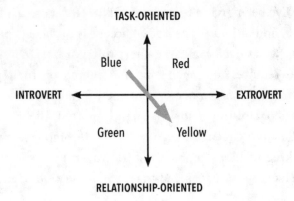

drive straight off the road. If they're asked why they didn't speak up about it, they'll explain that nobody asked. What dictates their chosen approach is probably their own interest.

While they do value quality, they have very low expectations of others. Their sense that process is more important than the goal causes them to disassemble every step into such tiny components that nobody else will be able to understand what they're really up to. No detail is too small to be viewed from every angle.

Their stone-faced demeanor can also induce a great deal of insecurity in others: *Why does he never smile?*

Well, maybe he's smiling on the inside, and maybe that will have to do. Maybe he's not smiling because he didn't catch the joke. Or maybe the joke wasn't funny, or didn't appeal to him because it was somehow inherently implausible. Whoever heard of a speaking giraffe, anyway?

Dry, dry, dry.

Some Blues are funny, of course. It's not as though they can't have a sense of humor. It's just that their jokes will operate on a frequency that ordinary people, generally speaking, can't even tune themselves to. When Blues make fun of themselves, they can be so clever about it that nobody else keeps up.

Blues don't always respond when spoken to. If you ask them a question, it'll help if it's both relevant and meaningful in terms of its content. Otherwise, the Blue might just stare you down: *You really ought to know this.* However, they won't actually say it. They'll just look at you, as though you were less evolved than they are. You didn't prepare; you didn't check the facts; you're just being sloppy with the important stuff. You fail to appreciate that the devil *is* in the details.

Blues refuse to deviate from the instructions in the manual, even when it's common knowledge that the manual is obsolete: *There must be a reason why that's what the book says.* It's like the old joke I heard when I was doing my military service: *If the map doesn't match the terrain, there must be something wrong with the terrain.*

Everybody but the Blues goes crazy when they do this. However, one color suffers great pain from this behavior, far more than any other, and this color is—you guessed it!—Yellow. For them, the loss of energy will be so severe that we had better take a good look at the dangers involved.

Blues Make Yellows Go Bananas

I won't be making the claim here that Blues are somehow wrong to act this way. This isn't a matter of right or wrong; it's a matter of reactions to behaviors contrary to your own. Yellows are everything Blues are not, and they don't have many of the properties Blues do have.

If you've recognized yourself in the descriptions I've given

THE BLUE ENERGY VAMPIRE (FOR THE YELLOW)

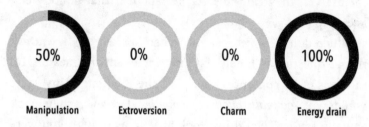

of Yellows so far, you'll know what I'm talking about. You feel energized by communication, positivity, open-mindedness, and free exchanges of crazy ideas. You have no need to plan every last step you take, and you prefer to have some leeway for improvisation.

When you encounter a Blue individual who constantly questions everything you say, and everything you *don't* say, for that matter, you may find yourself overcome by a kind of panic. I've heard Yellow individuals describe it as being slowly choked by a noose they can't even see.

Your ideas, your sudden inclinations, your way of thinking out loud, all of these are deconstructed and pulverized in a hailstorm of questions and scrutiny. You might start to feel like you're witnessing your own autopsy.

Yellows need space. They need opportunities to express themselves, be happy, have fun, and go a little crazy. Naturally, they realize that there's more to life than this and that you do also have to take some things seriously—they're not fools. However, getting in the car to take an unplanned drive to Germany and having your Blue travel partner tell you, *That's fine, in five hours and twelve minutes we'll arrive at a museum of the rhetoric of Adenauer in the old German Demo-*

cratic Republic, and I've always wanted to visit it, that's simply unacceptable.

A Blue can drain a Yellow's batteries so quickly that even Elon Musk couldn't figure out how to recharge them. It depletes them completely.

A genuine Blue and a top-scoring Yellow will have virtually nothing in common.

Yellows open their mouths without thinking first, while Blues think everything over carefully, even when they're just responding to a simple question.

Yellows hate details, because they focus on the big picture; Blues love diving into those same details, because it's the only logical approach to take.

That's right. Blues prefer logic and reason, even though they're not emotionally dead (they only seem that way sometimes), while Yellows are all about being guided by emotion. They wear their feelings on their sleeves, and they're unable to hide anything from anyone.

Yellows tend to live in the future and can see and even feel their visions vividly, while Blues approach life from a purely historical point of view. You can only analyze things that have already happened. The future doesn't even exist, so thinking about it is just a waste of time.

Yellows love to be around people, the more the better, while Blues prefer to work alone, in solitude.

Yellows see nothing but good and blue skies, while Blues tend to focus exclusively on errors and problems.

I could keep going, but let's move on instead and take a look at what we can do about this unfortunate and energy-draining combination.

Yellow Makes a Plan to Escape Death by Boredom

What you need here is a good plan.

Let's say you're a very Yellow person but have a Blue brother, whom you're very fond of. You're almost hilariously different, and nobody can really explain how you both ended up like this. However, you're firmly determined to get through to him and make him realize that his—as you see it—negative and critical attitude is suffocating you.

What you mustn't do is lunge into some sticky emotional outburst and give him a heavy dose of tears and wailing. His only response will be to stare at you as if you'd lost your mind. How you feel will simply not matter, because the truth, as he sees it, is beyond dispute.

Besides, he will be committed to maintaining his rational outlook, and this will mean you'll be transmitting on the wrong frequency. You might as well try to speak to a native Greenlander in Farsi.

Here's how you should go about it instead.

Plan a lunch, dinner, coffee—any situation where you can reasonably expect to have his full attention. You prepare a set of clear arguments and written notes. Why written? Because the written word is always more trustworthy than the spoken word. If you've brought notes, a Blue will think of you as more credible.

How you make your case will be absolutely decisive.

You'll give detailed explanations of how you experience your brother's constant nitpicking and sullen views of reality. Note: You explain your emotions, *but you do it in a rational way.*

What do I mean by that?

You explain that his critical views cause you stress, because, apparently, you secrete a lot of cortisol when he points out all the flaws of your new kitchen. But you *remain entirely calm* while telling him this.

You could say that you know he loves you, but that his way of A, B, and C—feel free to read out loud from your notes—can cause you to doubt this fact.

You also shouldn't hesitate to let him know that there is research that shows that the relationships of siblings can be very complicated in adulthood and that both parties need to work on them in order for the relationship to flourish. If you have a printed copy of that study available, it's a good idea to present it to your brother.

I think you get the point. You need to depart quite a lot from your genuine self in order to get a Blue to listen to you, but it can definitely be worth it.

But here comes the next step: Your brother will ask you for examples. Giving some vague response to the effect that it happens all the time or that he'll have to trust what you're saying will destroy the fragile trust you just gained.

You need to be well prepared and give him something like this:

When we redid the kitchen and spent lots of money and time on it, your first comment was that one of the cupboard doors was crooked.

When I told you about my plans for higher education, you immediately pointed out that I hadn't considered every university in existence.

When I told you about my long-planned trip to Austria, you started asking me about details that simply didn't matter to me, and in the end you made me cancel the whole trip out of sheer frustration.

He might well ask when exactly these things occurred. If he does, give him the most precise dates you can. Remember what the weather was like that day, and add that to the mix, too.

At this point, you'll be able to repeat—still in a very calm, sensible voice and still with as little emotive content as you can manage—that these examples, on each occasion, made you feel (a) drained, (b) stressed, and (c) miserable. But stay calm.

Now ask him for feedback on the case you just made.

If you did it all right, you're about to have a sensible, rational conversation about the finer subtleties of strong emotions.

Perhaps your energy levels will go back to normal. After all, you want to feel happy, energized, and positive, don't you?

Inside the Yellow Mind

Here we go.

I saved the best for last. We're about to move on to the ultimate in energy loss. Although a Yellow can certainly adapt to a Blue, the question of whether a Blue can do the same to a Yellow remains unanswered. Can a Blue actually adapt to the needs of a Yellow?

Let's take a closer look.

The example from the preceding pages is actually missing an important component. What's missing is the question of whether a Yellow can genuinely make their way all the way over to the Blue corner. My answer is that this is doomed to failure if the Blue doesn't feel like playing along. The distance from 100 percent Yellow to 100 percent Blue is simply too vast.

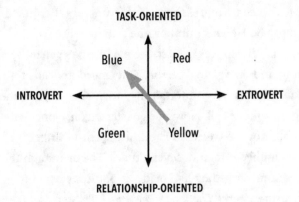

However, if the Blue is prepared to participate, there is some chance of success. Whether the Blue wants to take part in a conversation like this or not will depend on whether there's some problem he's interested in solving.

Just like any successful salesperson knows, it's very difficult to sell something that doesn't solve a problem. Regardless of what product or service you represent, if it doesn't solve a specific problem your target market actually experiences, there's simply no need for said product or service.

So what's the problem Blues have with Yellows?

I'm glad you asked.

A few years ago, my wife's phone rang and I happened to see who was calling. It was her friend Helen. I ran over to my wife with the phone, and she gave the screen a quick look before giving off a frustrated groan and asking me to answer it for her. I did as she asked.

Very soon, I understood her reluctance. My wife may not be Blue in the slightest (it's me who has a lot of those traits), but she is deep Red, and that makes her rather intolerant when it comes to digressions. Unfortunately, I think digressions must be Helen's number one talent in life.

As usual, Helen was in a terrific mood. She's generally a very inspiring and energizing person. One anecdote leads on to the next, and she's a very entertaining storyteller, as was the case during this phone call. Now, she got started on a long, entertaining account of the weekend she'd just spent with her husband, Hasse. I laughed out loud, several times. The main highlight was the restaurant visit they had made on Saturday evening.

The atmosphere! The food! The wine! The service! It was an absolute foodgasm!

Helen moved on to instructing me and my wife: *You have to go!*

Ah! A recommendation from somebody who actually had the goods! I felt very into the idea. Naturally, I told her we would try the restaurant. I mean, after that wonderful pitch, what choice did I have? It sounded incredible. So I asked the obvious question: *What's the name of the place?*

Helen's quite an interesting case of Yellow, since she's so unaware of her own behavior. Her contortions as she attempted to conceal the fact that she didn't know the name of the restaurant were actually quite funny. How on earth were my wife and I supposed to get to enjoy all these otherworldly delights if we didn't know the restaurant's name?

At one point, she called Hasse in to help, but he's also a Yellow, so what did he know?

I tried a new approach: *Do you know* where *the restaurant is?*

Her response: *Södermalm.*

In case you don't know Stockholm, perhaps I should point out that trendy Södermalm is a whole neighborhood that consists of virtually nothing but restaurants. Every last commercial premise seems to have been turned into a diner of some sort.

You know, Helen told me, still sounding as delighted as ever, *we went there by taxi—I was in the back, and Hasse was the one who spoke to the driver. I was on Instagram the whole time, too, so I actually have no idea.*

In any case, she added, *you have to go!*

I answered, dutifully, that we would go, of course. But my interest had waned a little at this point, I must admit. I had been looking forward to having the same experience that Helen and Hasse had, but things weren't looking too promising anymore.

Before I lost her attention completely, I tried lobbing a last question her way. I asked her, *What did you eat, then?*

It was curtains at that point. She started blabbering something about how Hasse had probably had the fish, but she had the meat. But that wasn't really the important part; it was the sauce—*THE SAUCE*—some kind of sherry-based thing, or perhaps it was a peated whiskey base. In any case, *you simply have to go*!

I couldn't call Hasse to ask him, either, because I wasn't convinced he'd actually been there that night. I gave up. In fact, the whole conversation left me frustrated. Helen inflated my expectations to heavenly heights and then punctured all my hopes with just two sentences.

What a disappointment!

I ended up not even mentioning it to my wife. I couldn't bear having to explain it all to her.

Do I need to point out the obvious here? Blue people have major issues with this kind of thing. Personally, I have a lot of Blue *and* Red, as well as *some* Yellow, in my profile, so I survived the encounter. However, a purely Yellow individual is a Blue's worst nightmare. The Yellow will open their mouth and spout off the most ridiculous things, all day long. None of it will seem to make any sense. When the Yellow speaks, they can sound energetic and inspiring, but their stories will be all over the place.

One moment they'll be discussing the current economy, and the next they'll be explaining what hipster coffee really is. Before you know it, they'll have moved on to the neighbor's problems with his daughter, only to somehow, miraculously, unexpectedly, return to the dawning recession, or bull market, or whatever it was.

All within four minutes.

How did that even happen?

You tell me.

Yellows don't reflect on these things; they simply express anything their brain comes up with, the very moment it occurs to them. Thinking and speaking are somehow one and the same to them. To the Yellow's own mind, they're just a freethinker, but others might get the idea that the Yellow's on some kind of drugs. As usual, this isn't a matter of right and wrong—there's a problem here.

Yellows hate details. They never open the manual. They simply tear the new machine out of the box and press the start button. They quite often break things the very first time they use them, because they can't be bothered to find out how anything works.

They lose things. They don't necessarily have poor memories, but they can certainly appear to. They misplace their brand-new, expensive smartphones whenever something else catches their attention. Their minds are like enormous mega-phones that are pointed the wrong way. Impressions just wash over them, and while their capacity to take in huge amounts of information and pick up on the big picture is impressive—this is an ability they share with Reds—it all ends up in the same tub. It's like emptying out everything you own in a single drawer. Everything is in there, but there's no system for sorting it all into some kind of meaningful context.

They're easily offended. But at the same time, they run their mouths so much, and with such poor control, that they often accidentally say really mean things about others. They rarely do this on purpose, and they don't hesitate to apologize to people they actually hurt. They're relationship-oriented, after all, and they're prepared to go quite far to stay on good terms with everyone, but they can't change their natures. It's going to happen again, and when it does they'll have to apologize, again. They do this with such deafening charm that their insulted friends will occasionally feel guilty for having been . . . insulted.

And so it goes.

What does this mean for the people around them? And what does it mean, specifically, for the Blues in their lives? How far should they let their energy reserves drop before they try to do something about it?

Ferrets on Speed

Well . . . A Blue will view a Yellow a little like a robot would view a ferret on speed. They watch them zip around like crazy, but they won't quite know what to make of it all.

If you're mostly Blue, you'll appreciate structure and or-der. You'll need clear processes and functional systems.

THE YELLOW ENERGY VAMPIRE (FOR THE BLUE)

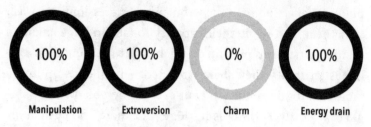

100%	100%	0%	100%
Manipulation	Extroversion	Charm	Energy drain

You'll crave time for reflection and trust your thoughts more than your feelings. Naturally, this doesn't imply that you don't have any emotions, but it does mean that you'll prefer to keep them under lock and key, especially in front of other people.

Letting one or more Yellows run amok around you can trigger some very serious stress reactions. All they do is talk, and they never get anything done. They're always making plans but never do anything about them. They talk about the future as though it were already here, and you have a very hard time understanding what exactly it is they want.

They laugh at everything you value.

Your need for details and data, for precision and exactness, will never be fulfilled, and your normal reaction will probably be to just withdraw from them completely.

You won't be able to keep up with all their unpredictable twists and turns, because your brain doesn't work like theirs does. Spur-of-the-moment decisions and sudden reactions are like a foreign language to you.

Every time you ask them for something specific, they give you an answer that doesn't seem to contain anything at all. Nothing solid, all fluff. Yellows are experts at blowing hot air at you, but what you need are facts.

Unless you've already decided everybody who has the slightest hint of Yellow in them is a fool, you'll probably end up in a state of hopelessness, perhaps even depression. Things look pretty bad.

How to Avoid Drowning in Nonsense

You find Yellows to be hopeless, but now you're sitting there, needing to get closer to one of them. Perhaps it's a business relationship; perhaps it's even your relationship with your boss.

Just like in the previous examples, it's all about approaching the person on their terms. It's absolutely pointless to go to the Yellow with an Excel sheet where you've scored your last nineteen conversations. What you need is, basically, to move towards the light. To head towards the Yellow.

We start with body language. Very few people can consciously control their body language. Deceiving somebody with fake body language takes both insight and training. However, everybody reads it. Whether consciously or subconsciously, they receive the signals. Yellows in particular. They don't always know *what* they're reacting to, just *that* they're reacting.

You're usually quite reserved. You often sit in your chair, with your back held straight, probably reclining slightly, with your hands in front of you on the table. One hand might be holding a sheet of paper with all your notes on it. Your security blanket. You sometimes sit still like this for a long time, too.

To a Yellow, this signals coolness and dismissiveness. It will make them hostile to you. They won't listen to your message. You won't reach each other.

What you need to do is practice some adjustments. For

instance, an active change of posture. Rather than leaning back all the time, you should sometimes lean forward, over the table. Sometimes you'll gesture with one hand; other times you'll do it with the other. When you speak to the other person, you point to them as follows:

You direct your whole hand towards them, with your fingers open and pointing forward. However, you turn your hand palm up. This signals positivity, friendliness, and support for the person you're addressing.

I see you. I hear you.

Your face.

I'm sure you smile and even laugh when somebody tells a good joke, but in an ordinary conversation you might not find too much to smile at.

Yellows smile all the time, though. Sometimes they even smile when they receive bad news. Don't worry about why—it's just how they work.

No, smiling on command or even trying to laugh when there's nothing really worth laughing at isn't easy. But if you want a Yellow's attention, you'll need to signal to them that you have a positive attitude. You'll simply have to practice your smiling in front of a mirror. Enlist the help of somebody you have complete trust in, and practice smiling without looking like you have a stomachache.

A big smile and a good laugh will release lots of positive endorphins, and they'll generally serve you well as icebreakers. They signal good intentions.

So make sure to smile.

Now that you're going to deliver your message, you have to do it without reading your notes verbatim. I'm fully aware that you've probably got everything you need to say written down.

However, you should practice the lines to the point where you don't need to refer to your notes. Make eye contact with the person you're speaking to, for at least five seconds straight. Look away, and then meet their gaze again. Keep doing that.

Don't tell them, *All you ever do is joke around, and I can't take you seriously at all*. This would constitute some very serious criticism of the Yellow in question, and it wouldn't be received well.

Don't tell them, *There's no way I can work in this place when the workflow is this haphazard and the processes are this subpar*. This, too, would be highly critical, and a very unfortunate start to a conversation. There's also this rather obvious point: The Yellow doesn't care about routines and processes anyway and will switch off immediately.

No, nothing that resembles actual criticism, however well deserved, will work.

What you do instead is inflate the Yellow's ego a little.

Tell them, *You know, you truly are an inspiration for many of the people here. It's impressive to see the way you share your vision with others*.

Note that this isn't lying. You haven't said that *you* are inspired by them, only that *others* are. Not everybody has the same difficulties you do with Yellows. You might add something about really wanting to know how they do it.

Next, you grit your teeth and listen to the Yellow's modest attempts at humility, which will really be all about reinforcing what you just said.

What you're trying to do, however, is explain what you need in order to succeed better at your work.

Say this: *I'd like to be a part of your vision, and I'd like to better develop my tasks in line with your inspiring plans. In order to succeed at that and achieve amazing results, I need some input, like X, Y, and Z.* (You know what you need, of course.)

The Yellow will agree to this and head into a long harangue of untested ideas and potential illusions.

When the silence returns, you repeat: *I'd like to be a part of your vision, and I'd like to better develop my tasks in line with your inspiring plans. In order to succeed at that and achieve amazing results, I need some input, like X, Y, and Z.*

You might very well get the same response as last time. If that happens, you simply repeat yourself until you're absolutely sure the Yellow has heard you. Remember that they're terrible listeners. And they think out loud.

Go for the solution. But for God's sake, keep listening.

Offer to take notes, and write down everything the two of you agree on. This is the only way to make any of it happen, because the moment you leave the room, the Yellow will already have forgotten half of what you said.

This is probably all you can do, and there are no guarantees that it will actually work.

Can this always be fixed? In my early years as a consultant, I would probably have insisted, *Yes, with some motivation and effort, it can be fixed.* These days, I'm not so sure.

Although a combination of knowledge and good intentions can take you a long way, there are some bridges that are very difficult to cross. Sometimes things end up getting better; sometimes they go very wrong. People sometimes part as enemies.

If you find yourself involved in something that reminds you of one or more of these four cases, I wish you the best of luck. The time and effort you invest could very well be rewarded, but you can't presume that the other party will view things the same way as you do.

You'll simply have to decide what it's worth to you. How much are you prepared to sacrifice to get where you want to go? You see, there will be a cost involved.

And remember this: We're all the jerk in somebody's story.

However, I can tell you that if you follow the advice I've given you here, methodically and with care, you'll at least only lose a minimum of energy in your interactions with the Yellows in your life. And you'll be feeding them more energy, so this really is a win-win approach.

General Intel on All of the Above

Here are some things I need to point out about the DISC theory:

- Not everything in a certain individual's behavior can be explained in terms of the DISC theory.
- There are other theories that explain human behavior.
- There are other pieces of the puzzle besides the "colors" that can be used to chart different behavioral patterns.
- The DISC theory is based on psychological studies, is used all over the world, and has been translated into fifty or so different languages.
- Around 80 percent of all people exhibit a combination of two colors that dominate their behavior. About 5 percent of people exhibit behavior that's

dominated by a single color. Others are dominated by three colors.

- The most common varieties are fully Green behavior and Green combined with another color, which is the most common of all. The most unusual is fully Red behavior, or Red combined with another color.
- There may be gender-determined differences.

There will always be exceptions to everything I have given examples of in this book. People are complicated—Red individuals can be humble, too, and Yellows can cultivate the ability to listen attentively to others. There are Green individuals who deal with conflict head-on, because they've learned to, and many Blues who actually know when it's time to stop verifying that the documentation is actually accurate.

I wanted to show you the challenges the different colors face because things occasionally sour between us, even when there are no real problems and nobody has actually behaved badly. We are who we are, and it's as simple as that.

Things can go wrong even when people behave fully decently to each other, and this can leave everybody involved drained.

However, as you've seen, it doesn't always have to be that way.

With a bit of imagination, a generous helping of self-knowledge, and a dose of willingness to take responsibility for the situation before it gets out of control, you can bring about something that seems like a miracle. I've seen it happen countless times. Somebody decides that they've had enough. They decide to take action.

Will *you* be that person? Will *you* step forward, speak out, and state loud and clear:

This isn't working, but I want to be part of the solution! Who's with me?

I think you will be. And when you do those things, you'll see the smiles appear on everybody else's faces. You'll see their hope return. You'll notice their nods of agreement. They want to deal with these energy vampires, too.

Yes, we're with you.

That'll be quite something.

In Closing

Whatever you set out to do, it'll work out better if you're full of positive energy. The people around you are probably the ones who are best positioned to quickly recharge your batteries—or drain them, for that matter.

When I wrote my first book, *Surrounded by Idiots,* my original idea was to shine a light on a phenomenon that drains us all of energy: seeking to understand those who can't be understood. We respond differently to the same situations, after all, and certain kinds of individuals simply cause us difficulties. They become energy vampires without even knowing it.

These were the people I decided to call idiots, albeit in a tongue-in-cheek way. Those people. Naturally, there were some who felt that my choice of title for that book was unfortunate. They reacted poorly to the wording and didn't get the joke, I suppose. The first emails from readers complaining about the title actually worried me, in all honesty. For a little while, they became my own energy vampires. However, these days, I just smile at it all. After the book spent a few years on the best-seller lists, a handful of angry critics stirred up a storm in the media, accusing both myself and my book of being idiotic. Look at that, more energy vampires! I soon learned to smile at that, too.

It also struck me that the same situation can result in very different reactions, depending on how you look at them. Some of us might gain energy from a certain event, while the very same event drains others completely dry. This is very interesting, and the real subject of the book *Surrounded by Idiots* was actually energy vampires.

This book is best seen as a further development of that idea. I've tried to take a more comprehensive approach to the different kinds of people who surround us, while also illuminating some phenomena that you might react more or less positively to. You see, I firmly believe that we are often our own worst energy vampires. I hope that I have awakened your curiosity enough to make you explore what this looks like in your own specific case.

When it comes to the energy vampires in your life, there are always choices available to you. You could choose to keel over in the face of their assaults on your mind or you could choose to do something about them. Sometimes you simply have to clear the bad air in order to let the new, fresh air in.

The world is definitely a complicated place, and it would be naive to think that you'll never face any problems of some kind.

I also feel that it's become more common for small problems to be left alone to grow into big ones. Perhaps this attitude is a First World problem; I won't deny that this can be the case. You forgot the charger for your phone? Disaster looms! Throwing a fit when the bus shows up two minutes late might seem reasonable when you're short on time, but in many parts of the world people are grateful when the bus shows up at all.

Sometimes I might accidentally glance at the headlines of some gossip rag that's trying to steal my attention with exaggerated doom and gloom. It's not a great way to start the day when you want to feel optimistic.

I might waste hours and hours doing the wrong things, which ends up causing me a great deal of stress four hours later. This is a genuinely awful way to be managing my time, which drains me completely and leaves me grouchy later that evening, when I'd rather be spending time with my wife than sitting at my desk.

And, of course, it could be caused by somebody whose behavior runs counter to everything I believe in. Whether it happens to be a domineering bully or a passive-aggressive work avoider, it will impact me either way. Why don't they get it?

One thing that really helps in situations like these is taking a look in the mirror: *Why am I reacting this way? Is there something inside me that's causing this, or am I actually dealing with an energy vampire?*

If I see a useful way to adjust my perception of what's going on, I try to do that. Sometimes the problem is actually my own attitude. This morning, for example, I had a three-hour drive ahead of me. I wanted to spend this time listening to an interesting lecture on neuroscience, but for some reason the car system refused to pair with my phone. I couldn't listen to the lecture, and so I spent ten minutes swearing over that, instead. Could I have acted differently? Certainly.

But in order to do that, I would need presence of mind.

When I run into somebody who does nothing but spout hot air in my face, it drains me completely. Although I am trained to deal with this, I'm just as likely to lose my patience as anybody else. When this happens, I need to remind myself that my tongue is occasionally too sharp for my own good. There's no need for me to be making enemies.

This also requires me to be *there*, in the moment, in the purely mental sense.

I need to take a few deep breaths and give myself a reminder:

I can't change anybody else. But I can change myself.

In my own close circle of loved ones, there is some extremely Red behavior, some passive aggression, some victimhood, some distinctly narcissistic tendencies, and something else that I can't quite pin down (heh, I bet that got your attention!).

When I end up in a situation where these behaviors are triggered, I try to remind myself who I am dealing with. Also, I make sure that I'm not expecting anything other than the usual outcomes. Then, of course, I adapt accordingly. Sometimes I stick a smile on my face; sometimes I raise my shields and do my best not to take offense. Then I simply do the very best I can.

If I can't evade the narcissist, I solve the problem by simply agreeing to everything they say. I don't say or do anything that I know from experience is likely to trigger a conflict. Even though I'm not at all afraid of conflict, it would be a pointless interaction that wouldn't lead to anything useful. Except, that is, for energy loss on my part.

When I need to handle somebody with the martyr mindset, whose attitude to life I have long since learned is never going to change, I "umm" and "aah" and nod, but I don't offer them any agreement. I don't contradict them, either, but I don't encourage them to tell me any more stories about the injustices of the world.

On the occasions when I run into a person who has displayed a strong passive-aggressive tendency, I do the exact same things that I have advised you to do: I'm clear about my expectations, I don't comment on annoyed faces, and I sprinkle in praise whenever possible. If I can, I also try to do favors for the person in question. You never know when you might need a favor returned.

However, and this is the most important thing: I don't expect anything but their usual behavior from them. I can't change any of them, but I can take responsibility for how I handle them, and for my own reactions.

Your Expectations Determine Your Everyday Experiences

I'm the first to agree that you should set proper, ambitious goals for most of the things you do. I'm one of those people who won't give up easily, assuming I know what I'm going after. Without fail, I will do anything (okay, almost anything) in my power to get to where I want to be. I daresay that the things I have achieved so far have been mostly due to my dedication. Of course, plenty of people have helped me along the way. I have a couple of old friends who cheer me along and support me and who genuinely want the best for me.

My wife, Christina, however, is my most important energy source. She's the reason why I spend evenings, nights, and many weekends working at my desk rather than relaxing in the garden. Or in bed. When I work, I have a hard time sleeping. So, naturally, I've enjoyed help and support, and that's not even including all the people who were involved in creating the book itself. They are too many to mention here, but I owe them all my gratitude. Since my wife is the extremely Red person in my life, I can also rely on her to let me know whenever I start slipping up.

However, I am responsible for keeping myself moving in the right direction. It's my job.

Getting up early and sitting down at the desk, or taking an early flight somewhere. Spending some evenings with my computer on my lap. Having long, involved conversations with my loved ones to resolve problems and challenges I can't afford to ignore. The list of things a person who wants to achieve something has to contend with can be a very long one.

That's enough boasting for now. I promise, I am working towards a point here.

You see, things weren't always like this for me. In my case, it took twenty years of professional life to realize that not everybody I met was trustworthy or reliable. That I had to rely more on myself than I do on others. In hindsight, it really seems bizarrely naive.

Some people I've spoken to have suggested that being naive is a good thing, a sign of innocence. Something beautiful that should be encouraged. However, I disagree completely. I rather think that being naive is just being gullible.

I've long since lost count of the times I ended up in trouble when I was younger, and the only explanation for some of the things that happened to me is that I was terribly naive. At times, I have had a childish, or even foolish, faith in my own ability. Sometimes I've been bad at estimating the time required for something and imagined that there was enough when there wasn't. Repeatedly, I have taken the things some people said to me as truths, without having any idea if they were just leading me on or not.

No, after you reach a certain age, being naive just won't do. Naivety is too costly for adults.

When you set your goals and define your visions, it's a good idea not to be too naive. Big ambitions are necessary, but believing that everything is going to be smooth sailing is actually just naive. What I'm saying here isn't that your goals must always be realistic—I actually think that would only limit you in the end.

However, you do need to realize and accept that the world will place a bunch of obstacles in your path and that your job is to get past these obstacles and keep moving towards the life you dream of.

A bully gets in your way. You start getting sloppy about managing your time. A colleague talks constantly during all your meetings, and your team never makes any progress. Someone in your family stubbornly refuses to talk about important stuff. Your social media use grows excessive, and you end up having trouble sleeping at night. Your partner takes the credit for all the things you do around the house.

There are plenty of things that can hinder you on your path towards your new, I hope bold goals. A single obstacle from the ones I mentioned earlier might not slow you down too much. But when the energy vampires are lining up outside your door, you really need to do something about it. You have to draw the line somewhere and set clear boundaries for what you're prepared to put up with. You're going to need every drop of energy you have.

The trick is to address each situation separately, take a look at the corresponding chapter in this book—and then start acting. One step at a time. Even a small step in the right direction is better than no step at all.

Accept that some things will take time to fix. That's how the world works.

You need to be in tune with your own expectations. They will impact how you experience the things that happen around you.

Buying lunch at McDonald's means you'll be feeding yourself a mass-produced burger that looks like somebody just sat on it, along with some mealy fries. Strangely enough, this won't be a disappointment to you as long as you weren't expecting anything else.

However, if you were to go to a real restaurant and order their recommended burger of the day, which costs four times as much as the McDonald's burger, and the food you received looked just like it does at McDonald's, you'd be very upset. You were expecting an experience, after all. Same burger, different expectations.

When you set your goals, you should think big. Think even bigger. Really *dream*. I want to encourage you to do that.

However, you need to accept that the road to your goal will lead past countless challenges. *Don't* be naive.

Naivety will make you give up after just a setback or two: *What? Is dealing with energy vampires this much work? In that case, I won't bother.*

No, no. Be a realist when it comes to your journey towards your goal. For example, accept that some people won't be on your side.

Let's suppose you've unwittingly involved yourself with a narcissist. This person isn't going to be happy if you're suddenly getting lots of attention from everybody else. It might make them feel less special. And so they will try to knock you down a peg or two. When you realize this, you will feel disappointed, disillusioned, and probably sad. It's not a nice feeling, but as you've seen, there are ways of handling a person like that.

Some will claim to be supportive of all your efforts but secretly hope that you're going to fail.

This doesn't necessarily make them evil. It could just be that they compare themselves to you and that your success makes them feel like failures. Perhaps they're simply struggling with self-esteem issues. They'd feel better about themselves if you crashed in a ditch and stayed there awhile.

Accept that most of the people you took to be your friends aren't going to be cheering for you with all their hearts.

Everyone who achieves success notices an interesting phenomenon: *Once I found success, my circle shrank significantly.*

I've gone through the exact same thing when I reached some of my major goals. Is it a shame? Yep.

Don't be naive. Accept that this is how the world works. But don't get the idea that it's your job to change it.

Some people really are only in your way. Like the long list of energy vampires I've described to you in this book. These people will try to hinder your progress in all kinds of ways; some will try to manipulate you; others will just try to frustrate you until you want to give up. They're really out there, and it would be naive to believe that you, however good-natured, gifted, and deserving you might be, are somehow blessed and won't have to confront them.

That would be very, very naive.

What Use Was All This to Me during Those Difficult Years at the Bank?

As you may recall, I started this book with a story about my time as a newly hatched bank employee, somewhere in Sweden. This was a time in my life that was plagued with a slew of troubles, but it was also a time when—as I have since realized—I was surrounded by several energy vampires.

Looking back at those specific years, I realize that there was a passive-aggressive individual who worked closely with me (we called her the coaster—she didn't appreciate that!). She was the one who was bitten by the ladybug and needed two weeks of sick leave to recuperate. Her behavior had me grinding my teeth on a regular basis. Witnessing her antics triggered some kind of quiet rage in me.

What I ought to have done was make sure somebody—our branch manager, I guess—was documenting all the things she wasn't getting done and blocking her escape routes. If I had done that, even the union might have agreed that there was a problem with her performance.

I was also impacted by the behavior of a hopelessly dramatic individual (we called him the Bermuda Triangle, because anything you gave him would disappear without a trace) who would try to grab attention whenever the opportunity presented itself. Whenever he saw a celebrity enter the bank branch, he seemed to lose his mind. It could take half a day for him to calm down, but by then the damage would already be done. He would have stirred up so much chaos that hardly anybody managed to get anything done that day.

In his case, I should have played along more. I shouldn't have argued with him in front of the other members of the staff. I'm sure he thought I was the energy vampire, as I kept trying to get him to stop talking about himself and stop wearing those shirts with the neon polka-dot print . . .

At the same office, we also had a person who displayed narcissistic traits (we didn't have a nickname for her—she mostly filled us with a vague sense of dread). She spent more time conspiring and trying to get people fired than she did on actual work. Her position, for some unclear reason, was apparently secure, although she was the most recently hired member of the staff. I suspect—but this is pure speculation—that this may have been because she was in a relationship with the branch manager. He always behaved like an absolute fool around her, and he let her get away with anything she liked.

I don't know what I should have done about her. I was never really on her radar, but if I had been, I should have tried to get off it as soon as I realized what was going on.

That's quite a lot for a single workplace, really. And of course, it's not as though they were all absolutely hopeless all the time. The tendencies were there, though.

It's quite easy to romanticize your own history and convince yourself it wasn't so bad. However, the truth is, I didn't enjoy those years at all. It made me perform way below my potential, which still pains me, despite the fact that I've lived half a lifetime since then.

I wish that somebody would have taken the time to sit me

down and explain some things about some of my colleagues. They could have told me that some of those people were genuine energy vampires and given me some tips on how to deal with them.

That would have helped a lot. I would have been able to avoid some pretty hopeless situations, and I would have found the courage to confront some of them.

None of this happened, but the time I spent there is still a big source of inspiration for me as I seek to communicate my experiences to others. You see, my hope for you is that you'll be able to avoid as many of these problems as possible.

This book is my gift to you. Okay, not in the sense that you got it for free, but I've invested an incredible amount of time and effort into it and I sincerely hope it will help you move towards your goals.

If it does, please get in touch and let me know! You can reach me at thomas.erikson@surroundedbyidiots.com.

Some Final Advice from the Author

I learned this from a colleague in the business: Take a blank sheet of paper. Draw a line down the middle of the sheet. On the left side, write down the names of all the awful people you have to deal with in your everyday life, whose impact on you seems negative in some way, shape, or form.

On the right side, write down the names of all the people you appreciate for being good to you and who help make your life worth living. The energy providers. The people who support you and make you feel good. These are the people who tend to go unthanked when you're busy being frustrated about the ones on the left side of the sheet.

When you meet one of the people from the left side, expect them to be difficult. Toss your naivety aside. Listen to them when they get started on whatever it is they do that bothers you. That subject they just can't keep from going on about. Those comments they just can't keep to themselves. Those rude behaviors they seem to enjoy so much.

Now look at the list on the right side. The one with all the good names on it. Remind yourself to give these people a call a little more often. Why not schedule a coffee with them, so you can tell them how much you appreciate them for being there for you?

Because if there's anything we tend to miss, this is it: showing our gratitude and joy for having those good people in our lives. We miss it because we're too busy dealing with the people we don't enjoy as much.

Don't fall into this trap. Life is too short for you to fail to spend time on the good people. The energy providers.

Take care, my friend.

Thomas Erikson
Svartå, October 2021–August 2022

References

Burchard, Brendon. *How NOT to Set Goals (Why S.M.A.R.T. Goals Are Lame)*. Accessed October 20, 2021. https://www.youtube.com /watch?v=54aFTZ9POw4.

Clear, James. "Procrastination: A Scientific Guide on How to Stop Procastinating." Accessed October 29, 2021. https://jamesclear.com /procrastination.

Doran, George T. "There's a S.M.A.R.T. Way to Write Management's Goals and Objectives." *Management Review* 70, no. 11 (1981): 35–36.

Eurich, Tasha. *Insight: The Power of Self-Awareness to Succeed in an Increasingly Delusional World*. New York: Crown, 2017.

Index

Blue people (DISC theory)
(*continued*)
  narcissists and, 192
  perfectionists and, 41, 44, 46–47
  procrastination by, 249–50
  Red people and, 291–93, *292*
  task-oriented, 105–6
  Yellow people and, 305, *306, 308*,
    309, *313*, 317–19, *318*
body language, 123, 129, 157, 176,
  302, 319–21
  drama queens and, 83–84, 90
boredom, 93, 179, 285, 310–12
bosses/leadership, 4, 6, 12, 50–51,
  250, 294–95, 319
  bullies and, 108–9, 111–17
boundaries, 176–78, 332–33
brain, 34, 245–46
bullies, 52–53, 91–92, *92*, 103–4,
  172, 332
  communication with, 109–10,
    112–15
  Ferrari/Toyota metaphor, 96–98
  Kenny example, 99–102
  narcissists compared to, 93,
    184–85, 187
  psychopathy of, 93–98, 102, 106–7
  in workplaces, 98–103, 108–17
Burchard, Brendon, 232–36

cancel culture, 183
change, 19, 137, 300, 329
chaos, 32, 36, 38, 103
charm, *24, 120, 296, 301, 308, 318*
  of bullies, *92*, 93–95
  of drama queens, *59*, 62, 84–90
  of narcissists, *180*, 194
childhood, 134, 162–63

choice/s, 56, 96–97, 153, 165, 238,
  245–46, 252, 327
Clear, James, 251
comfort zones, 75, 169–74
communication, 36, 151–52, 222–23,
  223, 224–25, 227, 269, 279–80
  with bullies, 109–10, 112–15
  drama queens and, 60, 69–72,
    74–76, 85–86, 89–90
  with know-it-alls, 216–18
  with narcissists, 185–86, 194–200
  passive-aggressive, 118, 129–30,
    144–45
  with Red people, 297–99
  self-awareness and, 229–30
  with whiners, 206–7
  Yellow people and, 139, 307–23
compassion, 34, 151, 164, 250
competence, 82, *223*
competition, 79, 182–83
complaining, 149–50, 159, 189,
  203–8, 298
compulsion, 28–31, 38–39, 59
confidence, 43, 96, 120, 182, 184–85,
  194
conflict, 48, 103, 108, 126, 152,
  194–95, 329
  drama queens and, 62, 84, 86
  Green people and, 46, 138,
    293–94, 300
  passive-aggressive people and,
    130, 132
consequences, 83, 245–46, 250,
  252–53, 255
  long term, 6, 269–70, 272
control, 18, 113–14, 282–83
  perfectionists and, 23–24, 33–34,
    40, 45–46

About the Author

Thomas Erikson is a Swedish behavioral expert, active lecturer, and best-selling author. For more than twenty years he has been traveling all over Europe delivering lectures and seminars to executives and managers at a wide range of companies, including IKEA, Coca-Cola, Microsoft, and Volvo.

Surrounded by Idiots has been a Swedish runaway best seller since it was first published in 2014. It has sold over 3 million copies worldwide and been translated into forty-nine languages.

Read the entire
Surrounded By Series
By Thomas Erikson

surrounded
by
narcissists

How to Effectively Recognize, Avoid,
and Defend Yourself Against
Toxic People (and Not Lose Your Mind)

thomas erikson

Bestselling Author of *Surrounded by Idiots*

Turning Obstacles
into Success
(When Everything Goes to Hell)

surrounded
by
setbacks

thomas erikson

From the 2-million copy bestselling
author of *Surrounded by Idiots*

surrounded
by
bad bosses
(and lazy employees)

How to Stop Struggling,
Start Succeeding,
and Deal with Idiots at Work

**thomas
erikson**

Bestselling Author of
Surrounded by Idiots

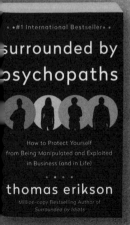

• #1 International Bestseller •

surrounded by
psychopaths

How to Protect Yourself
from Being Manipulated and Exploited
in Business (and in Life)

thomas erikson

Million-copy Bestselling Author of
Surrounded by Idiots

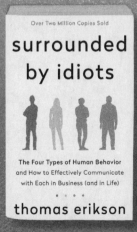

Over Two Million Copies Sold

surrounded
by idiots

The Four Types of Human Behavior
and How to Effectively Communicate
with Each in Business (and in Life)

thomas erikson

How to Slay the
Time, Joy, and Soul Suckers
in Your Life

surrounded by
energy
vampires

thomas erikson
Bestselling Author of *Surrounded by Idiots*

ST. MARTIN'S
ESSENTIALS